State, Market, and Religions in
Chinese Societies

Religion and the Social Order

An Official Publication of the Association for the Sociology of Religion

General Editor

WILLIAM H. SWATOS, JR.

VOLUME 11

State, Market, and Religions in Chinese Societies

Edited by

Fenggang Yang and Joseph B. Tamney

BRILL

LEIDEN • BOSTON

2005

This book is printed on acid-free paper.

Library of Congress Cataloging-in-Publication Data

State, market, and religions in Chinese societies / edited by Fenggang Yang
and Joseph B. Tamney.
    p. cm. — (Religion and the social order, ISSN 1061-5210 ; v. 11)
    Includes bibliographical references and index.
    ISBN 90-04-14597-4 (pbk. : alk. paper) 1. China—Religion. 2. Religion and
politics—China. I. Yang, Fenggang. II. Tamney, Joseph B. III. Title. IV. Series.

BL1802.S72 2005
200'.951—dc22

                                                                    2005047126

ISSN 1061–5210
ISBN 90 04 14597 4

PRINTED IN THE NETHERLANDS

CONTENTS

PREFACE

William H. Swatos, Jr.

In his 1993 Paul Hanly Furfey Address to the Association for the Sociology of Religion's annual meeting, N. J. Demerath, III, took up the "major shift that occurred in religion's perceived political prominence, especially following key events in 1979" (1994: 105). Jay went on to write a book to share the findings of the project that he outlined in his address (Demerath 2001), and it is fitting that in this, his Presidential, year at ASR we should see the Association's "Religion and the Social Order" series revived and renewed through a look at how religion is faring among one of the populations from that project: the Chinese. We do so courtesy of the collaborative work of ASR's 2004 president, Joseph B. Tamney, and his program chair for that year's meeting, Fenggang Yang. They have put together a series of chapters that explore in depth the many-faceted sides of religious expression among Chinese living in Asia.[1] Buddhists, Confucians, Daoists, Christians all enter a new market, albeit more heavily regulated than what we are used to in the West, to construct new expressions of age-old faith traditions. The results are fascinating and significant to our understanding of the variety of religion-and-society relationships that can develop across time and space among cultural groups. I am happy to offer this book as a "new beginning" for this series.

As I do this, I also want to express not only my own appreciation but also that of the Association to David Bromley, who first conceived this series and served as General Editor for a decade. Beginning in 1991, with an overview volume on new developments in theory and research, edited by Bromley himself, the series continued with an examination of changes in the Roman Catholic Church since the Second Vatican Council, under the editorship of Helen

---

[1] This collection will eventually be complemented by a special issue of *Sociology of Religion*, which they will also co-edit, that will contain articles about the conversion to Christianity of Chinese people in the United States, with special focus on the methods used by churches to attract Chinese converts.

Rose Ebaugh, through a two-part volume on new religious movements, co-edited by Bromley and the late Jeffrey K. Hadden, to additional offerings, among others, on quasi-religions, deviance and religion, the problem of 'authenticity' in religion, concluding with a volume recapping the definition-of-religion question. Throughout the series demonstrated high quality scholarship and professional dedication. As we move into a new era of publication with Brill, we can look back with gratitude to David for the not always easy years of service he gave to the Association and its members.

With respect to the present volume, most of the chapters included here were presented at the 2004 ASR annual meeting or at the 2004 annual meeting of the Society for the Scientific Study of Religion, and both organizations provided support to authors from 'greater China.' Additionally, the Henry Luce Foundation, the Institute of Sino-Christian Studies in Hong Kong, and the Culture Regeneration Research Society USA provided support for the development of the sociology of religion in China in 2004 in ways that were directly relevant to this volume. On behalf of the editors and myself, I wish both to acknowledge the support of these organizations and affirm our gratitude to them and to our colleagues who worked in the summer sociology of religion programs.

Finally, I am grateful to our contributors for sharing their research with us in this forum and for a spirit of outstanding cooperation in working to bring it to completion in a timely manner.

I look forward to sharing with you next year a collection under my own editorship on a variety of issues related to contemporary pilgrimage issues (*cum tourismus*), and invite our membership particularly to consider offering other work and expertise toward this series.

REFERENCES

Demerath, N. J., III. 1994. "The Moth and the Flame: Religion and Power in Comparative Blur." *Sociology of Religion* 55: 105–17.
———. 2001. *Crossing the Gods*. New Brunswick, NJ: Rutgers University Press.

INTRODUCTION

Joseph B. Tamney

The religious situation of the people in Chinese societies is in ferment. The essays in this book describe in detail some of the religious changes taking place in these societies. To give some relevant background information, I will discuss three topics here by way of introduction: the nature of the religious market in Chinese societies, contemporary religious changes in this market, and the relation between Chinese governments and religion.

The Religious Market in Chinese Societies

In practice, the Chinese living in The People's Republic of China (hereafter, China), Singapore, and Taiwan are, for the most part, divided among four religions: folk religion, Buddhism, Christianity, and Daoism.[1] The market analogy implies the assumption, which is increasingly justified, that these religions compete for the allegiance of Chinese people. I assume that most readers of this volume will have a general knowledge of Christianity, hence will comment briefly only on the other religious traditions that are discussed in the chapters that follow.

Folk Religion

Until recently almost all Chinese people practiced folk religion. Like all forms of this religion, the Chinese version has no central authority to establish what is orthodox belief or practice. There is thus much variation among practitioners, but several general points can be made.

People use folk religion to get this-worldly benefits, such as health or wealth, by gaining access to natural forces or the cooperation of

---

[1] Islam is an important religion among mainland Chinese, but this religion is not considered in this collection of essays, inasmuch as it has not shown a significance among other Chinese populations.

gods. If people learn of new gods or forces that are providing benefits to other devotees, folk religionists might borrow these religious entities and incorporate them into their own religion. While one's destiny is predetermined, one's luck can be influenced by seeking the help or advice of the supernatural. Fortune telling, spirit-mediums, and geomancy are used for this purpose.

Folk religionists are not part of religious congregations. They go to one or more temples or religious specialists until they have received help with their problems. Visits to folk temples often occur at times of personal crisis. The individual goes to ask help from favorite deities. No clergy may reside at the temple. When the individual has performed a ritual, he or she leaves. Ancestor worship is an important part of Chinese folk religion. Rituals, which are usually carried out in the home, are performed to honor the ancestors, to help them improve their lot in the other world, and to ask for help with practical problems. Chinese folk religionists accept values that are associated with Confucianism, most notably filial piety; thus it is believed that only when husbands, wives, and children play their proper roles in the patriarchal family structure would there be balance, peace, and harmony in the home.

During the last two thousand years, folk religionists have borrowed beliefs and practices from Buddhism and Daoism. Many of them believe in the doctrines of karma and rebirth (discussed below) and ask help from the Buddha and other revered Buddhist figures. The Daoist belief in the need to balance the forces of ying (gentility, the feminine) and yang (ferocity, the masculine) is also influential among folk religionists, leading many of them, for instance, to follow dietary rules that are meant to balance hot and cold elements in the body as a way to a healthy life. The balance of tastes in sweet and sour dishes is an example of the influence of Daoist beliefs.

Death rituals are especially important to ensure a pleasant existence in the next life. Upon death, the ying part of the person returns to the soil, while the yang part begins wandering the earth. Ideally the yang energy or force would be appeased and made available for help by a proper burial. Family problems are often "interpreted to be, in part, the work of dead ancestors who because of neglect by their kinsmen, inflicted harm in order to gain attention to their own predicament" (Eng 2003: 40).

Folk religion has a communal aspect. Some rituals celebrate local gods. These events bring the members of small villages and towns together and often occur in conjunction with communal fairs and annual festivals. Traditionally Chinese clans would each have a hall in which were housed ancestral tablets, and where the ancestors would be worshipped on festive occasions such as the Chinese New Year. The chapter in this book by Chi-shiang Ling discusses how the many ideas that compose folk religion have been spread among the common people through morality books.

Since the thirteenth century, folk religion has in different times and places crystallized into sects. These groups are voluntary and organized. The sects are consciously syncretistic, borrowing from folk religion, Confucianism, Buddhism, and Daoism. They promise followers salvation, usually as meant in the Buddhist or Daoist tradition. Although never more than a minority of the population, some sects have been able to spread across the regions of China. The imperial governments always defined the sects as heterodox. Hence they were considered dangerous to the state and were suppressed. Paul Yunfeng Lu's chapter is about a very popular sect, Yiguan Dao.

Buddhism

Buddhism offers the hope of a better life, and ultimately nirvana. A follower must seek wisdom. Of basic importance is to understand that suffering (a constant state of being unsatisfied) is the normal condition, but that one can escape this experience. The wise person comes to understand that everything is impermanent, that a sense of self is an illusion, and that the root cause of suffering is craving for things, people, feelings, and so on. With wisdom comes the ability to lead a virtuous life, and this accomplishment makes it easier to perform the rituals, especially meditation, the practice of which will eventually allow the person to live unattached to anything, nirvana.

Many Buddhists believe in the law of karma and the fact of rebirth. Supposedly our fortune is the result of the relative amount of good and bad deeds performed previously in this life as well as in previous lives. Acceptance of this belief has allowed Buddhists to explain injustice. It also offered people another way to perceive the Buddhist way of life, as one of amassing many merits in the course of daily life. For those who believe in karma, merit-making is an important preoccupation. Buddhists are told that they can earn merit by giving alms to the monks, helping finance temple building, following the ethical rules, performing acts of charity, and so forth. Another

related belief that appears among Buddhists is that it is possible to
transfer merit to the dead. Such a belief would have obvious attraction to those who practice ancestor worship. Given the traditional
Buddhist beliefs, there was no urgent need to "save" people.

> Generally Buddhists accept that after death people are reborn and that
> the quality of the new life is determined by the law of karma. The
> karma-rebirth orientation means that everyone has endless time to
> reach nirvana and that people can accept Buddhism only when their
> karma is good (Tamney and Chiang 2002: 181).

Most Chinese Buddhists follow the Mahāyāna, rather than the
Theravāda or Tibetan, form of Buddhism. (Thomas Borchert's chapter, however, concerns Theravāda Buddhists among a minority ethnic community in southwestern China.) Among the Mahayanists the
bodhisattva is the ideal, that is, someone who is on the verge of
achieving enlightenment but puts off personally entering nirvana in
order to help all sentient beings achieve this goal. Mahāyāna Buddhism
also puts less stress on the need to avoid this-worldly activities in
order to be saved. The attitude of nonattachment can be cultivated
while performing normal activities. Thus Mahāyāna is less elitist than
Theravāda Buddhism, in which the ideal of a monastic life as a necessary means of achieving enlightenment has been prevalent. Chinese
Mahāyānists have accepted such "Confucian virtues as filial piety,
congenial and harmonious family life, loyalty, moderation, and self-
discipline" (Chen 1964: 209); only filial piety was really an addition
to the Buddhist way of life.

Mahāyāna Buddhism, in turn, can be divided into Ch'an (in
Japanese, Zen) and Pure Land versions. The former emphasizes the
need to meditate. Pure Land Buddhism promises followers that they
will be reborn in the Western Paradise, which may be understood
metaphorically or literally. The most important Pure Land ritual is
the repetition of "Amitabha," the name of a manifestation of Buddha.
Amitabha became enlightened and caused to come into existence a
paradise where all who prayed to him could go after death and live
happily; in this "Western Paradise" the road to nirvana is supposedly easily traveled. Pure Land Buddhists, in effect, put their faith
in Buddha to save them.

Prior to the communist victory in China, Buddhist monks were
divided into: "wild monks," who did not follow the rules concerning
fasting and abstinence; "call monks," who worked in the village tem-

ples and who were called to perform rites for the dead; and the Buddhist elite, many of whom lived in monasteries and who followed the rules for living as a monk (Welch 1968: 234–5, 253). Eighty per-cent of the monks fell into the "call" category. In the village temples, monks often engaged in exorcisms, fortune telling, faith healing, and the performance of funeral rituals. Thus in Chinese societies, Buddhism has been experienced as little different from folk religion. Until recently, the monks were awarded little prestige (Chan 1953; Yang 1961: 33; Tamney and Hassan 1987: 42–3).

Kenneth Chen suggested that in the 1930s, there might have been about four million Buddhist lay people, of whom 60–70% followed the Pure Land tradition (1964: 460). By this time, meditation had "degenerated into habitual quiet sitting," and the recitation of Amitabha into "pure formalism without meaning or vitality" (Chan 1953: 65). The main occupation of the monks and nuns was performing folk rituals, especially death rituals, for some money. Writing about 1950, Wing-tsit Chan arrived at this harsh conclusion: "There can be no escape from the unpleasant fact that the sangha [the Buddhist order] is a congregation of ignorant and selfish people to whom religious observance has no spiritual significance" (1953: 80).

Daoism

Religious Daoism is distinguished by its devotion to the pursuit of longevity, indeed of physical immortality. Various methods have been developed to achieve this goal. One approach is to lead a virtuous life; here, the influence of Confucianism is obvious. In previous cen-turies, some Daoists devoted themselves to alchemy, producing elixirs from gold or cinnabar. Another approach uses techniques to preserve the life force within the body by performing breathing exercises, or doing calisthenics, or learning to keep the sperm during intercourse. Long life has also been pursued through meditation practices that were influenced by Buddhism. Daoists also emphasize the impor-tance of the right diet; people need to have a balanced diet, the specifics of which are based on the understanding of ying and yang. Daoists have been important preservers of knowledge about Chinese folk medicine.

Daoism has influenced Chinese popular culture. Many groups have developed special exercise routines that are meant to strengthen the person by harnessing *chi* (a material force), and these are based on

Daoist sources. Similarly the martial arts, whose specialists are often the subject of Chinese movies, are rooted in Daoist writings. Daoism has also long been an inspiration to Chinese artists. Daoist philosophy and religion have coexisted with Confucianism in the lives of the Chinese elite. An old saying is that the elite is Confucian by day and Daoist by night. That is, they are good bureaucrats at work, but go home and paint or write poetry.

Daoism as it is commonly practiced is hardly distinguishable from folk religion, except that the monks of Daoism are better organized than are the spirit mediums of folk religion.

> Daoism as an inherent and 'locally born and bred' religion in China, absorbed many beliefs and customs during its formation, and in its maturity continues to interact with folk religious activities. Daoism has absorbed so many classics and ideas of different schools that the *Daoist Canon* is a great encyclopedia of Chinese indigenous culture. People are even at times unaware that the religious services they attend are Daoist. (Liu 1993: 235)

The fate of popular Daoism in the first half of the twentieth century was similar to the situation of popular Buddhism at that time. While some Daoist monks and nuns lived in monasteries and led celibate lives, others lived in village temples and combined Daoist and folk beliefs and rituals. This book's chapter by Graeme Lang, Selina Chan, and Lars Ragvald describes a similar situation in the village temples that they recently studied. Der-Ruey Yang's chapter has a brief history of Daoism; he also describes how contemporary Daoist temple priests in China survive economically by cooperating with shamans, thus reproducing the symbiotic relationship between Daoism and folk religion that existed during imperial times.

Contemporary Religious Changes

During modernization, at least two processes are occurring. First, all world religions are undergoing religious purification, that is, the world religions are being purified of folk beliefs and practices (Tamney 1980). Thus in Chinese societies, folk religion, Buddhism, and Daoism are becoming increasingly differentiated forms of religion. Second, all religions are dividing into adherents who resist modernization, the traditionalists, and those who want to accommodate modernization, the modernists. The most notable East Asian example of this process is the development of reform Buddhism, which is discussed below. Reformers seek to differentiate and modernize Buddhism. But recently even Daoist leaders in Singapore "have taken steps to shake off its [Daoism's] negative, superstitious image and make its customs and practices more relevant to the Singapore of today" (Chen 1998: 56). As one would expect, these processes occur more frequently among more educated followers of a religion (Tamney 1980; Tamney and Chiang 2002; Eng 2003). The chapters in this book by Graeme Lang, Selina Chan, and Lars Ragvald, Chi-shiang Ling, Paul Yunfeng Lu, Der-Ruey Yang, Fenggang Yang and Dedong Wei, and Anna Sun include consideration of the effects of modernization on religions in Chinese societies.

Religious Trends

Singapore has the best statistics about religion, since they have included a question about religion in every census since 1980. The pattern of change is quite clear: Folk religion is declining, Christianity is growing, and Buddhism seems to be on the upswing as well. The decline of folk religion is dramatic. In the census, if respondents said they were Daoists or practiced ancestor worship, or belonged to a Chinese sect, they were put into the same category, which I am calling "folk religion." In 1980, 38.2% of Chinese people aged 10 years or older identified with folk religion. In 2000, 10.8% of the population 15 years or older (the government changed the criterion for inclusion in the census) identified with folk religion (Tamney and Chiang 2002: 159). Moreover folk religionists were older than other religious groups in 2000, suggesting the probability of further decline. Affiliation with Christianity among the Chinese in Singapore increased, from 10.6% in 1980 to 16.5% in 2000. The change in identification with Buddhism among the Chinese in Singapore is also impressive. In 1980, the census reported that 34.2% of the Chinese were Buddhists; the figure for 1990 was 39.3%, and for 2000, 53.6%. Thus it was especially during the 1990s that affiliation with Buddhism grew. (In addition, 18.6% of the Chinese did not claim any religious affiliation.) Of course, given that Singapore is a city-state, with a well-educated population, it cannot be assumed that trends in other Chinese societies will resemble Singapore's experience.

The Taiwanese government does not collect statistics about folk religion, but the government believes that the practice of this religion has declined (Republic of China 1994). Despite the fact that folk religion is declining, its public practice has increased in Taiwan. The end of martial law has created an environment in which folk specialists such as spirit mediums can be more public. Moreover this change coincides with a growing affluence that allows Taiwanese to give financial support to all religions, including folk religion. Finally, spirit mediums are receiving more formal training, which may have made them more socially acceptable (Jordan 1994). Although the numbers are less reliable than those for Singapore, Buddhism also seems to be growing in Taiwan (Tamney and Chiang 2002: 165).

After the communist victory on the mainland, many Christians were among those who moved to Taiwan. Both Catholicism and Protestantism grew rapidly between 1950 and 1965. However since then, Christianity has stagnated. Christians are probably about 4 percent of the population (Sha and Shen 1996: 135). They tend to live in the cities and to be relatively well educated. "Thus there are a substantial number of intellectuals, making the Church primarily a 'white-collar' church reaching out to intellectuals. Just how to reach out to the working class is a challenge which the church is faced with today" (Sha and Shen 1996: 140).

On the mainland, the greater tolerance of religion over the last twenty years has apparently resulted in the revival of all religions. For example, there is supposedly a "renaissance of traditional culture in the villages," which includes practices such as animal sacrifice and fortune telling (Pomfret 1998: 17). However it is difficult to tell if a higher percentage of the people are practicing folk religion than before the communist victory. Buddhism has also undergone a revival. There are now at least 200,000 Buddhist temples, 150,000 monks and nuns, and 30 colleges (Wei 2001). Undoubtedly the growth of Christianity in China has been spectacular since the beginning of the reform period. While only about one percent of the population is Catholic, and they are mostly poor (Madsen 2004: 104), rapid growth has occurred among Protestants, especially in rural areas among poor and illiterate people (Kindopp 2004b: 135).

Reform Buddhism

The reform movement in Buddhism is the result of state policies, which will be discussed in the next section, of challenges from Christianity, of the increasing contact of Chinese Buddhists with

Western Buddhism, and of the modernization of Buddhism in Chinese societies. In both Singapore and Taiwan, growth is associated with greater outreach efforts and more involvement in charity work (Eng 2003; Shiau 1999). The goal is to appear "modern" and thereby to attract more members. "Within the [Singaporean] Chinese community, Reformist Buddhism has emerged to challenge Christianity's claims to modernity"(Eng 2003: 280). Fenggang Yang and Dedong Wei describe an example of the reform process in China in their essay.

An ideal type of reform Buddhism (Eng 2003; Tamney and Chiang 2002) has these elements:

– An emphasis on creating an earthly Pure Land; engaging in social welfare programs and efforts to protect the environment
– More attention to outreach efforts, such as monks appearing on television, organizing college campus groups, and running summer camps for college students (Sha and Shen 1996: 133)
– A stronger role for the laity, including women; establishment of lay Buddhist groups
– More impersonal rules for monasteries to ensure the recognition of individual merit
– Provision of social activities such as sports events or cooking classes
– Developing ties to global Buddhism; reform Buddhism presents itself as not simply a parochial 'Chinese' religion but as part of global Buddhism
– An emphasis on personal spiritual development, especially by studying the scriptures and practicing meditation.

The last element is especially important. As Eng put it, a new generation of Singaporean Chinese sees "their religious needs as personal, no longer tied to the religious needs of their families or community. Thus, religion, to many of them, is a personal quest for spiritualism" (2003: 7). Supposedly 65% of the Chinese Buddhists in Singapore regard themselves as part of the reform movement (Eng 2003: 1).

Christian Growth

Christian growth in Chinese societies has resulted from many factors. On the one hand, the competition has been weak. Folk religion is not centrally organized and has been slow to respond to modernization. As previously discussed, until the rise of reform

Buddhism, this religious group had been perceived as indistinguishable from folk religion. In China, the deepening disillusionment with Communism has meant that this ideology no longer functions as an alternative to religion. On the other hand, Christian groups have had ready access to resources, which have been used to establish schools and medical facilities. This achievement has gained support, and sometimes converts, for Christianity. Moreover until the development of reform Buddhism, the only religious groups actively evangelizing were Christian ones.

An interesting question is whether China will follow the Taiwanese (growth followed by stagnation) or the Singaporean pattern (continual growth). In Taiwan, Christian growth has been hampered by two factors that do not apply in China. First, the modernist Presbyterian Church has played a leading role in the development of Taiwanese Christianity, but this church is not as strongly evangelistic as other Christian groups. Second, whereas about 80% of the Taiwanese speak either Taiwanese or Hakka, many Christian congregations are Mandarin-speaking (Sha and Shen 1996). In contrast, Christianity in Singapore has had several advantages, notably the facts that English is the main language in the school system and in the business world and that Singapore has been open to Western influence since the founding of the country in the 1960s.

Christianity has traditionalist and modernist wings. The latter are sometimes referred to as liberals or, in the case of Protestantism, mainline. Traditionalist Christians can be divided into fundamentalists and evangelicals; the former more strongly resist modernization than the latter. To confuse matters more, there are Christians who combine this religion with elements of Western folk religion, especially emphasizing the importance of religious experience, healing, and prophecying: On the one hand, there are the Pentecostals, who combine a fundamentalist attitude toward the Bible with folk practices; and on the other hand, there are the charismatics, who accept modified versions of the folk practices, and who theologically range from being comparable to evangelicals to being similar to modernists (Tamney 2002; Tamney and Chiang 2002: 170–1).

Much of the Christian growth in China is in rural areas. (Fenggang Yang and Jianbo Huang provide a history of a rural church and document its impressive growth during the reform era.) In part, this is a result of the weaker government surveillance outside the cities and big towns. Undoubtedly the promise of miracles, especially healing, is a very attractive feature of rural, traditionalist congregations (Hunter and Chan 1993: 174; Deng 1996: 115). Similarly indigenous Christian groups follow in the Pentecostal tradition and are among the fastest growing churches in China (Xu 2004: 109–10). For instance, the True Jesus Church combines obvious Western religious elements, such as devotion to Jesus, with leaders who are a version of traditional Chinese spirit-mediums (Rubinstein 1991: 138). However Chen Cunfu and Huang Tianhai described "a new type of Christian" appearing in urban areas (2004: 189). The new Christian works in the emerging free market part of the economy, and is affluent and well educated. It will be interesting to watch how this new Christian affects the religious institution.

Christian growth is not occurring equally among the types of Christians. Protestants are increasing faster than Catholics. Although adequate statistical information about this matter is lacking, informed opinions suggest that among the Protestants, growth is greater among the traditionalists, and especially among Pentecostals/charismatics (Rubinstein 1991: 155; Hunter and Chan 1993: 174; Wong 1996). The Reverend Stephen H. T. Hsu, who is Secretary for Evangelism at The Presbyterian Church in Taiwan, told me in a personal interview that growing congregations are charismatic, with more informal services that incorporate lively music. It is interesting that the form of Christianity that includes folk elements is so successful.

Whereas the most compelling challenge for Buddhism is to modernize, the main issue for Christianity is indigenization. Structurally, Christian churches have completed or nearly completed this task; the churches are now in the hands of the local people. Culturally, there is much to be done. Christianity is still seen as a foreign religion. Among the main issues are

> the Christian assumption of an evil human nature, which runs counter to Mencius's doctrine [of innate goodness], the idea of eternal damnation, which is denied by Buddhism, and the Christian demand for people's total commitment, which is contrary to the Chinese experience with weakly bounded religions (Tamney and Chiang 2002: 177).

Of course, an image as foreign can help among people who are critical of what they see as the backwardness of their traditional culture. But in the long run, being perceived as foreign would seem an undesirable handicap. In this regard, it is interesting that in Singapore, the Chinese who usually speak English at home have been more

likely to become Christians, than those Chinese who usually speak
Chinese at home. In 2000, while 40% of the English-speaking Chinese
were Christian, only 9% of the Chinese-speaking identified with this
religion.

Confucian Revival

Anna Xiao Dong Sun's chapter describes the new interest in
Confucianism on the mainland. Despite the absence of this tradition
from the educational system in China for over 50 years, and thus
the general ignorance about Confucianism, it seems inevitable that
people would be at least curious about it, once the reform era com-
menced. However there are signs that Confucianism is losing its
stature in other Chinese societies. During the 1980s, the Singapore
government introduced a compulsory religious studies program into
secondary schools; parents could choose the specific tradition their
children would study; the government had hoped that most of the
Chinese pupils would be in the Confucian studies option, but it
proved to be relatively unpopular; in part because of this, the program became voluntary and has been rarely chosen (Tamney 1996).
During the 1990s, the Taiwanese government changed the college-
level course in which students studied Confucianism from manda-
tory to an elective. Given the overwhelmingly important role of
Confucianism in Chinese history, there will no doubt be a continuing
interest in the tradition. Moreover, as Sun points out, there is a
movement to emphasize not only the ethical components of Confucianism, but also the religious aspects of this tradition. To gain
relevance, however, Confucianism will probably have to be modernized. Chi-shiang Ling's chapter describes how the Confucian content of the morality books is being adapted to a modern society,
which is part of a broader movement to make Confucianism more
appealing to modern people (Tamney and Chiang 2002). An interesting question is: How will a revived interest in Confucianism affect
the fate of religions in Chinese societies?

Church-State Relations

Modernization supposedly includes the structural separation of church
and state. A modern state guarantees human rights, which include
religious freedom. For instance, in the United States the constitution

prevents the government from favoring any one religious viewpoint or from interfering with a person's religion. Moreover, modern states are founded on secular goals such as promoting public health, social welfare, and economic prosperity. Of course, a complete separation of church and state is not possible. In cases of conflict, modern states control religious beliefs and organizations to ensure that religions serve the public good (Smith 1970: 85–6, 116).

In the present world, there are a variety of church-state relationships. Iran approximates a theocracy, although the tension between hardliners and reformers suggests that the situation is unstable. Some relatively modern states subsidize churches, most notably Germany and Spain, but also Italy and the United Kingdom.

For over a thousand years, the imperial Chinese government regulated religions. Religious groups were required to register with the state. Institutional Buddhism, Daoism, Islam, and, in some centuries Christianity, were recognized. Roaming monks, who were not associated with recognized temples, and members of sects were considered dangerous and were often suppressed. In practice, "the behavior of local authorities toward unregistered religious groups often varied from disinterested neglect to violent crackdown, depending on the locality" (Bays 2004: 27). Thus for over a thousand years, China had state-supported religious organizations that were pressured to serve the political goals of the ruling elite.

The most destructive form of a state-church relationship in modern times occurred during the period of the Cultural Revolution (1966–76) in China. Religious organizations, except those that went underground, were in effect abolished. Religious activities were forbidden, and church assets were seized. Moreover an elaborate propaganda campaign sought to convince people that all religions were backward and doomed to disappear with modernity.

At present, the Chinese government recognizes only five world religions—Buddhism, Catholicism, Islam, Protestantism, and Daoism. Freedom of religious belief and the performance of 'normal' religious activities is guaranteed by the government. However: "'Superstitious' activities, such as fortune-telling, divination, exorcism, and healing are expressly forbidden" (Spiegel 2004: 51). All religious organizations must belong to the appropriate government-controlled organization that has been established for each recognized religion. For instance, all Protestant churches must join the Three-Self Patriotic Movement, and all Catholic parishes, the Catholic Patriotic Association.

These organizations control the appointment of clergy, the running of places of worship, the publication of religious material, the training programs for clergy, and so on.

> Official control extends even to the realm of beliefs. Political authorities impose boundaries for acceptable religious doctrines, denouncing beliefs that emphasize evangelism, supernaturalism, or salvational doctrines that challenge the government's religious policies or contradict its projected symbolic order, which depicts all of Chinese society as unified under Chinese Communist Party CCP) rule (Kindopp 2004a: 3).

For example, official Catholic clergy are pressured to endorse government policies on abortion even though they are not consistent with orthodox Catholic doctrine. State policies during the reform era are more fully discussed in the chapters by Fenggang Yang and by Jianbo Huang and Fenggang Yang.

There are reasons to believe that the current policies in China regarding religion might change. First, local governments are finding religious organizations to be useful in achieving secular goals. For instance, religious sites are being developed as a way of stimulating tourism and thereby contributing to economic development (see the chapters in this book by Graeme Lang, Selina Chan, and Lars Ragvald, by Thomas Borchert, and by Fenggang Yang and Wei Dedong). Moreover the central government wants to enlist the private sector in coping with welfare problems. As part of this strategy, the state may allow religious groups to participate in the privatization of welfare (*Christianity Today* 2003). Second, China is increasingly enmeshed in global society and, as a result, might feel more pressure from foreigners to change. Third, globalization will expose more and more Chinese citizens to liberal, Western societies, and this might increase internal demand for the liberalization of religious policies (Chan 2004). Fourth, the current policies are a compromise between the conservatives and the progressives within the Communist Party (Chan 2004: 66) and are therefore unlikely to remain unchanged over time. Fifth, the policy of forcing all followers of the same religious tradition into a single group is contrary to the dividing of all religions into traditionalist and modernist versions. In China, there are two types of Christian churches, those that are officially recognized and those that are not; the latter are often called "underground churches," even though there are unofficial churches whose practices are publicly known. Most Christians are in the unofficial churches (Kindopp 2004a: 5). Among Protestants this split coincides with the division between traditionalist (unofficial) and modernist (Spiegel 2004: 48; see also Madsen 2004: 104–5). The current official structure is unrealistic for the Christians and will become increasingly so for the other religious traditions as they modernize.

Singapore is an alternative, non-Western model for China. The Singapore government expects the religious institution to contribute to society in two ways: first, by teaching the right values, and second, by getting involved in welfare work. When he was Prime Minister, Lee Kuan Yew said there are many reasons why "the established religions—not fake religions, new fangled cults, but orthodox religions" are allies of the government: "If nothing else, all religions are against addiction to drugs . . ." (*Straits Times* 1988). The government also wants religions to help in the effort to encourage families to take care of their elderly, and generally in privatizing welfare. For instance, the government financially assists welfare homes run by religious groups, and it gives grants to the Singapore Buddhist Free Clinic.

At the same time, the government regulates religion closely. There are several reasons for this. First, the Singaporean government seeks to eliminate any serious political opposition; the leaders do not want any version of Christian Liberation Theology or Islamism to become the basis of a political movement. Second, the government always worries about ethnic tensions resulting in social unrest; because religion and ethnicity are intertwined in Singapore, the regulation of religion is a means of controlling ethnic relations. Thus The Religious Harmony Act, which was passed in 1992, prohibits religious groups from engaging in politics and in aggressive evangelizing (Tamney 1996; Eng 2003).[2]

Will China become more like Singapore? Or, will China become closer to the church-state differentiation model? In any case, as several chapters in this book demonstrate, church-state relations in China are changing. "Into what?" is an interesting question.

---

[2] Since the lifting of martial law in 1987, church-state relations in Taiwan have also been more and more approximating the modern model (Katz 2003).

REFERENCES

Bays, Daniel H. 2004. "A Tradition of State Dominance." Pp. 25–39 in *God and Caesar in China*, edited by Jason Kindopp and Carol Lee Hamrin. Washington, DC: Brookings Institution Press.

Chan, Kim-kwong. 2004. "Accession to the World Trade Organization and State Adaptation." Pp. 58–74 in *God and Caesar in China*, edited by Jason Kindopp and Carol Lee Hamrin. Washington, DC: Brookings Institution Press.

Chan, Wing-tsit. 1953. *Religious Trends in Modern China*. New York: Columbia University Press.

Chen Cunfu and Huang Tianhai. 2004. "The Emergence of a New Type of Christian in China Today." *Review of Religious Research* 46: 183–200.

Chen, Kao. 1998. "Taoism at a Crossroads." *Straits Times* (Singapore), 18 April, 56.

Chen, Kenneth K. S. 1964. *Buddhism in China*. Princeton, NJ: Princeton University Press.

Christianity Today. 2003. "About-face on Charities." November, 34–5.

Deng, Zhaoming. 1996. "China." Pp. 91–129 in *Church in Asia Today*, edited by Saphir Athyal. Singapore: Asia Lausanne Committee for World Evangelization.

Eng, Kuah-pearce Khun. 2003. *State, Society, and Religious Engineering*. Singapore: Eastern Universities Press.

Hunter, Alan and Kim-kwong Chan. 1993. *Protestantism in Contemporary China*. Cambridge: Cambridge University Press.

Jordan, David K. 1994. "Changes in Postwar Taiwan and their Impact on the Popular Practice of Religion." Pp. 137–59 in *Cultural Change in Postwar Taiwan*, edited by Stevan Harrell and Huang Chun-chieh. Boulder, CO: Westview Press.

Katz, Paul R. 2003. "Religion and the State in Post-war Taiwan." *China Quarterly* 174: 395–412.

Kindopp, Jason. 2004a. "Policy Dilemmas in China's Church-State Relations." Pp. 1–22 in *God and Caesar in China*, edited by Jason Kindopp and Carol Lee Hamrin. Washington, DC: Brookings Institution Press.

———. 2004b. "Fragmented Yet Defiant: Protestant Resilience under Chinese Communist Party Rule." Pp. 122–45 in *God and Caesar in China*, edited by Jason Kindopp and Carol Lee Hamrin, 122–45. Washington, DC: Brookings Institution Press.

Liu, Xiaogan. 1993. "Daoism." Pp. 229–90 in *Our Religions*, edited by Arvind Sharma. New York: HarperSanFrancisco.

Madsen, Richard. 2004. "Catholic Conflict and Cooperation in the People's Republic of China." Pp. 93–106 in *God and Caesar in China*, edited by Jason Kindopp and Carol Lee Hamrin. Washington, DC: Brookings Institution Press.

Pomfret, John. 1998. "Rural People Put their Faith in Religion." *Guardian Weekly* (Manchester), 6 September, 17.

Republic of China. 1994. *The Republic of China Yearbook 1994*. Taipei: Government Information Office.

Rubinstein, Murray A. 1991. *The Protestant Community in Modern Taiwan*. Armonk, N.Y.: M. E. Sharpe.

Sha, James and Andrew Shen. 1996. "Taiwan, ROC." Pp. 130–42 in *Church in Asia Today*, edited by Saphir Athyal. Singapore: Asia Lausanne Committee for World Christian Evangelization.

Shiau, Chyuan-jeng. 1999. "Civil Society and Democratization." Pp. 101–15 in *Democratization in Taiwan*, edited by Steve Tsang and Tien Hung-mao. Hong Kong: Hong Kong University Press.

Smith, Donald Eugene. 1970. *Religion and Political Development*. Boston: Little, Brown.

Spiegel, Mickey. 2004. "Control and Containment in the Reform Era." Pp. 40–57 in *God and Caesar in China*, edited by Jason Kindopp and Carol Lee Hamrin. Washington, DC: Brookings Institution Press.

Straits Times (Singapore). 1988. "PM Response to a Question About Cheng Affair." 24 August, 18.

Tamney, Joseph B. 1980. "Modernization and Religious Purification: Islam in Indonesia." *Review of Religious Research* 22: 207–18.

———. 1996. *The Struggle over Singapore's Soul*. Berlin: Walter de Gruyter.

———. 2002. *The Resilience of Conservative Religion*. Cambridge: Cambridge University Press.

Tamney, Joseph B. and Linda Hsueh-ling Chiang. 2002. *Modernization, Globalization, and Confucianism in Chinese Societies*. Westport, CT: Praeger.

Tamney, Joseph B. and Riaz Hassan. 1987. *Religious Switching in Singapore*. Singapore: Select Books.

Wei Dedong. 2001. "The Development and Characteristics of Contemporary Chinese Buddhism." Unpublished paper.

Welch, Holmes. 1968. *The Buddhist Revival in China*. Cambridge, MA: Harvard University Press.

Wong, James. 1996. "Singapore." Pp. 188–211 in *Church in Asia Today*, edited by Saphir Athyal. Singapore: Asia Lausanne Committee for World Evangelization.

Xu, Yihua. 2004. " 'Patriotic' Protestants: The Making of an Official Church." Pp. 107–121 in *God and Caesar in China*, edited by Jason Kindopp and Carol Lee Hamrin, 107–21. Washington, DC: Brookings Institution Press.

Yang, C. K. 1961. *Religion in Chinese Society*. Berkeley: University of California Press.

CHAPTER ONE

BETWEEN SECULARIST IDEOLOGY AND DESECULARIZING REALITY: THE BIRTH AND GROWTH OF RELIGIOUS RESEARCH IN COMMUNIST CHINA[1]

Fenggang Yang

[I was] overwhelmed by the total secularization of a society and culture that once placed high value on religious shrines, festivals and symbols. During our visit [to China in 1974] we saw almost no evidence of surviving religious practice. . . . We saw no functioning Buddhist temples. Some of those we visited had been converted to use as tea houses, hostels or assembly halls; others were maintained as museums. . . . Some Chinese with whom we talked were curious about religion. They were amazed to learn that educated persons in the West continue to believe and practice religion. For them, they said, the study of scientific materialism had exposed the logical fallacies and absurdities of religion. (MacInnis 1975: 249, 251–52)

Merely three decades ago, China appeared to be the most secularized country in the world. Not a single temple or church was open for public religious service, and people appeared to believe wholeheartedly in atheism, as reported by this American observer. At the turn of the twenty-first century, however, China may have become one of the most religious countries in the world. All kinds of religions, old or new, conventional or eccentric, are thriving. American and other Western media often feed images and stories of spectacular revivals of various religions and reckless crackdowns on religious organizations by the Communist government. The growth of various religions and the government's religious policies are important research topics both for understanding China and for theoretical development in the social scientific study of religion, which have received limited scholarly attention (e.g., Hunter and Chan 1993; Madsen 1998; Overmyer 2003; Kindopp and Hamrin 2004).

---

[1] An earlier version of this chapter was published in *Sociology of Religion* 65(2) 2004: 101–19, the official journal of the Association for the Sociology of Religion.

However, between the atheist ideology and repressive religious policy of the government on the one hand and the desecularizing reality of thriving religions on the other hand, religious research in China
has emerged as a third entity playing complicated but increasingly
important roles in China's religious scene. This chapter focuses on
the changing scholarship of religious research.[2] What are the roles
of religious research in China under the rule of the Communist
Party? Is the scholarship merely part of the atheist propaganda and
for the purpose of controlling religion? Or is it serving the interest
of religions? What are the predominant theories, perspectives, or
approaches in religious research? How are these changing and why?

I will show that during the last two decades of the twentieth century, the birth and growth of religious research in China have been
dramatic. In a sense it parallels the paradigm shift in the sociology of
religion in the United States (Warner 1993), in which the new paradigm offers a more objective, scientific, and consequently more balanced approach to religion than the old paradigm that favors
secularization as religion's destiny (Stark and Finke 2000). Religious
research in China remains limited and restricted in many ways.
However, scholarship has shifted away from ideological atheism—a
radical form of secularization theories—to a more scientific, objective approach that affirms both the positive and negative functions
of religion. This intellectual history has three distinct periods: the
domination of atheism from 1949 to 1979, the birth of religious
research in the 1980s, and the flourishing of the scholarship in the
1990s. Religious research in Communist China was established for
the purpose of atheist propaganda and religious control, but it grew
into an independent academic discipline that has become more
responsive to the desecularizing reality.

1949–1979: Religious Research as Part of Atheist Propaganda

In the ideological lexicon of the Chinese Communist Party (CCP),
atheism is a basic doctrine, which manifests in two major forms:
scientific atheism and militant atheism. Scientific atheism, as an

---

[2] In this chapter religious research includes all scholarly research on religion,
such as studies of religion in social sciences, humanities, and theology. 'Religious
studies' in the North American context often refers to a discipline, as in such named
departments in some universities, which tends to be in the humanities, such as historical and textual studies.

offspring of the European Enlightenment movement, regards religion as illusory or false consciousness, non-scientific and backward; thus atheist propaganda is necessary to expunge religion. In contrast, militant atheism, as advocated by Lenin and the Russian Bolsheviks, treats religion as the dangerous opium and narcotic of the people, a wrong political ideology serving the interests of antirevolutionary forces; thus counter-force may be necessary to control or eliminate religion. Scientific atheism is the theoretical basis for tolerating religion while carrying out atheist propaganda, whereas militant atheism leads to antireligious measures.

In practice, almost as soon as it took power in 1949, the CCP followed the hard line of militant atheism. Within a decade, all religions were brought under the iron control of the Party: Folk religious practices, considered feudalist superstitions, were vigorously suppressed; cultic or heterodox sects, regarded as reactionary organizations, were resolutely banned; foreign missionaries, considered part of Western imperialism, were expelled; and major world religions, including Buddhism, Islam, Catholicism, and Protestantism, were coerced into patriotic national associations under close supervision of the Party. Religious believers who dared to challenge these policies were mercilessly banished to labor camps, jails, or execution grounds.

Within such a political environment, academic research on religion was no more than a means for atheist propaganda. A Chinese scholar who lived through that period states:

> Scholarly research on religion was considered an important means for atheist education to the masses of people, thus it stressed the differences and conflicts between theism and atheism, and between idealism and materialism. (Dai 2001: 41)

Religious research was indeed an almost forbidden field because of the political risks involved (Wu 1998: 3). Any religious research could be easily labeled as pure scholarship (i.e., an irrelevant subject and a waste of resources), or with feudalist-capitalist content (i.e., reactionary substance), thus subject to reproach and penalty.

In the 1950s and 1960s, very few publications about religion appeared in China. Among these, most were edited collections of source materials from the ancient past. Some made comments on ancient scriptures such as the Daoist *Taiping Jing* (Taiping Scripture) and the Buddhist *Tan Jing* (Chan Sutra), and the sole criterion of evaluation was whether the text was for the peasant revolution, which was good, or for the feudalist ruling class, which was antirevolutionary

and reactionary. It is said that the supreme leader Mao Zedong
spoke positively about *Tan Jing* (Huang 1998b: 135; Dai 2001: 42),
which was attributed to an illiterate peasant monk Hui Neng (638–713
C.E.), who was the key founder of the Chinese sect of Chan Buddhism.
Following such a hint, some scholars ventured to apply Marxism-
Leninism-Maoism to the analysis of Chinese Buddhism. The most
notorious work of this type was the *Collection on Buddhist Thoughts in
Han-Tang* by Ren Jiyu (1962; also see Chen 1965), which won Mao's
favor. In 1963, Ren was called in to meet with Mao, and then
entrusted to establish a religious research institute. This was to become
the Institute for the Study of World Religions at the Chinese Academy
of Social Sciences. The designated task of the institute was to apply
Marxism-Leninism-Maoism systematically to explore the essence and
causes of religion for the purpose of defeating theism. However,
started in 1964 but interrupted by the Cultural Revolution, it did
not become functional until 1978. Ironically, in the 1980s and 1990s,
this Institute played a leading role in the process of shifting away
from completely opposing religion to affirming religion.

During the Cultural Revolution (1966–1976), even the little freedom for writing about Buddhism vanished. In pre-1949 China, there
were three major Buddhist magazines, which were closed out one-
by-one in 1953, 1955, and 1958. *Modern Buddhism* magazine, which
was started in 1950 and was put under the patronage of the patriotic
China Buddhist Association, also stopped publication in 1964. From
1967 to 1974, not a single article on religion was published in journals, magazines or newspapers in the People's Republic of China
(Huang 1998a: 102). It was during this period that the American
observer Donald MacInnis (1975) visited China, reporting a totally
secularized society with empty churches and temples and willing atheist young people. What he saw was only on the surface, which was
maintained by a terrifying dictatorship (also see FitzGerald 1967;
Bates 1968; Welch 1969; Huang 1971; Strong and Strong 1973):

> During the Cultural Revolution, under the slogans of 'class struggles
> are the guiding principle' and 'completely break up with conventional
> ideas', religion was listed as part of the four olds [old ideas, old cul-
> ture, old customs and old habits] and of feudalism, capitalism and
> revisionism that should be eradicated. Religious beliefs of the great
> masses were said to be reflections of class struggles in the sphere of
> ideology and signs of political backwardness and reaction; religious
> believers were subject to crack-downs as 'ox-monsters' and 'snakedemons',

resulting in many framed and fabricated cases. Religion was a realm
of heavy catastrophes. The Religious Affairs Administration was dis-
solved; religious cadres were censured for their crime of following the
wrong political line. All religious venues were closed. Many religious
artifacts were destroyed. Religious research completely halted. The criticism of theism quickly became in practice the theoretical declaration
for struggling and eliminating religion in society. (Dai 2001: 43)

Therefore, scholarly research on religion completely ceased to exist.
The few scholars who had written about religion in the past were
muted, and many of them suffered physical and psychological tor-
tures, as did many religious believers.

However, militant atheism and merciless suppression failed to erad-
icate religion in Chinese society. Although religious organizations
were disbanded, churches and temples were closed and clergy were
dismissed, many believers went underground—keeping one's faith to
oneself or gathering in homes amidst vigilant secrecy. Instead of
declining, religions persisted and resurfaced as soon as the suppression policy relaxed.

The 1980s: The Opium War

Following the death of Mao Zedong in 1976, Deng Xiaoping emerged
as the paramount leader of the CCP and at the end of 1978 launched
the economic reforms and open-door policies. Deng Xiaoping himself had little to say about religion, except mentioning it in passing
when addressing ethnic relations, such as Tibetan problems, or international relations, such as Buddhist exchanges with Japan (in order
to win investments and loans). Nonetheless, as political pragmatism
was prevailing over ideological dogmatism, religious policy also changed
from complete eradication to limited toleration (MacInnis 1994). In
order to mobilize people of all walks of life for the central task of
economic development, beginning in 1979, a limited number of
Christian churches, Buddhist temples and other religious sites were
allowed to reopen, bringing religious life back to the public scene.

Following a brief period of confusion in religious policies, the CCP
Central Committee formulated "The Basic Viewpoint and Policy on
the Religious Affairs during the Socialist Period of Our Country"—
which has become known as Document No. 19 and has been the
basis of the religious policy since then. This document concludes that

religion in socialist China has five characteristics (*wu xing*): it will exist for a long time; it has masses of believers; it is complex; it entwines with ethnicity; and it affects international relations. Therefore, religious affairs should be handled with care; religious believers should be rallied for the central task of economic construction; religious freedom should be guaranteed as long as the believers love the country, support CCP's rule, and observe the socialist laws. It acknowledges the mistakes of militant atheism. But it also clearly reaffirms the atheist doctrine: religion will eventually wither away and atheist propaganda should be carried out unremittingly.

Document No. 19 reports the reality of religious persistence: From the early 1950s to the early 1980s, the number of Muslims increased from over 8 million to over 10 million. Catholics increased from 2.7 million to over 3 million. Protestants increased from 0.7 million to about 3 million. Buddhism and Daoism have also persisted, although no enumeration was provided. Given that the whole population has about doubled from 1950 to 1980, the absolute number of religious believers has increased, but the proportion of believers in the whole population of the country has decreased (RAB 1995: 56). This was noted in the document, and later by some officials as well, as a partial victory of atheist propaganda.

However, after so many years of pervasive atheist education and fierce suppression, the persistence of religion itself was very puzzling. Document No. 19 simply states that there may be psychological and social roots for religion to continue to exist in socialist society. But what are such roots? What is the nature of religion? Document No. 19 set the basis for tolerance and restriction policies, but it also set off debates on the nature and roots of religion.

Initially, the debate was around the opium thesis. "Religion . . . is the opium of the people." This statement by Karl Marx in his "Critique of Hegel's *Philosophy of Right*" (1844 [Marx and Engels 1975: 38]) was once regarded by the CCP as the foundation of Marxist atheism. After this position was reiterated by Party ideologues around 1980, other theorists, under the cloud of thought liberation (*jiefang sixiang*), spoke out in challenge. Many scholars and ideologues were drawn into the debate (see He 2000; Gao 2000; Dai 2001). The leftists insisted that the opium thesis was the cornerstone of a Marxist view of religion, whereas the liberals offered counter arguments within the parameters of upholding orthodox Marxism, making painstaking efforts with delicate rhetoric. The liberals argued,

– the opium statement was only an analogy, and an analogy is not a definition;

– the opium analogy by Marx should not be understood in complete, negative terms, because opium was used as a pain reliever at Marx's time;

– this analogical statement did not represent the complete view of Marxism on religion since Marx, and especially Engels, made other important statements on religion; and

– before Marx other people had already compared religion to opium, so this was not a uniquely Marxist view.

Gradually, liberal thinking prevailed, especially attracting younger scholars. Many leftists also softened, or even completely abandoned, their original position. A striking example is Lü Daji, as will be discussed later, who eventually turned away from Marxist atheism in favor of scientific neutrality and objectivity.

This debate has been referred to as the 'opium war' because of the involvement of numerous scholars and ideologues from both sides. It also stimulated interest in religion among young scholars. The most important contribution of the opium war debate was probably that it legitimized religious research as a discipline. The Institute for the Study of World Religions at the Chinese Academy of Social Sciences expanded. Some provincial academies of social sciences also established religious research institutes, including Shanghai in 1980, Yunnan in 1984, and Tibet in 1985. Several specialty journals for religious research were launched, including the *Journal for the Study of World Religions* (Beijing, 1979), *Religion* (Nanjing, 1979), *Sources of World Religions* (Beijing, 1980), *Scholarly Reseach on Religion* (Chengdu, 1982), *Contemporary Religious Research* (Shanghai, 1989), and several other journals for internal circulation. Meanwhile, several major universities, including Fudan University, the People's University of China, and Beijing University, formed a section for teaching and studying religion, most of which were based within philosophy departments. Books about religion began to be published, including introductions or general surveys of various religions, and historical studies of Chinese Buddhism, Daoism, Islam, and Christian missions (e.g., Ren 1981; Gu 1981; Jiang 1982; Tang 1982; Ma 1983; Zhang 1986; Yu 1987; Zhang and Liu 1987; Luo 1988; Qin 1988–1995). The overall tone of the publications gradually changed from completely negative criticism of religion to a more balanced evaluation.

The 1990s: The Culture Fever

The economic reforms and thought liberation policies in the early
1980s set off a series of intellectual or cultural movements, including the scar literature, which condemned the evils of the cultural
revolution and other leftist political campaigns; the humanist literature, which called for the return of humanity against political bru-
tality, and the hazy poetry, which questioned the orthodox or clear-cut
artificial normality. Various Western philosophies and social theories, such as existentialism, psychoanalysis and Nietzscheanism, were
reintroduced, and they aroused fascination especially among college
students and young scholars. Meanwhile, modernization and democratization, which were old themes of the May Fourth and New
Culture Movement in the 1910s and 1920s, sparked new enthusiasm.

Within the new social and cultural climate, cultural comparisons
of the East and West became hot (see Gu 1999). The culture fever
(*wenhua re*) excited the whole intelligentsia and spilled over to the
public, climaxing in the student-led democracy movement in 1989.
After the Tiananmen Square Incident on June 4th, 1989, when the
democracy movement was violently crushed by the government, political discussions muted, but cultural debates continued. Catching the
waves of the culture fever, religious research expanded its horizon.

In the late 1980s, some vanguard scholars began to argue that to
understand culture and cultures, it was necessary to study religion as
part of culture and to study the relationships between religion and
other cultural components, including folklore, literature, arts, music,
philosophy, science, morality, politics, economy, laws, and so on (e.g.,
Ge 1987; Fang 1988; Zhuo 1988; see also He 2000). In the 1990s,
the cultural approach to religion made vivacious waves. Several new
journals were launched, including *Buddhist Culture* (Beijing, 1989) and
the *Review of Christian Culture* (Guiyang, 1990). The well-established
journal *Sources of World Religions* was renamed *World Religious Culture*
in 1995. By the late 1990s, several more book-form journals appeared,
including *Religion and Culture* (Hangzhou 1994) and the *Journal for the
Study of Christian Culture* (Beijing 1999). Meanwhile, several publishers brought forth culture series of books: Religious Cultures Popular
Readings by the Qilu Press,[3] Religious Cultures by China Construction

---

[3] Including such titles as *Aspects of Buddhist Culture, Aspects of Christian Culture* and
Aspects of Islamic Culture.

Press,[4] and Religion and the World translation series by Sichuan People's Press.[5] A newly established publisher was even named the Religious Culture Press.[6]

Culture is an all-encompassing and esteemed term in the Chinese context. The importance of the cultural approach to religious research is two-fold. First, when religion is studied as a cultural phenomenon, its ideological incorrectness becomes unimportant and its scientific incorrectness obscure, eliminating two key criticisms of religion by the militant and scientific atheisms respectively. Culture has its own significance and its own life. Religion as part of culture has its own reasons for existence and its own logic. Therefore, religion cannot be reduced to social or psychological factors. Studying religion as culture, therefore, is necessary and respectable. Second, the cultural approach makes religious research wide reaching and consequently academically rewarding. Scholars of both religious research and other disciplines can now write and publish about religion and its related aspects of culture and society, such as the arts, philosophy, literature, education, politics, archeology, and science. The topics are indeed limitless, and the new book series and new journals provided outlets for such scholarly studies. The effervescence of cultural discourses of religion in effect pushes leftist ideologues to the margins, for the stifled reiteration of atheism and antireligious position, still backed by certain Party and government officials, appeals to few people in the market of ideas.

During this period, some scholars became openly sympathetic to religion in general or to a particular religion. The phenomenon of cultural Christians (*Wenhua Jidutu*) is the most interesting development in this regard. In the past, Chinese intellectuals as a whole were most resistant to and critical of Christianity, which was perceived as a foreign religion and a means of Western colonialism and imperialism (Yip 1980; Lutz 1988). In the 1990s, however, quite a number of Chinese scholars began to publish about Christianity with sympathy and empathy (see ISCCC 1997; Chen and Hsu 1998; An 2000; Zhuo 2001). Some of them have even openly or semi-openly taken

---

[4] Including *A Hundred Questions of Christian Culture, A Hundred Questions of Buddhist Culture, A Hundred of Questions of Islamic Culture*, etc.

[5] Including a variety of scholarly books in humanities and social sciences.

[6] Interestingly, it is under the direct control of the State Religious Affairs Bureau. More interestingly, it has published Christian apologetics and Buddhist sutras.

up the Christian faith. These scholars are commonly based in universities and research academies in the disciplines of philosophy, history, and literature. They have translated Western books of Christian
theology, philosophy and history into Chinese, published books and
articles to discuss various aspects of, or in relation to, Christianity
or Christian culture, and lectured on university campuses to intro-
duce Christianity. It is the cultural approach to religion that has
legitimized such activities in academic settings, for they can claim to
be studying and introducing Western culture, not religion per se.
Because of their prolific publications and enthusiastic promotion of
Christianity, these cultural Christians have been dubbed as China's
Apollos by outside observers (see ISCCC 1997).[7] Amid the culture
fevers, these cultural Christians have stirred up a Christianity fever
among the college-educated urbanites while underground house
churches spread with zeal in the rural areas. Many college students
and intellectuals have been drawn into Christianity initially through
reading the publications of the cultural Christians rather than through
contacts with the church or Christian believers.

   Lately, some people began talking about a comparable phenomenon of cultural Buddhists within academia. Actually, there have been
more Buddhist studies scholars who have been openly sympathetic
or adherent to Buddhism. Although cultural Christians and cultural
Buddhists are not necessarily converted religious believers, precisely
because of their nonbeliever status they are often considered in a
better position to speak positively, and critically as well, about religion. They can, and do, claim academic neutrality and objectivity
when they talk about positive contributions of religions to social stability and morality. Religious leaders appreciate such expressions. On
the other hand, however, some of these scholars have also advocated
reformation in theology and religious organizations, which is not
always pleasing to religious leaders.

   Lü Daji, a scholar at the Chinese Academy of Social Sciences
who exemplified the shift of approach to religion, says,

> In reviewing the path of scholarship on religious research since 1949
> we may say this: there was no other theory or concept but 'religion

---

[7] According to the book of Acts (18:24–28) in the New Testament, Apollos is a
Jewish teacher and follower of John the Baptist, but became an enthusiastic and
effective preacher of the Christian gospel before his Christian baptism.

is reactionary politics' that was more fettering to scholars of religious research; and there has been no other theory or concept but 'religion is culture' that is more liberating to scholars of religious research. (quoted in He 2000: 85)

Defining Religion: From the Marxist to the Scientific

Religious research in China has changed from virtual nonexistence from the 1950s to the 1970s to flourishing in the 1990s. Moreover, the predominant perspective in the scholarship has clearly shifted from antagonistic atheism up to the early 1980s to a more objective and consequently affirmative understanding in the 1990s. This dramatic shift crystallized in the efforts to define and redefine religion by Lü Daji (1989, 1998), who has become one of the most respected theorists of religious research in China.

During the 'opium war' debate in the early 1980s, as described earlier, the leftist camp was based primarily in Beijing at the Institute for the Study of World Religions (ISWR) at the Chinese Academy of Social Sciences, and the liberal camp was loosely clustered in Shanghai, although there were liberals in the North and leftists in the South as well. Lü Daji has been a research fellow at the ISWR since it became functional in the late 1970s. He was one of the major representatives of the Northern leftist camp, who followed Lenin's emphasis that the opium statement was the cornerstone of the Marxist view of religion. By the end of the 1980s, however, Lü publicly moved away from that position. Still insisting on following the line of Marxism, Lü took a statement of Engels as the key to define religion. Engels, the cofounder of Marxism, says in *Anti-Dühring* (1877), "All religion . . . is nothing but the illusory reflection in men's minds of those external forces which control their daily life, a reflection in which the terrestrial forces assume the form of supernatural forces" (1939: 353). Following this line but expanded to include elements from Durkheim and other scholars, Lü offered this definition:

> Religion is a kind of social consciousness, an illusory reflection in people's minds of the external forces which control their daily life, a reflection in which terrestrial forces assume the form of superhuman and supernatural forces, and the consequent believing and worshipping behaviors toward such forces; it is the normalized socio-cultural system that synthesizes this consciousness and these behaviors. (Lü 1980: 80–81)

This is clearly an atheist definition for it presumes gods being illusory. But it has also clearly moved away from Leninist radicalism.
His book, *A General Theory of Religious Studies* (1989), was widely praised
by scholars of religious research and won an award.

About a decade later, Lü (1998: 74–75) has further discredited
Engels' statement. First, Lü said that the statement was a value judgment, biased by a strong atheist position, thus unacceptable as a
scientific definition. The scientific definition should be value-neutral
or value-free, and should not negate at the onset the existence of
god or gods. Second, this statement was only about the notion of
god, not about the whole religion, which should include the social
organization as well as the religious ideas. Therefore, a new definition
of religion was formulated:

> Religion is a kind of social consciousness regarding superhuman and
> supernatural forces, and its consequent believing and worshipping behav-
> iors toward such forces; it is the normalized and institutionalized socio-
> cultural system that synthesizes this consciousness and the behaviors.
> (Lü 1998: 81)

By then, Lü did not insist that this was a Marxist definition. Instead,
he stated that this was a scientific definition with reference to various theories of religion, including both Marxist and non-Marxist
ones. More important, by then it did not matter anymore whether
or not the definition was Marxist. He contended, "we should not
indiscreetly negate a view or blindly accept a stand" (1998: 81). He
even expressed appreciation of theism for its liberating effects to
primitive people (1998: 88), which had become a shared view among
most scholars of religious research. Obviously, this new definition of
religion and the corresponding new attitude have come a long way.
What is more interesting, instead of being reprimanded by the authorities for his open departure from Marxist doctrines, Lü's definition
has been widely praised by scholars of religious research for its
scientific nature and liberating effect.

Factors for the Dramatic Shift

The most important factor for the dramatic shift of perspectives of
religious research in China is the desecularizing reality. In 1982,
Document No. 19 acknowledged the persistence of religions, yet con-
currently claimed a partial victory for the proportional reduction of

believers in the population, and confidently proclaimed the eventual victory of atheism. As soon as the suppressive policy relaxed, however, religious revivals burst through the vast land. A report based on a government census of religions provides the following statistics (Li 1999): Catholics grew from 2.3 million in the early 1950s to 3 million in 1982, to 4 million by the end of 1995. Protestants grew from 0.7 million in the early 1950s to 3 million in 1982, and to over 10 million by the end of 1995. The Muslim ethnic minority population more than tripled from 5 million in the 1950s to 18 million. Buddhist and Daoist believers cannot be enumerated due to the lack of a membership system but seem to have increased in multitude as well.

If these numbers seem extraordinary, the reality is even more astonishing. Every scholar of religious research in China and overseas China watcher believes that the estimates published by the Chinese government are severe undercounts (Overmyer 2003). For instance, there could be as many as 80 million Protestants by the mid-1990s (Chao and Chong 1997). While the Communist Party has failed to reduce the number of religious believers in reality, some officials seem to have taken comfort in reducing the numbers at least in the official records.[8] However, first cannot be wrapped in paper. The reality cries for proper recognition and serious understanding. Whereas officials may be reluctant to face the challenge of the reality due to a belief that their political fortune is at stake, some scholars in academia have made the effort to reveal and reflect upon the desecularizing reality. When this is done in a proper tone, and at the right moment, it can be rewarding for their academic career. Religious believers and those prospective converts are eager consumers, thus books, journals and magazines on various religions are popular. Religious research scholars, once despised by other scholars for their obscure scholarship far removed from reality, have now won respect,

---

[8] Ye Xiaowen, the Head of the State Religious Affairs Bureau, in a speech to the Chinese Communist Party Central School in 1996, acknowledged problems of receiving inaccurate counts of religious believers. A major problem is because of this rule of the Chinese political game: the numbers come from the cadres, and the cadres come from the numbers. More exactly, Ye says, regarding religion, it is "the negative numbers come from the cadres, and the cadres come from the negative numbers" (2000: 9). In other words, local officials who report negative growth of religious believers are more likely to get promoted, consequently there has been the chronic problem of serious undercounts of religious believers.

sometimes even celebrity stardom, among intellectuals as well as ordinary religious believers. Obviously, the desecularizing reality provides
social grounds for the change of perspectives in religious research.

The possibility of academic rewards for serious scholarship leads
to the other important factor for the paradigm shift, namely, the
relaxed political climate for scholarly research. Although Chinese
academia today is not completely free from political restrictions, the
free space of scholarship has been significantly enlarged. Opposing
views among scholars in various disciplines have become normal.
Despite periodical purges and repressions of the most outspoken dissenters against the official positions of the CCP, disagreements on
government policies, and their underpinning theories as well, have
become common among scholars as well as the masses. Scholars are
usually left alone to perform academic research and publish scholarly writings as long as there are no open and direct criticisms of
certain government leaders and policies. Moreover, ironically, a
scholar who got singled out by the authorities for a reprimand almost
always gained more respect both in academia and by the public.

Although the dramatic shift of religious research scholarship in
China has developed quite independently with its own internal dynamics, the change has also been facilitated by international exchanges.
Since the early 1980s, some scholars have made tremendous efforts
to translate Western classics into Chinese and publish them in China.
The most influential translation series in religious research is Religion
and the World published by Sichuan People's Press under the editorship of Professor He Guanghu, a highly respected scholar previously at the ISWR before joining the faculty of the People's University
of China. Another highly influential translation series is the Daofeng
collection of Christian thought published by the Daofeng Press in
Hong Kong under the editorship of Dr. Liu Xiaofeng, who has
become a star pursued by many young intellectuals and college students. These and other translated classics have inspired ideas, concepts, and theories for the dramatic shift of perspectives. Meanwhile,
some Western scholars have visited China, and many Chinese scholars have spent time in North America and Europe. Some Western
scholars and foundations have also provided resources for cooperative research projects inside China. These international exchanges
have helped Chinese scholars engage with Western scholars, consequently helping to expand the horizons of religious research scholarship in China.

By the late 1990s, religious research became a solidly established discipline with a significant accumulation of scholarly works and networks. Nationally, about 500 people were believed capable of doing serious research and scholarly writing about religion (Wu 1998). Additionally, several prestigious universities have established departments of religious studies. In 2000, there were over 60 institutes focusing on religious research and over 60 journals on or of religion. In the last five years of the twentieth century, a total of over a thousand books on religion had been published, and over 100 articles on religion were published every year. The number of such publications is increasing (Cao 2001). Overall, given the critical mass of scholars, outlets for publications, and networks, religious research has become a self-sustaining discipline. Such a status of the discipline, backed by the significant level of academic freedom, has made it possible to theorize independently without much fear of political ramifications and the consequent administrative reprimands.

Dancing Under the Shadow of Shackles

The discipline of religious research in China has become lively and interesting. Mainstream scholars have gained considerable freedom and shown significant creativity. They are dancing with many new ideas. However, they are still dancing under the shadow of shackles. This can be seen clearly in the uneven development of different subfields within the discipline. Two contrasts are noticeable: the uneven development of Buddhist studies versus Christian studies, and the uneven development of historical studies versus contemporary studies.

Publications and conferences in Buddhist studies far exceed Christian studies. Over 1000 books on Buddhism were published between 1979 and 1998 (Wu 1998: 30), whereas less than 200 books appeared on Christianity, the majority of which were translations of Western works (Wu 1998: 16). The very few historical studies of Christianity in China, especially those which appeared in the early 1980s (e.g., Gu 1981, 1985), tended to stress the imperialistic nature of Christian missions. In the 1990s, historical studies of pre-1949 Christian universities offered more objective and balanced evaluations (see Shen and Zhu 1998).

Meanwhile, over 60 conferences specifically on Buddhism took place from 1980 to 1988; also there were many other conferences

with Buddhism as one of the major subjects in discussion (Huang
2000: 251). In 2000 alone, ten conferences on Buddhism were held
covering topics ranging from Buddhist Arts, Tiantai and Chan Sects,
Mi-Le Culture, 120 Birthday Commemoration of Master Hong Yi,
to the mutual adaptation of Buddhism and socialist society. By comparison, conferences on Christianity have been fewer and have often
encountered difficulties in obtaining permission from the authorities.

Two reasons account for this contrast between Buddhist studies
and Christian studies. First, there are more historical and textual
materials of Buddhism available to China's scholars than those of
Christianity, so it is easier to research and write about Buddhism.
Second, the political risk in publishing about Buddhism is less than
about Christianity. A book or article on Christianity is more likely
to be censored or banned from publication than one on Buddhism.
Certain persons, events, and issues regarding Chinese Christianity
are still off limits for open discussion or publication. This is a reflection
of the skewed policies of the CCP toward different religions, which
deserves a focused analysis, but is beyond the scope of this chapter.
It will suffice to say here that some leaders in the CCP and the government tend to favor Buddhism (and Daoism) as a Chinese native
religion over Christianity as a foreign religion, hence wish to impede
the rapid growth of Christianity.

The lack of studies of contemporary religions in Chinese society
is another indication of the shackles. The majority of publications
are historical studies, whether on Buddhism, Christianity, or any
other religion. Empirical research on contemporary religions is
extremely rare. Several reasons may account for this. First, availability
of historical materials is far more abundant than contemporary data.
Second, there is a greater political risk in discussing issues of contemporary religions. This is the greatest obstacle (Wu 1998: 39–40).
Contemporary religious phenomena are often politically sensitive due
to their direct association with social stability and government policy. The research offices of the CCP and the government have conducted investigative studies of contemporary religions for policy-making
purposes. Occasionally, these studies were contracted out to academic institutes. But the authorities clearly prefer issuing internal reports
to publishing the findings in journals or books. In cases where publication is permitted, it is closely scrutinized; interesting information
is often taken out from such publications. In addition to political
risks, scholars are also discouraged by such publication limits, for
the academic principle in China is the same—publish or perish.

In 1999, the Chinese government officially banned Falun Gong and other qigong groups, along with over a dozen heretical sects of Christian background. They were labeled as evil cults that endanger the health of the masses and disturb the stability of the society. Responding to this anti-cult political campaign, many scholars of religious research have shied away from speaking against the specific Chinese cults; instead they have danced around the issues by publishing books and articles about cults or new religious movements in the West (e.g., Dai 1999; Luo 2002). A few scholars have argued tacitly that the natural enemy of cults is conventional religions, so the solution is to allow the growth of those religions (e.g., Jiang and He 2000). Meanwhile, some scholars and universities have seized this opportunity to call for allocating more resources for the study of contemporary religious phenomena. This appeal seems to be receiving its due attention from government officials as well as scholars. Contemporary Western books in the sociology of religion are being translated and published in China. Some scholars have started to gather empirical data systematically. A symposium was held in October 2003 in Beijing focusing on the methodological issues surrounding the study religions in China today. In July 2004, several Western sociologists of religion taught a Summer Institute for the Scientific Study of Religion in Beijing.

However, there are important obstacles for studying contemporary religion in China. One significant obstacle is the lack of a sophisticated methodology. Most religious research scholars in China today migrated from other disciplines of the humanities, especially philosophy, literature, and history. They commonly lack training in social scientific methodology. Meanwhile, few social scientists are interested in religious research; even if some are interested, they lack the necessary knowledge of religion to conduct religious research. Relatedly important, social scientific research projects of contemporary religion usually require larger funding, and such funding is very scarce and extremely difficult to obtain in China. Religious research scholars in China do seem eager to learn sociological methods and to find international collaborators.

Despite such difficulties and uneven developments, the relationship between academia and the government on religion has become more interactive. While the Party and the government often set limits for academic research, scholars often test the limits and push to expand the boundaries. Some research projects have even made evident impacts on religious policies. One example is the research team at the Shanghai Academy of Social Sciences, which published their empirical research findings and a rereading of Marxist works in the book *Religious Problems in the Era of Socialist China* (Luo 1987). It argues that religion and socialist society can be compatible, and they should adapt or accommodate to each other. The book immediately stirred up debates: some ideologues wrote in direct opposition on the basis of atheism, but more scholars spoke in favor or offered support (see Wei 2000; Ng 2000). Eventually, in 1993, the authorities officially adopted the language of mutual adaptation, although with its own twists in the policy application to guide religions to adapt actively to socialist society.

The ideological core of CCP remains atheistic and anti-religious, as continuously expressed by Ye Xiaowen, the tsar of religious affairs: "we always hope to effect a gradual weakening of the influence of religion" (2000:5). However, religious research scholars decreasingly follow the Party line. In the current sociopolitical contexts, Chinese scholars can be dancing with many new ideas; only the shadow of shackles keeps most of them self-restrained from directly challenging established religious policies.

Conclusion

Religious research in China has developed from nonexistence to a growing, self-sustaining discipline. The predominant perspective has shifted away from the completely anti-religious, atheist position to the more objective, scientific approach. Between 1949 and 1979, religious research was only to serve atheist propaganda. The opium war debate about the nature of religion in the early 1980s gave birth to the discipline, and the culture fevers since the late 1980s significantly expanded the horizons of the scholarship. Despite repressive policies toward religion and restrictive policies toward academia, religious research has become increasingly autonomous and responsive to the desecularizing reality. By the late 1990s, Marxist dogmatism has evidently given way to scientific principles, which require neutrality and objectivity, thus making it possible to affirm both the positive and the negative functions of religion.

The dramatic change of religious research in China has developed independently with its own internal dynamics. But international scholarly exchanges have evidently facilitated the change by providing ideas, theories, collegial support, and material resources. In the era of increasing globalization, religious research in China is poised to expand and destined to merge into the global streams of religious scholarship. Given continuous evolvements without sudden disruptions, religious research in China is likely to unveil new empirical findings and to engender further theoretical development in the sociology of religion within and beyond its borders.

References

An, Ximeng. 2000. "Wenhua jidutu shi shenme ren?" ["What are the Cultural Christians?"], *Sijie zongjiao wenhua* [*World Religious Culture*] (Beijing) 2000: 36–7.

Bates, M. Searle. 1968. "Churches and Christians in China, 1950–1967." *Pacific Affairs* 41: 199–213.

Cao, Zhongjian, ed. 2001. *1999–2000 zhongguo zongjiao yanjiu nianjian* [*Annual of Religious Research, 1999–2000*]. Beijing: Religious Culture Press.

Chao, Jonathan and Rosanna Chong. 1997. D*angdai zhongguojidujiao fazhanshi: 1949–1997* [*A History of Christianity in Socialist China, 1949–1997*]. Taipei: China Ministries International Publishing.

Chen, Cunfu and Edwin Hsu. 1998. "Wenhua jidutu xianxiang de zonglan yu fansi" ["An Overview and Reflection on the Phenomenon of Cultural Christians"]. *Regent Journal* 1998: 2–3.

Chen, Kenneth. 1965. "Chinese Communist Attitudes towards Buddhism in Chinese History." *China Quarterly* 22: 14–30.

Dai, Kangsheng, ed. 1999. *Dangdai xinxing zongjiao* [*Contemporary New Religions*]. Beijing: Dongfang Press.

Dai, Kangsheng. 2001. "Xin zhongguo zongjiao yanjiu 50 nian" ["50 Years of Religious Research in New China"]. Pp. 38–57 in *Annual of Religious Research in China, 1999–2000*, edited by Cao Zhongjian. Beijing: Religious Culture Press.

Engels, Friedrich. 1939. *Herr Eugen Dühring's Revolution in Science (anti-Dühring)*. New York: International Publishers.

Fang, Litian. 1988. *Zhongguo fojiao yu chuantong wenhua* [*Chinese Buddhism and Traditional Culture*]. Shanghai: Shanghai People's Press.

FitzGerald, C. P. 1967. "Religion and China's Cultural Revolution." *Pacific Affairs* 40:124–29.

Gao, Shining. 2000. "Zongjiaoxue jichu lilun yanjiu licheng" ["Historical Development of the Basic Theoretical Research in Religious Studies"]. Pp. 73–8 in *Annual of Religious Research in China, 1997–1998*, edited by Cao Zhongjian. Beijing: Religious Culture Press.

Ge, Zhaoguang. 1987. *Daojiao yu zhongguo wenhua* [*Daoism and Chinese Culture*]. Shanghai: Shanghai People's Press.

Gu, Changsheng. 1981. *Chuanjiaoshi yu jindai zhongguo* [*Missionaries and Modern China*]. Shanghai: Shanghai People's Press.

———. 1985. *Cong malixun do situlaideng* [*From Matteo Ricci to Stuart*]. Shanghai: Shanghai People's Press.

Gu, Edward X. 1999. "Cultural Intellectuals and the Politics of Cultural Public Space in Communist China (1979–1989)." *Journal of Asian Studies* 58: 389–431.

He, Guanghu. 2000. "Zhongguo zongjiaoxue lilun yanjiu huigu" ["Theoretical Development of Religious Research in China"]. Pp. 79–91 in *Annual of Religious Research in China, 1997–1998*, edited by Cao Zhongjian. Beijing: Religious Culture Press.

Huang, Lucy Jen. 1971. "The Role of Religion in Communist Chinese Society."
      Asian Survey 11: 693–708.
Huang, Xianian. 1998a. "20 shiji de zhongguo foxue yanjiu" ["Buddhist Studies in
      20th Century China"]. Pp. 95–113 in *Annual of Religious Research in China, 1996*,
      edited by Cao Zhongjian. Beijing: China Social Sciences Press.
————. 1998b. "1949–1964 nian woguo de chanxue yanjiu" ["Chan Buddhist
      Studies in our Country in 1949–1964"]. Pp. 114–36 in *Annual of Religious Research
      in China, 1996*, edited by Cao Zhongjian. Beijing: China Social Sciences Press.
————. 2000. "1997–1998 nian zhongguo dalu foxue huiyi zongshu" ["Buddhist
      Studies Conferences in Mainland China, 1997–1998"]. Pp. 232–61 in *Annual
      of Religious Research in China, 1997–1998*, edited by Cao Zhongjian. Beijing:
      Religious Culture Press.
Hunter, Alan and Kim-Kwong Chan. 1993. *Protestantism in Contemporary China*.
      Cambridge: Cambridge University Press.
ISCCC (Institute for the Study of Christian Culture in Chinese]. 1997. *Wenhua jidutu
      [Cultural Christians]*. Hong Kong: ISCCC.
Jiang, Jinsong and He Bing. 2000. "Zhengtong zongjiao shi xiejiao de tiandi"
      ["Orthodox Religions are the Natural Enemy of Evil Cults"]. *The Religious
      Cultures in the World* (Beijing): 2000: 6–7.
Jiang Wenhan. 1982. *Zongguo gudai jidujiao ji kaifeng youtairen [Christianity in Ancient
      China and Jews of Kaifeng]*. Beijing: Knowledge Press.
Kindopp, Jason and Carol Lee Hamrin, eds. 2004. *God and Caesar in China*. Washington,
      DC: Brookings Institution Press.
Li, Pingye. 1999. "90 niandai zhongguo zongjiao fazhan zhuangkuang baogao" ["A
      Report on the Development of Religion in China in the 1990s"]. *Journal of
      Christian Culture* (Beijing) 1999: 201–22.
Luo, Weihong. 2002. *Shijie xiejiao yu fan xiejiao yanjiu [A Study of Cults and Anti-cults
      in the World]*. Beijing: Religious Culture Press.
Luo, Zhufeng, ed. 1987. *Zhongguo shehuizhuyi shiqi de zongjiao wenti [Religious Problems
      in the Socialist Era of China]*. Shanghai: Shanghai Social Sciences Press.
————, ed. 1988. *Zhongguo dabaikequanshu zongjiao juan [China Encyclopedia, Religion
      Volume]*. Beijing: China Encyclopedia Press.
Luo, Zhufeng, ed. 1991. *Religion under Socialism in China*. Armonk, NY: M.E. Sharpe.
Lutz, Jessie G. 1988. *Chinese Politics and Christian Missions*. Notre Dame, IN: Cross
      Roads Books.
Lü, Daji, ed. 1989. *Zongjiaoxue tonglun [A General Essay on Religious Studies]*. Beijing:
      China Social Sciences Press.
————, ed. 1998. "Zongjiao shi shenme?—zongjiao de benzhi, jiben yaosu, jiqi
      luoji jiegou" ["What is Religion?—The Essence, Elements and Logical Structure
      of Religion"], Pp. 58–91 in *Annual of Religious Research in China, 1996*, edited by
      Cao Zhongjian. Beijing: China Social Sciences Press.
Ma, Tong. 1983. *Zhongguo yisilan jiaopai yu menhuan zhidu shilue [A Brief History of
      Chinese Islamic Denominations and Sects]*. Ningxia: Ningxia People's Press.
MacInnis, Donald. 1975. "The Secular Vision of a New Humanity in People's
      China." *Christian Century* (March 12): 249–53.
————. 1994. *Religion in China Today*. Maryknoll, NY: Orbis Books.
Madsen, Richard. 1998. *China's Catholics*. Berkeley: University of California Press.
Marx, Karl and Friedrich Engels. 1975. *On Religion*. Moscow: Progress Publishers.
Ng, Peter Tze Ming. 2000. "From Ideological Marxism to Moderate Pragmatism,"
      Pp. 405–22 in *China Review 2000*. Hong Kong: Chinese University of Hong
      Kong Press.
Overmyer, Daniel L., ed. 2003. *Religion in China Today*. Cambridge: Cambridge
      University Press.

Qin, Xitai. 1988–1995. *Zhongguo daojiao shi [A History of Daoism]*, 4 vols. Chengdu: Sichuan People's Press.

RAB (Religious Affairs Bureau). 1995. *Xin shiqi zongjiao gongzuo wenxian xuanbian [Collection of Selected Documents on Religious Affairs in the New Period]*. Beijing: Religious Culture Press.

Ren, Jiyu. 1962. *Han tang fojiao sixiang lunji [Collection on Buddhist Thought in Han-Tang]*. Beijing: The People's Press.

———. 1981. *Zongjiao cidian [Dictionary of Religion]*. Shanghai: Shanghai Dictionary Press.

Shen, Dingping and Weifang Zhu. 1998. "Western Missionary Influence on the People's Republic of China." *International Bulletin of Missionary Research* 22: 154–9.

Stark, Rodney and Roger Finke. 2000. *Acts of Faith*. Berkeley: University of California Press.

Strong, S. and J. Strong. 1973. "A Post-Cultural Revolution Look at Buddhism." *China Quarterly* 54: 321–30.

Tang, Yongtong. 1982. *Sui tang fojiao shi gao [Manuscripts of the History of Sui-Tang Buddhism]*. Beijing: Zhonghua Publishing.

Warner, R. Stephen. 1993. "Work in Progress Toward a New Paradigm for the Sociological Study of Religion in the United States." *American Journal of Sociology* 98: 1044–93.

Wei, Dedong. 2000. "Zongjiao yu shehuizhuyi shehui xiang shiying lilun yanjiu huigu" ["A Review of the Theoretical Research on the Compatibility of Religion and Socialist Society"], Pp. 66–72 in *Annual of Religious Research in China, 1997–1998*, edited by Cao Zhongjian. Beijing: Religious Culture Press.

Welch, Holmes. 1969. "Buddhism since the Cultural Revolution." *China Quarterly* 40:127–36.

Wu, Yungui. 1998. "Woguo zongjiaoxue yanjiu xianzhuang yu fazhan qushi" ["The Current Status and Trends of Religious Research in our Country"]. Pp. 3–42 in *Annual of Religious Research in China, 1996*, edited by Cao Zhongjian. Beijing: China Social Sciences Press.

Ye, Xiaowen. 2000. "Dangqian woguo de zongjiao wenti—guanyu zongjiao wuxing de zai tantao" ["Current Issues of Religion in our Country—A Reexamination of the Five Characteristics of Religion"], in *Annual of Religious Research in China, 1997–1998*, edited by Cao Zhongjian, 1–27. Beijing: Religious Culture Press.

Yip, Ka-che. 1980. *Religion, Nationalism, and Chinese Students*. Bellingham: Center for East Asian Studies, Western Washington University.

Yu, Songqing. 1987. *Ming qing bailianjiao yanjiu [A Study of White Lotus Sect in Ming and Qing]*. Chengdu: Sichuan People's Press.

Zhang, Sui. 1986. *Dongzhengjiao he dongzhengjiao zai zhongguo [The Orthodox Church in China]*. Xuelin: Xuelin Press.

Zhang, Li and Liu Jiantang. 1987. *Zhongguo jiao' an shi [A History of Missionary Cases in China]*. Chengdu: Sichuan Academy of Social Sciences Press.

Zhuo, Xinping. 1988. *Zongjiao yu wenhua [Religion and Culture]*. Beijing: The People's Press.

———. 2001. "Discussion on Cultural Christians in China." in *China and Christianity*, edited by Stephen Uhalley, Jr. and Xiaoxin Wu, 283–300. Armonk, NY: M. E. Sharpe.

CHAPTER TWO

THE CROSS FACES THE LOUDSPEAKERS: A VILLAGE CHURCH PERSEVERES UNDER STATE POWER

Jianbo Huang and Fenggang Yang

On a sunny Sunday in winter 2002, hundreds of villagers congregated at a humble church well blended into the surrounding mud-colored houses. Atop the entrance gate stood a tall cross in bright red. Peaceful hymn singing flowed through the windows and filled the air. It was another ordinary Sunday in this remote village in the northwestern Province of Gansu. Shortly after ten o'clock, Elder Liu stood up, walked to the pulpit on the raised platform, and began preaching. His voice was soft and clear in the quiet sanctuary.

Suddenly, a shrill sound pervaded the church. It came from the loudspeakers on top of the Village Committee Office across the street. The secretary of the village branch of the Chinese Communist Party was making announcements to the whole village: A command had come down from the town government—each household must provide two laborers to plant trees on the nearby Guatai Mountain; an oil seller would be coming in the afternoon and anyone who wanted to buy should come to the Village Committee Office. The announcements were repeated several times. Following a brief pause for a minute or so, the loudspeakers began to broadcast earsplitting Qinqiang, the local-style opera known for its high-pitch singing in the local dialect.

The broadcasting drowned out Elder Liu's preaching. However, the soft-spoken preacher continued without a pause, and no congregant appeared to be distracted or disturbed. About half an hour later, when the sermon concluded, the Qinqiang opera also stopped. Then the congregation started singing praises to God joyfully and wholeheartedly.

After the service, we asked people about the intrusive broadcasting. Uncle Fu, a long-time church member, responded with a smile. "We've become used to it. It's been like this for years. Actually, it's become better now than it was a couple of years ago when the

Laoshuji was still around." *Laoshuji* means the 'old secretary' of the Wuzhuang branch of the Chinese Communist Party.

Actually, Wuzhuang Christians have had to get used to the intruding sounds of the loudspeakers, which signify the state power that pervades every corner of the country, even down to this faraway village in remote Gansu Province. Indeed, these village Christians feel genuinely grateful for the improved political condition nowadays. Having lived through the more difficult years of attempted eradication and suppression, they have learned to live in peace without giving up their faith. This chapter describes how the Wuzhuang Christian Church has persevered despite state restrictions and intrusions, just like the red, tall cross atop the church that silently yet sturdily faces the loudspeakers on the roof of the Village Committee Office. The congregation has managed to survive as a government-approved, open church since 1982.

A Brief History of the Wuzhuang Christian Church

Wuzhuang is a remote village in the southeast corner of Gansu bordering Shaanxi Province.[1] From Lanzhou, the capital of Gansu, it takes more than five hours by train to reach the city of Tianshui, and one more hour to get to the village by local train or two more hours by bus through the spiraling mountain roads. It takes about 18 hours by train from Tianshui to Beijing.

However, Wuzhuang is located at the birthplace of Chinese civilization. The village is in the Wei River valley at the foot of Guatai Mountain. Guatai is believed to be the very place where Fuxi, a legendary forefather of the Chinese people, first conceived the eight diagrams (*ba gua*) of yin and yang, which became the foundation of *Yijing* (*I-Ching*) and of many schools of thought. On the top of Guatai Mountain, a Fuxi temple has existed for an innumerable number of years. Fuxi worship has been a folk tradition of the surrounding villages for countless generations.

On the east side of Guatai Mountain, looking down at Wuzhuang, people find that the most eye-catching sign is the tall cross in bright red atop the Christian church near the center of the village. To its

---

[1] Wuzhuang is a pseudonym, meaning the 'Wu Village,' where more than eighty percent of its residents share the Wu surname. Pseudonyms are used for all Wuzhuang residents.

left is the Village Committee Office compound, followed by the Wuzhuang Elementary School. Scattered around these buildings are over five hundred houses spreading out in the valley.

Christianity was first brought to the Tianshui area by British missionaries of the China Inland Mission at the end of the nineteenth century. In 1898, the Wuzhuang Christian Church was formed by over thirty converts. They built their first chapel two years later. By 1920, its membership had grown to nearly 200, and they built a brick building with a large sanctuary. Meanwhile, they helped to spread Christianity to the surrounding villages. By 1949, when the People's Republic of China was founded by the Chinese Communist Party, over 1,100 Christians worshipped at eleven village churches in the valley, including more than 200 believers in Wuzhuang.

In the 1950s and 1960s, waves of political campaigns washed over Wuzhuang again and again. In 1958, the church buildings were confiscated and occupied by the village government as its office and as the elementary school. While many Christians stopped worship activities, some believers continued to gather at homes discreetly. In 1962, as the political climate became less tense, about 40 members came together and began Sunday worship services at the then elementary school. The building was used by the school on weekdays and by the church on Sundays. Beginning in spring 1964, however, all religious activities were banned in the whole of Tianshui Prefecture, as well as in many other parts of the country. During the Cultural Revolution (1966–1976), several Wuzhuang Christian leaders were persecuted as 'anti-revolutionaries' (*fan geming*), 'landlords' (*dizhu*), or 'wealthy peasants' (*funong*). Several people were jailed, including Deacon Wu Ende, who was in prison from 1966 to 1973.

In the 1970s, Wuzhuang Christians clandestinely gathered at homes in the night. In summer 1975, two young men got baptized in the Wei River behind the village, the first baptisms in two decades. Many more people followed in their footsteps in the next few years. After secretly celebrating Christmas in 1978, they began Sunday worship services in daytime, semi-openly, although still illegally. By 1980, the number of Christians in Wuzhuang reached 300. In 1982, Wuzhuang Christians succeeded in getting back one of three church properties, the one that had been used as the Village Committee Office.[2]

---

[2] A new Village Committee Office compound was then erected across from the church; on top of its room, four loudspeakers were installed.

Wuzhuang Christianity began a period of rapid growth. By 2000, there were at least a thousand Christians in Wuzhuang, about a third of the total village population of 3,129.

The post-1949 history of Christianity in Wuzhuang is quite common in the People's Republic of China. After the establishment of the People's Republic of China, the Chinese Communist Party regarded foreign missionaries as part of Western imperialism and drove them out. Chinese Protestants were coerced to participate in the so-called Three-Self (self-administration, self-support, and self-propagation) Patriotic Movement. The goal of this movement was to cut ties completely with Christian organizations in the West. Noncompliant leaders were put into jails or labor camps. Beginning in 1957, denominational or sectarian systems were also abolished, and all Protestants had to attend union services under the leadership of the Three-Self Patriotic Movement (TSPM) Committee. The number of worshippers dropped. Many churches were subsequently closed. When the Cultural Revolution broke out in 1966, all religions were banned, and eradication measures were imposed. Secretly keeping a Bible was a crime. The remaining believers had to make public renunciations or were sent to jails or labor camps. However, some Christians who stopped attending the union services began to meet underground in the late 1950s. In the 1970s, while staying underground, Christianity began reviving in many parts of the country, especially in rural areas (Hunter and Chan 1993; Chao and Chong 1997; Leung 1999; Lambert 1999; Aikman 2003).

Under the new leadership of Deng Xiaoping, the Chinese Communist Party (CCP) set a new course to modernize China. It launched 'economic reforms and opening-up' policies at the end of year 1978. In order to rally the people for the central task of economic development, the pragmatic leadership began to loosen control over various aspects of social life, including religious life. A Protestant church in Ningbo City, Zhejiang Province, first reopened for religious services on 8 April 1979. Following this, churches began to re-open throughout the country. The national TSPM Committee was revitalized in 1980. Since then, the national and local TSPM committees have facilitated the reopening of many churches. In 1982, the TSPM committee of the Beidao District of the Tianshui Prefecture was established. In the same year, it helped the Wuzhuang Church to get back one of its properties. Since then, Wuzhuang Church has been an open church under the supervision of the TSPM Committee of Beidao District of Tianshui Prefecture. Nationwide, many Christians have refused to join the TSPM organization because they regard it as a means of government control. In the Tianshui area, however, as far as we know, underground Christians have not been many, or they were not as active and visible as in some other parts of the country.

The Village Church in the Reform Era

In 1982, religious toleration was formally reinstated in a new edict of the CCP—"The Basic Viewpoint and Policy on the Religious Affairs during the Socialist Period of Our Country"—which has become known as 'Document No. 19.' This central document has served as the basis for the religious policy since then. 'Document No. 19' acknowledges that religion will exist for a long time before eventually withering away and that religious believers should be rallied for the central task of economic construction. It states that freedom of religious belief should be guaranteed as long as the believers love the country, support CCP rule, and observe the socialist laws. Since 1982, CCP and the government have issued a number of circulars and installed various formal ordinances and administrative orders (Potter 2003). However, the basic policy remains the same—religious tolerance with restrictions.

The authorities try to control religion by allowing only five religions (Buddhism, Daoism, Islam, Protestantism, and Catholicism); by conferring legal status only to those churches, temples, and mosques under the supervision of government-sanctioned 'patriotic' religious organizations; and by certifying clergy. For Protestant Christians, the Protestant Three-Self Patriotic Movement Committee and the China Christian Council, whose personnel are shared, are the only legally recognized Protestant organizations. Any evangelist who is not accepted by the TSPM committee and certified by the government's Religious Affairs Bureau should not conduct religious services or organize religious activities. Moreover, no propagation of religion outside of approved religious premises is allowed. Violators of these regulations may face punishments from warnings and fines to prison terms.

Government-approved churches have to operate within the limits imposed by the government in exchange for being able to carry out open religious services. Many evangelical Christians do not accept the restriction on evangelism within the walls of the church and do

not want to be supervised by the TSPM committee, whose top leaders have been regarded as holding liberal theological positions (Chao
and Chong 1997). These Christians have mostly stayed underground
in spite of risking periodic raids and crackdowns by the RAB and
police. Meanwhile, other Christians find it beneficial to stay aboveground in spite of the restrictions. They find they can still manage
to hold most religious services satisfactorily. Moreover, without much
proselytizing effort beyond the religious premises, it seems that as
long as the church doors remain open, many people have found
their own way to the church. In fact, some seekers have come to
the church, knocked at the closed doors, and demanded to be taught
about the faith (Lambert 1999: 156; Yang *forthcoming*). This is happening in part because while public demand for religion has been
increasingly awakened during the market transition process, religious
organizations have been in short supply (Yang 2004). The Wuzhuang
Church has remained aboveground and has grown despite regula-
tory restrictions and state intrusions. It has dealt with regulations
and intrusions tacitly and creatively.

Resorting to State Regulation and Rhetoric to Protect Church Interests

Reform-era changes in inland provinces have lagged behind coastal
provinces. In the sphere of religious affairs, Gansu, like many inland
provinces, has been late in implementing the new policy of limited
tolerance toward religion. In the coastal provinces, churches began
to reopen in 1979. However, the Wuzhuang Church could not get
back any of the church buildings until three years later. After the
CCP circulated 'Document No. 19' in 1982, Wuzhuang Christians
took the circular to the local government bureaus and petitioned to
get the buildings back. Only after showing this CCP document did
the local government officials consent. In the process, the Beidao
District TSPM Committee mediated between the government bureaus
and Wuzhuang Christians, eventually reaching a compromise—return-
ing one of the three church properties.

   In the process of petitioning to reopen the church, besides lever-
aging with 'Document No. 19,' Wuzhuang Christians had to offer
persuasive justifications pleasing to the authorities. Above all, they
had to acknowledge repeatedly the legitimate authority of the Chinese
Communist Party. In their oral and written presentations, church
leaders had to praise the greatness of the past and present CCP
leadership, the glory of the CCP history, and the correctness of the

current CCP policies. Moreover, they have had to recite the officially imposed slogan "love our country, love our religion" (*ai guo ai jiao*), with 'love our country' preceding 'love our religion.' Underground Christians reject this official slogan as idolizing the state and regard TSMP church leaders as having betrayed the Lord Christ who should be the ultimate authority. In reality, many TSMP leaders do not feel comfortable singing such praises to the CCP and the state. Several leaders of the Wuzhuang Church expressed this discomfort. For the TSPM church leaders, repeating the slogan "love our country, love our religion" was like chanting a political mantra, which was for the simple purpose of avoiding political troubles while getting things going.

Wuzhuang Christians celebrated the return and reopening of the church with great joy. After 18 years (1964–1982) of prohibition and persecution, they rejoiced about a spiritual triumph given by God. In remarking on this victory, Wuzhuang Christians liked to recite these biblical verses: "God's thoughts are higher than man's thoughts, and His ways higher than man's ways" (Isaiah 55:9); "The king's heart is a stream of water in the hand of the Lord; He turns it wherever He will" (Proverbs 21:2). They have shown respect to the state power, but put their faith in the almighty God.

Adopting the Discourse of Anti-Imperialism

Wuzhuang Christians do not find all patriotic rhetoric difficult to say. Besides submission to the CCP and the state, patriotism in the official discourse also includes anti-imperialism. Wuzhuang Christians have had little difficulty about this. In petitioning for the return of their church buildings, the leaders handed to the authorities a copy of the church history as told by Elder Wu Shengrong, in which were recorded patriotic stories of the Wuzhuang Church in the 1920s.

> It was during the time after the sanctuary was completed in June of 1920, and before my father Wu Buyi [one of four founders of the church] passed away. A British missionary, Li Chunlei [the missionary's Chinese name], offered a donation of 200 *liang* of silver, and asked us to give the deed to the China Inland Mission. At that time, our Elder Wu Buyi realized that it was the imperialists' trick to control our church. We firmly refused it, so that their planned plot failed. That was probably the first case of all the churches [in this area] in which a foreign swindle effort was of no avail. Li Chunlei was shocked and ashamed, saying that it was the first time he was in this kind of situation since he came to China.

The description of this incident was well liked by the TSMP and CCP authorities, for it was later included in the official publications, *History of Christianity in Tianshui* and *History of Christianity in Gansu Province*, as an example of Chinese believers' patriotism in their struggles against Western missionaries.

That incident was the precursor of the Christian Independence Movement (*jidujiao zili yundong*), which spread throughout China in the second quarter of the twentieth century. The Wuzhuang Church History continues:

> In the year 1927, when the National Revolutionary Movement was at its climax, Brother Tong Lin-ge of Tianshui initiated the independence movement of the Chinese churches from the control of Western missionaries. He called Chinese believers to establish Chinese indigenous churches with four measures: Self-governing, self-supporting, self-evangelizing, and self-standing (*zili*, independence). So our village church became the 'Independent Christian Church of China' and formally cut off all ties with foreign missionaries. The imperialists' control of our church passed into history. At that time, Elder Wu Jietian went to Tianshui City and spent 40 *liang* of silver to have a gilt board made, on which was inscribed "Independent Christian Church of China," with signatures of the four founders—Wu Buyi, Wu Rongyi, Wu Farong, and Wu Jizhi. We held a grand ceremony, hanging up the gilt board and celebrating this magnificent feat. . . . In order to make the church sustainable on its own, Elder Wu Buyi also selected three young people—Wu Jietian, Wu Yongfu, and Wu Zhaofan—as Elders. They replaced the aged Elders to take care of this house of God.

The historical development of the Wuzhuang church is doubtlessly factual. It shows that Wuzhuang Christians have been very conscious of what the authorities like to hear, and have adopted the discourse of anti-imperialism to highlight their patriotic history. These are assets they have fully exploited to secure peace with the authorities.

In China today, the authorities treat Protestant and Catholic Christians with greater suspicion than other religious believers in regard to their political loyalty. Christians are still referred to as believers of a 'foreign religion.' After the Tiananmen Square democracy movement in 1989 and the collapse of the Soviet regime in the early 1990s, the Chinese communist authorities adopted strict measures against foreign hostile forces that seek to 'peacefully subvert the socialist system.' The significant role of the Catholic Church in the collapse of communist Poland has been frequently cited by Chinese officials in expressing their concern about Christians becoming a political force threatening to the regime. In 1991, the CCP circulated *Document*

No. 6—"A Further Notice to Better Deal with Religious Affairs." It declares that China faces two kinds of political threats related to religion. First, "overseas enemy forces have always been using religion as an important tool for their strategic goal of 'peaceful subversion,' infiltrating China and causing damage to our country." Second, "the separatists are also making use of religion, attacking the leadership of the Party and the socialist system, threatening the unity of the country and harmony among the ethnic groups." While Tibetan Buddhism and Uygur Islam are the references for the second threat, Protestantism and Catholicism are the focus of the first threat. Anti-infiltration has become a major concern of the authorities in regard to Christianity. Within this social and political context, to ensure continuous legal existence, Christian leaders at the government-approved churches must repeatedly reiterate their patriotism and political loyalty to the Chinese Communist Party.

"Giving to Caesar What Is Caesar's"

Adopting the patriotic discourse is not a temporary tactic on the part of Christians, but a permanent adjustment under CCP rule. Besides the anti-imperialist history, Wuzhuang Christians also stress that they do love the Chinese nation and are good citizens. They would quote what Jesus said, "give to Caesar what is Caesar's, and to God what is God's" (Matthew 22:21). An often preached message to the congregation is "all those who believe in the Lord are obedient to the laws and regulations." The current leader Elder Liu Guizhu said:

> The authorities often hold meetings to emphasize the importance of 'loving our country and loving our religion.' But as I see it, these meetings are nothing but formality and superficiality. In fact, if a person really believes in the Lord, knows God, and loves God, naturally he wouldn't do anything unlawful.

Uncle Fu, the longtime member, spoke in agreement:

> No matter whether it's turning in the public grain [a form of tax in rural China], or donating clothes and money to areas stricken by natural disasters, I can say that every time it was the [Christian] believers who were most cooperative and active. I have never heard of a single believer refusing to turn in the public grain.

Indeed, the accountant of the Wuzhuang Village Committee confirmed this: "These Jesus believers are all honest, good fellows, and really easy to deal with." Of course, Wuzhuang Christians are not exceptional in this regard. This pattern of civic obedience and social charity among Christians has been observed and reported by several studies published in China (Xu and Li 1991; Jing 1995; Wang 1987).

However, obedience to the government does not mean Wuzhuang Christians are willing to abandon their faith. Rather, it means that as long as they are given the space to practice their religion, they will be good citizens. While they are willing to "give Caesar what is Caesar's," they also insist to "give God what is God's." Actually, many Christians think that their faith in God should take precedence over anything else, including the state or nation. As the history of the 1960s and 1970s has demonstrated, Wuzhuang Christians could not accept the government's prohibition of practicing religion. They did break the 'law' during the eradication period when they secretly practiced Christianity.

During the reform era, the CCP has maintained a policy of religious tolerance within limits. However, some ideology-driven measures and officials continue to demand political loyalty above everything else, including religious piety toward God. An example is the authorities' demand to put patriotism before the faith. Li Dezhu, the Deputy Minister of the Central Unified Front Department of the CCP, said, "In regard to religion, when the national and the people's interests are violated, there is but one principle to follow: Stand by the interests of the nation and the people. No ambiguity is permitted on this point. No damage to the state is allowed with whatever excuses" (Li 1996: 13). Such a demand corners Christians in the government-approved churches into an impossible situation, forcing them to choose between compromising the faith and going against the authorities. This is one of the reasons many underground Christians have cited for their staying away from the government as much as possible.

Fortunately, Christians do not have to deal with this problem everyday. In the reform era, it seems that as long as Christian leaders reiterate patriotic slogans and express respect to the CCP authorities at formal occasions, they do not have to take the slogan 'love the state first' by heart or change anything in their religious beliefs and practices. An interesting anecdote is quite telling about the pragmatic solution of the tension between political loyalty and religious piety. The current leader of the Wuzhuang Church has been Liu Guizhu. Liu is the surname, and Guizhu the given name, which in Chinese literally means 'belongs to the Lord.' It is a name that Chinese Christians can immediately recognize for its Christian identity. However, the TSMP Committee of the Beidao District has listed Liu Guozhu as the leader of the Wuzhuang Church. Upon inquiry, the TSMP leader told us that Liu Guozhu is Liu Guizhu, the same person with two names. The pronunciations of Guizhu and Guozhu are close, but the written characters are very different, and the meanings or symbolisms very different as well. Guozhu in Chinese means 'a pillar of the state' or 'a pillar of the nation,' which is a commonly recognizable patriotic name. Among Wuzhuang Christians, Elder Liu is known only as Guizhu, the Christian identity. He also referred to himself as Guizhu when we talked with him. It appears to us that to accommodate the authorities' demand for patriotism, Elder Liu chose to use the patriotic name 'a pillar of the state/nation' for the formal registration of the church and for official occasions. However, at the church and in his daily life, he is the Christian Guizhu. This kind of acknowledgement of political loyalty may seem superficial, but that seems to be enough for government officials.

Keeping State Intrusions at Arm's Length

Government's control over religious organizations has been less effective in the rural areas than cities. Urban churches are more easily and closely supervised by government officials. For example, following official guidelines or hints, ministers at the churches in Tianshui City have avoided preaching on certain topics. Pastor Wei of the Beidao Church told us:

> There *are* some topics that are not suitable to talk about at the present. The Religious Affairs Bureau has given me hints against topics like the doomsday, the final judgment, and the creation of the world. I should talk about them as little as possible, if at all. But we hold that if it is in the Bible, we should talk about it. I am against the so-called 'construction of theological thinking.' That stuff belongs to the unbelieving type.

The 'construction of theological thinking' is a theological movement promoted by Bishop Ding Guangxun, the chief leader of the TSMP in the reform era. Bishop Ding has spoken on various occasions and published the *Collection of Ding Guangxun* in 1998. His central idea is to make Christianity compatible with the socialist society under Communist rule, which would be achieved by emphasizing the notion of love above anything else. Underground Christians have rejected this idea as giving up faith in Christ. Some aboveground church

leaders have resisted the movement as blurring distinctions between
Christians and non-Christians. Both underground Christians and
aboveground critics say that the importance of 'justification by faith'
should not be compromised for whatever reasons. "Without this core
belief, what kind of Christianity would it be?" Pastor Wei continued:

> Actually we have to do that 'construction of theological thinking' thing
> here. But we just hand some materials to those people in charge.
> That's all. We get pressures from the above. Somebody has reported
> me to the provincial government bureaus. But I'm not afraid of it. I
> was not afraid of that kind of stuff even when I was a young man.
> At worst, I would just quit.

As a young man, Pastor Wei was imprisoned and spent three years
in a 'reform-through-labor camp' in Xinjiang. After the TSMP was
reopened in 1982, Pastor Wei has been the Chairman of the Beidao
District TSPM Committee. While he was determined to resist this
particular ideological movement, his non-cooperation had obviously
generated heavy pressure on him. He has had to get psychologically
prepared to step down if the situation became worse.

In comparison, the leaders of the village church in Wuzhuang
have felt little such pressure. First of all, they really have no position to lose. Their leadership status has been attained very much
through members' trust nourished over a long time. Even if an official
title of Eldership or Deaconship were removed by an order from
above, that would not take away their influence and trust among
the members. Second, the TSMP and government officials have
made infrequent visits to this remote village. Therefore, the indirect
hints or even explicit guidelines of the RAB have made little impact
on the content or mode of the pulpit message delivered at the
Wuzhuang Church.

Nonetheless, Wuzhuang Christians conform as much as possible to
the requirements of the Religious Affairs Bureau and the Three-Self
Patriotic Movement Committee. This manifests itself in many routine
arrangements of church affairs. Here we provide a few examples.

First, acting on the order of the RAB, the TSPM has instructed
the churches to hold regular meetings to study state policies, regulations,
and laws. The Wuzhuang Church has followed the order by holding
a Thursday evening meeting every week. They post the meeting
schedule and intended content at the most visible place on the wall
of the chapel (not the sanctuary), so that when the TSMP or RAB

officials come to inspect they will feel reassured and satisfied. In reality, however, such study sessions have routinely turned into Bible study or testimony-sharing meetings. As a matter of fact, even the study sessions organized by the CCP for CCP members have frequently turned into chatting or gossiping meetings. Therefore, even if the actual contents of the Thursday evening study sessions became known to the officials, the officials are likely to treat it 'with one eye shut.' Some kind of formal compliance to the state requirements seems sufficient to avoid troubles.

Second, the authorities have imposed a 'three fixes' policy. All religious groups must have a 'fixed place' to hold activities. All churches or 'gathering points' must have 'fixed persons' in leadership and membership. And all clergymen must have 'fixed areas' of ministry and cannot conduct religious services in other places without prior approval. The 'three fixes' are to restrict evangelization across administrative borders. Uncle Fu told us:

> If our church people go out to other places to evangelize, if it is within the valley, they don't have to inform the authorities. If they go out of the valley, they have to inform the Beidao District authorities. If they go out of Beidao jurisdiction, they have to inform the Tianshui Municipal authorities. If they go out of Tianshui Prefecture, they have to inform the provincial authorities. Actually it is almost impossible to go beyond the province. The same is true for those missionaries who come to Wuzhuang.

Have there ever been visiting preachers to Wuzhuang? Uncle Fu said:

> Yes, but very few. They were mostly from the valley area. Occasionally the Beidao Church would also send somebody to lead the service, about one or two times a year. That's all.

Elder Liu Guizhu told us that this policy of restricting cross-border evangelists was not all bad. It could help prevent disturbances by heretical sects that have been very actively proselytizing. But Uncle Fu said:

> I think there's nothing good about it. We believers need to communicate with each other in order to grow spiritually. But generally speaking, we don't invite evangelists from other places, for someone [at the Wuzhuang Church] may report us to the authorities and that would get us into trouble.

Apparently, the Wuzhuang Church has observed this regulation even though they do not like it. However, we also learned that Wu Ende, the former deacon who was jailed for six years during the Cultural Revolution, had been traveling around the Tianshui Prefecture to evangelize. He has even traveled to areas in the neighboring provinces of Shaanxi and Ningxia, and as far as to Qinghai and Tibet. When we asked Uncle Fu about what the authorities have done to Wu Ende, he laughed:

> Him? The Three-Self Church can't order him. He is not an elder or deacon now, just a layman. Besides, he goes out with his silver needles to do acupuncture, and evangelizes along the way. The Religious Affairs Bureau can't do anything about him.

Apparently, the state power diminishes over village Christians who do not hold any official title or position and thus cannot be dismissed. Their evangelization cannot be controlled as long as they can keep it low profile without obviously violating the criminal code. In fact, tens of thousands of such nameless evangelists have been active in the vast rural areas since the 1970s. Believers call them 'brothers' and 'sisters,' 'uncles' and 'aunts' (Aikman 2003). These nameless evangelists have led the revivals in rural areas, which have multiplied the number of Christians in China in the last few decades. Wu Ende was just one of them.

Third, the most intrusive act from above to the Wuzhuang Church has been the appointment of an Elder. State regulations require church Elders and Deacons to obtain the approval of the higher level TSMP committee and the RAB. When the Wuzhuang Church was to elect Elders and Deacons in 1996, the Beidao TSMP under the instruction of the Beidao RAB handpicked a Wuzhuang believer, Wu Shenzhao, and appointed him as one of the three Elders. The TSMP and RAB wanted Wu Shenzhao keep an eye over the church and report any violation of regulations. He was used as a means of state control. The Wuzhuang Church acquiesced to the appointment. While the rest of the church leaders and lay members have been careful not to antagonize Wu Shenzhao, they have managed to circumvent his power and influence effectively by distancing themselves from him. Most of the church affairs have been decided by the senior Elder Liu Guizhu. Believers would not go to Wu Shenzhao for anything important to church life. Up to now, Wuzhuang Christians have been able to keep state intrusions at arm's length.

Wuzhuang Christians in the Village Power Structure

While the village church has managed to keep state intrusions from above at arm's length, Wuzhuang Christians have to face fellow villagers day by day. In this ancient village that has a majority of Wu families, clan ties are actually not very strong. The power of the village has been in the hands of the Chinese Communist Party cadres. Although Christians comprise one third of the village population, they have no share in the political power. They have intentionally stayed away from village politics in the hope that this would keep away interference with their religious practice from other villagers. However, their unbending beliefs set off open antagonism by the village Party chief. While their faith gave them the strength to endure silently the Party chief's abuses, the larger political atmosphere for social stability ensured their peaceful existence in the village.

Weak Clan Ties

Although over eighty percent of Wuzhuang residents share the surname Wu, traditional clan bonds or divisions have not been strong in Wuzhuang. Unlike other villages that have been documented by scholars (e.g., Jing 1996), Wuzhuang does not have any clan temple (*ci tang*) or long-term clan association. Actually, the Wu-named villagers do not think that they are descendants of the same ancestor. Therefore, the entry and growth of Christianity in Wuzhang met little resistance by traditional clan forces.

Since its early days, the church has had members with different surnames. Wu-named members and leaders at the church have been the largest proportion, but that is accidental and does not translate into clannish solidarity or division within the church. Actually, the only significant frictions in the history of the church were theological ones between the Calvinist rationalists and the charismatic oriented believers. The former inherited the traditions of the China Inland Mission, while the latter was influenced by the Jesus Family, a Chinese indigenous church that originated in Shandong and spread to this part of the country in the 1930s. Since the reopening in 1982, Wuzhuang Christians have been well united with no significant internal conflicts. This is probably because the Christians have been a weak segment of the village population and have faced constant external threats and pressures.

Powerful CCP Cadres

Without strong clan forces, the CCP authorities retain the actual political power. With a population of over three thousand, Wuzhuang is considered a large village and entitled to have five official positions. The most powerful is the Secretary of the CCP Village Branch (*cun zhishu*), followed by the Chairman of the Village Committee (*cun weihui zhuren*), the Vice Chairman of the Village Committee, the Director of Agricultural Production (*shezhang*), and the Accountant. The villagers are organized into eight Production Brigades (*shengchan dui*). Although about a third of the villagers are Christian, no Christian has ever held one of the five administrative positions, and only one of the current eight brigade leaders is a Christian. The Party Secretary position naturally requires CCP membership, and the CCP Constitution has been clear that CCP members must uphold atheism. CCP membership is not required to serve in other positions, but it is clearly preferred. The village leaders have always been chosen from among the 30 or so CCP members. The Party cadres at the village do not like to share power with Christians. First of all, they are not compatible in ideology. Second, Christians do not smoke or drink, which would make the CCP cadres feel uncomfortable on social occasions or at the dinner table.

However, Wuzhuang Christians have expressed little desire to take any of the official positions. According to church leaders, Christians have been afraid of being corrupted and committing sins against God if they step into the quagmire of power. They have also been afraid of being suspected of having political ambition. Under the current ideological and political conditions, Christians have to show no interest in politics at all to avoid inviting any trouble. They hope that if they pose no threat to others, others would not care about what they do in their private life. The only Christian leader of a Production Brigade told us that he did not want the position. "Nobody wanted it," he said, "there was neither power nor profit in it, only countless odd jobs to do and responsibilities to shoulder." He was approached by the Village Committee after it failed to find any one else. Only after repeated urging and persuasion by the village leaders did he accept the position. His reluctance to enter the village power structure is a means of self protection. Wuzhuang Christians have been content to have a marginalized status in the village power structure.

Antagonism and Assuagement of the Old and New Party Chiefs of the Village

Even though Wuzhuang Christians have tried hard to avoid problems, they have nevertheless stumbled into various troubles. The most difficult ones in the reform era involved the *laoshuji*, the previous Party Secretary of the village. His antagonism toward the church started in the mid-1980s, when he imposed a temple tax on all villagers but Christians refused to comply.

As mentioned before, Wuzhuang is located at the foot of Guatai Mountain, which has been the center of Fuxi worship. From the late 1950s to the early 1980s, the authorities banned it in the name of cleaning up feudal superstitions. In the early 1980s, however, villagers around Guatai Mountain revived Fuxi worship as a practice of traditional culture. The authorities endorsed this folk practice by recognizing the Guatai Mountain Cultural Antiquity Preservation Group (*guataishan wenwu baohu xiaozu*), which has been commonly referred to as the Temple Management Council (*miao guan hui*). The Temple Management Council organizes restoration projects and various collective activities. The local town, county, and prefecture governments even encouraged Fuxi worship by partially financing restoration of temple buildings and sponsoring opera troupes during the annual temple fair (*miao hui*) around the fifteenth day of the first month in the Chinese lunar calendar.

The authorities endorsed and supported folk practices for political and economic considerations. Economically, Fuxi festivals may attract tourists. Politically, Fuxi as the believed progenitor of Chinese civilization is appealing to overseas Chinese as well as intellectuals in China. The authorities hope to use Fuxi festival celebrations to increase solidarity among the Chinese people at home or abroad. Patriotic propaganda is clearly reflected in these slogans in the form of traditional couplets during the 2002 festival: "All teachings of Confucianism, Daoism, and Buddhism can civilize people; All sounds of the bells, drums, and hymns may praise patriotism." For local villagers, however, Fuxi is known not so much as the forefather of Chinese civilization, but as a tutelage god who can heal the sick and turn bad luck into blessings.

The Temple Management Council members come from the two villages closest to Guatai Mountain. Wuzhuang's *laoshuji* served as its president from its establishment in the early 1980s until his death in 1998. In 1984 or 1985, the Council decided to collect a temple tax or fee from every resident of the two villages. Naturally, *laoshuji* was responsible to collect this money in Wuzhuang. To his surprise, Wuzhuang Christians all refused. They told him that as believers of God they would not be involved in any idol worship. Uncle Fu explained to us: "If it were charity for disaster relief, we all would be willing to contribute. But we absolutely will not give any money for idolatry." Indeed, Wuzhuang Christians have noticeably stayed away from the festivals on Guatai Mountain. Their refusal angered *laoshuji*. He took it as a sign of the absence of submission to his power as the Party Secretary. He also felt a loss of face in front of his fellow Council members. In the following years, instead of collecting a separate temple tax from each household, *laoshuji* ordered it to be lumped together with other taxes and fees. Because there were so many items of taxes and fees without clear explanations, villagers commonly could not tell which item was for what purpose. Christians suspected that the lump sum taxes might include the temple tax, but they never could confirm it, thus they did not confront *laoshuji* regarding it. The only thing they could do was to pray to God to stop the whole Fuxi worship thing.

After the incident of tax resistance, *laoshuji* became openly antagonistic to Wuzhuang Christians. He intentionally and regularly turned on the loudspeakers on the roof of the Village Committee Office when the church was holding a worship service or some other gathering. He would broadcast revolutionary songs or Qinqiang opera in the highest possible volume. The loudspeakers became so annoying that a non-Christian young man threw some bricks at the loudspeakers. *Laoshuji* immediately ordered several people to take him to the Village Committee Office, and they beat him badly. The Christians simply kept quiet about the very intrusive loudspeakers.

In 1995, as church membership increased, the Wuzhuang Church renovated and enlarged the sanctuary, added a chapel, and replaced the worn-out mud walls of the yard with new brick walls. They also built a covered gate, on top of which they erected a tall cross in bright red. The cross faces the loudspeakers silently, yet sturdily. It is a symbol of perseverance and determination. The renovated church visibly outshined the Village Committee Office across the street. This made *laoshuji* unhappy. Moreover, adding oil to fire, a *feng shui* master in the village told him that the taller church gate overshadowed the Village Committee Office, which would bring bad luck to the Village

Committee. This made *laoshuji* depressed. He made several attempts to stop its erection or to destroy it. As Elder Liu Guizhu recalled:

> *Laoshuji* was unhappy about the brick walls and the new gate. He first asked us halt the construction. After its completion, he ordered us to tear the gate down. We did not follow his order. So he went up to the Commune and reported that the church had added new buildings in violation of state policies and regulations.[3] He asked the Commune government to send officials to Wuzhuang and to issue an order to tear down the walls and gate. Some Commune officials came and inspected the church. Surprisingly, however, they told *laoshuji* that having the new walls and gate was not a big deal. They ignored his request and left.

This enraged *laoshuji*. After that, in addition to turning on the loudspeakers, he sometimes stood in front of the Village Committee Office and swore at Christians as they were walking into the church. The Christians simply ignored his provocation and went to their gathering. During some evening services, *laoshuji* walked into the church and ordered the group to leave, accusing the crowd of disturbing the neighbors' sleep. The Christians simply acquiesced. "Because we believe the Lord will redress the injustices for us." Elder Liu continued:

> In July 1998, we invited an old pastor to lead our summer revival meetings. Many people came to the church. Some came from neighboring villages. One night it was indeed quite late. *Laoshuji* led several people, who came in and ordered us stop the gathering immediately. The congregants were very angry, but the old pastor told us not to do anything, just leave for the night, and come back the next day. About two months later, in October, *laoshuji* suddenly died.

"What happened to him?" we asked. Elder Liu continued in his calm and soft tone:

> Nobody knows. He was not very old, only around 60 years of age. His health had been very good. No illness and no accident. But suddenly he died. It took less than an hour [from showing symptoms to death]. It surprised people. We believers thought it was the Lord who redressed the injustices for us, so we were very thankful to God. He is the true

---

[3] Here the 'Commune' (*gongshe*) should be the 'town government' (*xiang zhengfu*). The Commune system was established in the 1950s under radical Maoism and abolished in the early 1980s under the leadership of Deng Xiaoping. The villagers habitually referred to the town government as the Commune government, which indicates that they did not see substantial changes in the administrative structure in the reform era.

and faithful God. Even nonbelievers felt that it was very strange. They said that it was because he offended our God. It was God's punishment of him. After that, many people became fearful [of the Christian God]. In the past some nonbelievers would curse us in front of us or behind our backs. But they dared no more.

Not only did average villagers seem to have learned the lesson of not insulting Christians, the new Party Secretary has also resorted to assuagement. On Christmas of 1998, he led all the village cadres to the church and conveyed greetings to Christians at this special occasion of their most important festival. He also brought a gilt board to the church, on which were inscribed the words 'everlasting friendship' (*youyi chang cun*). Under his new leadership, the loudspeaker has also come on less frequently.

Obviously, *laoshuji*'s hostility toward the church was not totally driven by the atheist ideology of the Chinese Communist Party. As a matter of fact, he was very much involved in the folk religious practice of Fuxi worship and even took the *feng shui* master's words seriously. But he went too far so that even the government did not want to back him. The nonintervention of the town government officials was because they did not see it necessary to risk antagonizing Christians by tearing the new gate and walls down. In the 1990s, the authorities put high priority on maintaining social stability.

The new Party Secretary's efforts of assuagement do not mean any change of the overall religious policy. As a new chief of the village, he needed to consolidate his power. He knew that Christians were cooperative citizens on civic matters. He understood that it would do no good to antagonize this large mass of Christian villagers. In addition, like many other non-Christian villagers, he might also hold some fear toward the Christian God. The goodwill visit and the gilt board were gestures intended to end the bad relations under the old Party Secretary.

Concluding Remarks

The survival and perseverance of the Wuzhuang Christian Church shows that reform-era China has held a religious policy of tolerance with restrictions, and that the restrictions have not been very effective in the remote village, far away from the city where government bureaus are based. In order to attain and maintain a status of legal existence, the church has had to resort to the patriotic rhetoric imposed by the authorities, conform to numerous ordinances and guidelines, and acquiesce to the appointment of a church elder by the Religious Affairs Bureau through the Three-Self Patriotic Movement Committee. The Wuzhuang Church has managed to keep state intrusions at arm's length. Wuzhuang Christians have exercised extraordinary forbearance. After all, the overall situation has indeed improved in comparison with the earlier decades under Communist Party rule. It is still far from the ideal of religious freedom. Nevertheless, the social space for religious practice has enlarged.

In the reform era, China's economy has developed fast. Industrialization and urbanization processes have expanded and accelerated in recent years. Overall, the inland provinces have been lagging behind the coastal provinces, but they have seen significant changes as well. Moreover, in the new century, the central government has begun strategically steering attention and investment to western provinces. Nowadays, many young villagers go to cities for jobs. Some have gone far away to the southwestern coast. According to church leaders and village cadres, nearly half of the village population might not be home most of the year, and those who stayed behind are mostly seniors and women. This is having an important impact on church life. Church attendance has declined since the late 1990s. Moreover, compared with the past, fewer people get baptized now.

The rapid urbanization has brought new challenges to the village church. In addition to the lack of young people and fewer new converts, state control has been strengthened as well. As telephones and cell phones have become available to the villagers, Elder Wu Shenzhao can report 'problems' instantly to the city's Three-Self Patriotic Movement Committee and the Religious Affairs Bureau. Instructions and orders from above also get to the village quicker. Meanwhile, a newly constructed highway and an extended railroad have shortened the distance between the village and the city. Soon after our research in spring 2002, the new highway near Wuzhuang opened. Instead of taking two hours by bus from Wuzhuang to Tianshui City, it now takes only twenty minutes on the highway. The villagers have welcomed it for greater convenience and better opportunities. However, it also means that it takes less time and effort for the RAB officials and police to get to Wuzhuang. In fact, according to the plan, Wuzhuang will soon join an urban district of the expanding Tianshui City.

Marketization is now well underway in most of China, which has led to further relaxation of state control over the private life of citizens. In the more market-driven coastal provinces, Christians and others seem to enjoy greater freedom in practicing their religion. Moreover, to follow international norms, the authorities have made 'rule by law' or 'rule of law' an official goal in deepening reforms. Although these reforms have been 'two steps forward and one step backward,' things seem to have been moving in the desired direction. Taking a broad and long-term view, we have seen, and will likely see more, progress toward greater freedom of religion in China.

References

Aikman, David. 2003. *Jesus in Beijing*. Washington, DC: Regnery Publishing.
Chao, Jonathan and Rosanna Chong. 1997. *A History of Christianity in Socialist China, 1949–1997*. Taipei: China Ministries International Publishing.
Hunter, Alan and Kim-Kwong Chan. 1993. *Protestantism in Contemporary China*. Cambridge: Cambridge University Press.
Jing, Jiuwei. 1995. "A Trip to West Yunnan." *Heavenly Breeze* (Nanjing) 154 of the joint edition: 1.
Jing, Jun. 1996. *The Temple of Memories*. Stanford, CA: Stanford University Press.
Lambert, Tony. 1999. *China's Christian Millions*. London: Monarch Books.
Leung, Ka-lun. 1999. *The Rural Churches of Mainland China Since 1978*. Hong Kong: Alliance Bible Seminary Press.
Li, Dezhu. 1996. "Hold on to 'Love our Country, Love our Religion; Unite and Make Progress' and Strengthen the Self-Construction of the Religious Organizations in order to Make Religion Compatible to Socialist Society." Pp. 11–14 in *Love Our Country, Love Our Religion; Unite and Make Progress—Symposium in Northeast of the Religious Organization Leaders*, edited by Central United Front Department. Beijing: Hua Wen Press.
Potter, Pitman B. 2003. "Belief in Control: Regulation of Religion in China." *China Quarterly* 174 (2): 317–37.
Wang, Jingwen. 1987. "The True Light of Christ Shining on the Mountain Village." *Heavenly Breeze* 60: 23.
Xu, Hongbin and Sun Li. 1991. "An Investigation of the Present Situation of Religion in Yixing." *Contemporary Studies on Religion* 6: 48–52.
Yang, Fenggang. *Forthcoming*. "Lost in the Market, Saved at McDonald's: Urban Chinese Converting to Christianity." *Journal for the Scientific Study of Religion*.
———. 2004. "Religion in Socialist China: Demand-Side Dynamics in a Shortage Economy." Paper presented at the Annual Meeting of the Society for the Scientific Study of Religion, Kansas City, Missouri.

CHAPTER THREE

THE BAILIN BUDDHIST TEMPLE: THRIVING UNDER COMMUNISM

Fenggang Yang and Dedong Wei

Bailin is a Buddhist temple located about 300 kilometers (186 miles) south of Beijing. Before 1988, only a dilapidated pagoda (stupa) remained standing alone outside the county seat of Zhaoxian in Hebei. It was an abandoned site of ancient relics that only a few overseas pilgrims occasionally came to visit to reflect upon its glorious past. This Buddhist site can be traced to the ninth century C.E., when an eminent monk, dubbed the Zhaozhou Monk because of the temple's location, developed a distinct tradition of Chan Buddhism—the Zhaozhou Chan. The temple might be traced even back to the second century, when a Buddhist temple was first built on this site. In any case, this Buddhist center began to decay in the late Qing Dynasty, if not earlier. At the start of the "Cultural Revolution" (1966–1976), everything but the stupa that housed the Zhaozhou Monk's ashes was destroyed.

The year 1988 was a turning point. A Buddhist monk, the Venerable Master Jing Hui, came with the mission to revitalize Buddhism in Hebei Province. In the decade and a half following, a number of buildings have been constructed one after another, including the Guan Yin Hall, the Bell and Drum Tower, the Meditation Hall, living quarters, and so on. The non-stop construction climaxed with the grandeur of Ten-Thousand Buddha Hall completed in 2003. Now, the Bailin Temple has become a fourteen-acre (80 *mu*) compound of magnificent buildings in the traditional Buddhist style of architecture. Within 15 years, a site of ruins has been transformed into a sublime Buddhist center with a beautiful monastic environment. The number of residential monks has reached around 150, whose outlook and ritual performance have impressed many domestic and international Buddhist believers. Witnesses say that no one has ever seen Buddhist revitalization occur with such speed.

Bailin has functioned as the center of Buddhist revivals in Hebei Province. By the end of 1987, the whole Province of Hebei had only two Buddhist temples open for religious services; their shabby halls and tatty living quarters were in desperate need of renovation, but the small income from devotees and tourism was not enough even to support the daily life of the few ailing monks who tended the temples. In the whole province, no more than 4,000 lay Buddhist believers had taken *guiyi* (*Chan* 1989–1),[1] a formal rite of conversion comparable to baptism for Christians.[2] From that point on, however, Buddhist growth in Hebei has been nothing but extraordinary. For example, within two days in May 1988, 461 people in the county of Renxian in Southern Hebei took *guiyi* rite under the Venerable Jing Hui (*Chan* 1990–4). On 8 January 1995, over a thousand people took the rite at the Bailin Temple (*Chan* 1995–2). Upon arriving in Hebei, Jing Hui became the president of the Hebei Buddhist Association. Under his leadership, more and more temples were reopened, restored, or rebuilt throughout Hebei Province. By the end of 2003, there were over 580 Buddhist monks and nuns stationed at over 280 Buddhist temples open for religious services.[3] Hebei suddenly became one of the provinces with a very active Buddhist Sangha (monks and nuns) and lay believers.

How did the Bailin Temple achieve such expansion within merely 15 years? How could it lead revivals throughout the whole province? How was this change possible in China today, where the ruling Chinese Communist Party continues to maintain a restrictive, even repressive, policy toward religion (Overmyer 2003; Kindopp and Hamrin 2004)? By examining the case of Bailin, this chapter seeks to explore the social and political factors for Buddhist revivals in China today.

---

[1] *Chan* magazine is the official publication of the Hebei Buddhist Association. The full texts of every issue have been online (http://www.chancn.com/magazine/index.asp (downloaded on September 13, 2004). Citations to this magazine will be noted by the year and issue number only.

[2] *Guiyi* is to "turn to and depend on" the three jewels—the Buddha, the Dharma (Buddhist teachings), and the Sangha (Buddhist clergy). The believer takes vows to follow the three jewels, be loyal to the three jewels, and is given a "Dharma name" by the officiating monk to signify the new Buddhist identity. Jing Hui and other Buddhist leaders in China often state that only those who have taken *guiyi* can be considered true Buddhists. Many Buddhist followers in China are not formal converts.

[3] See the official website of the Hebei Ethnic and Religious Affairs Bureau (http://www.hebmzt.gov.cn/HBreligion/index.jsp, downloaded on December 21, 2004). In addition to these temples designated for religious services, there are also former Buddhist temples designated as tourist sites.

The Leadership of the Sangha

Traditional Chinese Buddhism has been a Sangha-centered religion. Following the Mahāyāna tradition, the Sangha is composed of celibate monks and nuns living at the temple-monastery to carry out their own practices, attend to the statues of Buddhas and Bodhisattvas, and perform rituals for lay worshippers. Some of the lay believers may take the conversion rite of *guiyi*, but they do not belong to, or formally affiliate with, a temple. Lay believers who are attracted by the Sangha, especially by the abbot, may patronize the temple by making donations to the monks or for the construction of temple buildings. Most lay believers go to a temple to make personal requests, and their donations tend to be small and spontaneous. Therefore, a temple's existence and expansion depends less on the number of regular attendees at the temple and more on a few wealthy and generous donors. A charismatic abbot is thus critical for a temple's survival and growth.

Venerable Master Jing Hui is the indispensable magnet in the success story of the Bailin Temple. He is an entrepreneurial monk who has mobilized multiple resources for his endeavors to revitalize Buddhism. Born in 1933 in Hubei Province in South-Central China, he was abandoned by his parents in dire poverty when he was only 18 months old. Reared at a Buddhist nunnery, he became a novice monk at age 15. A few years later, he took refuge as a disciple of the Venerable Master Xu Yun, the most revered Buddhist monk in modern China. In 1956, the Chinese Buddhist Academy was established. Jing Hui entered the first class, and upon graduation he was admitted to its graduate program. His talents and diligence were recognized by his classmates and teachers. However, sharing the fate of most clergymen in the 1950s and 1960s, in due time Jing Hai was persecuted and sent to a camp for reeducation through labor. During the brutal Cultural Revolution period, Jing Hui was even forced to return to a secular life in his hometown in Hubei Province.[4] Not until 1979, when the CCP's religious policy changed from eradication to limited toleration, was he able to return to the religious life.

---

[4] Several people told us that Jing Hui even got married in those years. Jing Hui himself has avoided talking about it, neither confirming or denying it, although the rumor of his marriage has been circulating within some circles of Buddhist believers and scholars. If this is true, it is an embarrassment that would taint his reputation.

Before coming to Hebei Province, Jing Hui worked as the chief editor of the *Fa Yin* (*Voice of Dharma*), the official magazine of Buddhist Association of China. Working at the magazine and being involved in the operation of the Buddhist Association of China for nearly a decade, Jing Hui gained remarkable experiences and unusual access to various resources. First of all, this mannerly monk was able to develop personal relationships with various important people, including major monks, lay activists, foreign Buddhist leaders, and government officials in charge of religious affairs. The political, religious, and financial support of these people was essential for the revitalization of the Bailin Temple. The trust of Mr. Zhao Puchu (1907–2000), the President of the Buddhist Association of China from 1980 till his death, was especially important. Zhao was the unchallenged leader of Chinese Buddhism in the last two decades of the twentieth century. He also held important political positions, including being the Vice Chairman of the Chinese People's Political Consultative Conference, which is one level higher in rank in the Chinese political system than the director of the State Religious Affairs Bureau (RAB). The head of the State RAB indeed showed deference to Zhao on certain occasions.

Secondly, the nature of the work editing the magazine made it both necessary and possible for Jing Hui to become a scholar. This diligent monk managed to master an impressive amount of knowledge about Buddhist theories, ideas, and practices of various sects and major monks, and about modern developments of Buddhism in China and other societies. When the opportunity came, he knew what to do to revive Buddhism.

Finally, but most important, working in this important position helped Jing Hui develop a thorough understanding of political dynamics and policy subtleties. The chief editor of the official magazine is the ultimate gatekeeper of the information flow within the Chinese Buddhist community. He was responsible for publishing articles that were both appealing to Buddhist believers and also acceptable to the CCP authorities. Publishing a single politically incorrect article could result in his dismissal, as has happened to many magazines' chief editors in reform-era China. Some magazines were even closed due to one faulty article. At the same time, publishing articles of purely political propaganda may alienate Buddhist believers, or risk losing respect from fellow clergymen. In an interview in November 2004 at the Bailin Temple, Jing Hui told us:

Editing the magazine made me familiar with the state's policies and also made me master the means of propaganda toward the outside. It required a good grasp of policies in order to know what to do to get the best possible achievement. The work experience accumulated in those years is a very important resource for our current work. That resource comes not only from the prestige of the magazine, but through it I gained experience using the propaganda media, handling state policies in organizing religious activities, and coordinating with various departments and bureaus.

Then the opportunity came. In October 1987, he represented the Buddhist Association of China in accompanying a Japanese Buddhist delegation of over 100 people to visit the lonely stupa in Zhaoxian. Since 1980, some Japanese Buddhists had been coming on pilgrimage to the Zhaozhou stupa and other original temple sites of various sects (*zu ting*).[5] The 1987 pilgrims expressed the wish to restore the Bailin Temple. They had even raised some funds in Japan for the restoration work. Before the trip, Jing Hui evidently had read extensively about the Zhaozhou Chan and its temple. Upon seeing the site with his own eyes, however, he could not help but feeling very sad about the ruined condition of the once glorious temple. A burden arose in his mind to do something for its restoration.

Soon after, coincidentally, representatives of the Hebei Province's CCP's United Front Department (UFD) and the Religious Affairs Bureau (RAB) went to Beijing to invite Jing Hui to come to establish the Hebei Buddhist Association. Jing Hui said that at first he declined several times, but then was persuaded by Zhao Puchu, the President of the Buddhist Association of China. Zhao commissioned Jing Hui to go and establish the Hebei Buddhist Association and revitalize the Bailin Temple and the Linji Temple, another renowned Buddhist temple in Hebei Province. With Zhao's endorsement and evident support from people with some political clout, Jing Hui accepted the challenge and came to Shijiazhuang, the capital of Hebei Province, on 4 January 1988. On his second day, a meeting of Buddhists representatives was held. Almost all of the monks and nuns in the whole

---

[5] Mahāyāna Buddhism in China evolved into eight sects—Tiantai, Huayan, Sanlun, Weishi, Lü, Chan, Jingtu (Pureland), and Mi (esoteric), and various lineages or traditions developed within each sect. In modern times, however, Chinese Buddhists have often blended practices of different traditions (see Welch 1967, 1968). Japanese Buddhists appear to show more attachment to particular lineages or sectarian traditions.

of Hebei came, but the total number of the participants was only just over a dozen. These people elected Jing Hui to lead the steering committee to establish the Hebei Buddhist Association, and later officially elected him to be the President of the association.

Even before coming to Hebei, Jing Hui had attracted some highly educated young people as followers or disciples through the *Fa Yin* magazine. Following the 1989 Tiananmen Square incident, when the student-led pro-democracy movement was crushed by tanks, many college-educated young people began to turn to religion to search for personal salvation and national direction. A number of college graduates went on to become Buddhist monks and nuns. Jing Hui has attracted several such highly educated young people who became his disciple-monks.

Among Jing Hui's disciple-monks, the foremost is the Venerable Master Ming Hai. He majored in philosophy at Beijing University between 1987 and 1991. After the Tiananmen Square incident, he took *guiyi* in 1990, and two years later he had his head shaved and became a monk under Jing Hui. He has made significant contributions to the development of doctrine at Bailin, the construction of several buildings, and the organization of various activities. In 2004, Jing Hui formally passed on the title of Abbot of the Bailin Temple to the 37 year-old Ming Hai. Another important monk is the Venerable Master Ming Zhuang. He graduated from Zhongshan University in Guangzhou and became a monk under Jing Hui in 1995. In the following year, he began to play an active role in the summer camp, the key activity in Bailin's success, which will be described later. Now Ming Zhuang is in charge of running the summer camp and other activities specially targeting college-educated people. Overall, it is said that about a third of the Bailin Sangha have had a college education. These highly-educated, highly-dedicated, and highly-diligent young monks form the leadership core of the Bailin enterprises. Beginning in 1998, the Hebei Buddhist Academy (*foxueyuan*) was established and housed at the Bailin Temple. The more than one hundred novice monks at the Academy are also helping hands at the Bailin Temple. Together with their teachers, they comprise an outstanding Sangha community in China today.

A Marketable Brand of Buddhism

In late dynastic, or pre-modern, China, Buddhism became a religion very much detached from the world. The teachings focused on sufferings in the world and how to become free from these sufferings through chanting, rituals, and secluded meditation or 'sitting still' (*zuo chan* or *da zuo*). Most of the temples were monasteries in the deep mountains. Along with its increasing withdrawal from the world, Buddhism declined in Ming and Qing Dynasties.

However, throughout its long history, many Chinese Buddhists have emphasized helping others to achieve enlightenment and to engage the world. The Chan sect especially underscores gaining enlightenment in daily life. In modern times, some Buddhist laymen and monks hoped to reform traditional Buddhism and make it more relevant in social life. The most influential Buddhist reformer in the first half of the twentieth century was the Venerable Master Tai Xu (1890–1947). He advocated 'Buddhism in the World' (*renjian fojiao*). He also initiated such reforms as establishing Buddhist academies on the model of Christian seminaries and operating charity projects on the model of Christian missionary works. Whereas Tai Xu's experiments were criticized by most of his contemporary monks and nuns, in the second half of the twentieth century Buddhism in the World has influenced waves of revivals in Taiwan and diasporic Chinese communities.

One of the most notable contemporary leaders of reformed Buddhism has been the Venerable Master Hsing Yun (1927–), who developed the Foguangshan sect and led it in establishing many temples in Taiwan, Southeast Asia, and North America. He refers to his brand of Buddhism as 'Buddhism of Life' or 'Humanist Buddhism' (*rensheng fojiao* or *renben fojiao*). In March-April 1989, Hsing Yun made his first visit to mainland China, together with a 70-person delegation. Jing Hui, representing the Buddhist Association of China, was among the few who accompanied Hsing Yun and his delegation in their four-week pilgrimage journey throughout China. Afterwards, Jing Hui published an article to praise Hsing Yun for his strategic efforts in reviving Buddhism in the modern world (*Chan* 1989–2).

In the early 1990s, Jing Hui developed his own distinct brand of Buddhism—the Life Chan (*sheng huo chan*). To promote his ideas of Buddhism, Jing Hui launched a new magazine—the *Chan* magazine—

soon after his arrival in Hebei. Its intended audience is people interested in Chan Buddhism who may or may not be Buddhists. In the
"Life Chan Pronouncement" published in the *Chan* magazine in the
first issue of 1993, he states that learning Buddhism, practicing cultivation, and living life should be combined into an organic unity:

> The so-called Life Chan is to meld the spirit of Chan and the wis-
> dom of Chan into life, to realize the transcendence of Chan in life,
> and to manifest in life the realm of Chan, the spirit of Chan, and the
> wonder of Chan. The purpose of promoting Life Chan is to restore
> the lively nature of the Chan spirit, which is the result of melding
> Buddhist culture and Chinese culture. It is Buddhism with Chinese
> cultural characteristics. It is to apply the methods of Chan in the real
> life of the world in order to remove various problems, frustrations, and
> psychological obstacles in the life of modern people. It is to make our
> spiritual life more fulfilled, material life more dignified, moral life more
> righteous, emotional life more pure, human relations more harmo-
> nious, and social life more peaceful, so that we may approach the life
> of wisdom and life of perfection. (*Chan* 1993–1)

Jing Hui claims that his Life Chan is rooted in the long history of
Mahāyāna Buddhism, the Chan Buddhist sect, and the Zhaozhou
Chan tradition that was developed at the Bailin Temple in the ninth
century. He also acknowledges that it is continuation of the modern trend of 'Buddhism in the World' or 'Buddhism of Life.' In a
2002 talk in Hong Kong, Jing Hui further explains:

> The ultimate goal of Life Chan is 'a life of enlightenment, a life of
> dedication' (*jue wu ren sheng, feng xian ren sheng*). Where does this slo-
> gan come from? It is from the Zhaozhou monk's famous cases of the
> 'no-entrance gate' and the 'Zhaozhou bridge.' These eight words are
> the modern interpretation of the Bodhisattva spirit, are the popular
> understanding of the dual-path of compassion and wisdom. The spirit
> of the whole of Mahāyāna Buddhism can be condensed into these
> words, 'a life of enlightenment, a life of dedication.' In order to make
> it even more applicable in individuals' spiritual cultivation, in recent
> years I have further defined 'a life of enlightenment' and 'a life of
> dedication' as follows: 'A life of enlightenment' is continuous improve-
> ment of the quality of oneself... and 'a life of dedication' is contin-
> uous effort to harmonize self-other relations. The ultimate goal of
> compassion is to make all people in the world live harmoniously, love
> and care each other, and dedicate or sacrifice for each other. It is the
> harmonious life, the so-called 'everyone is for me and I for everyone.'
> (*Chan* 2002–6)

In 1993, Jing Hui created the Hebei Institute of Chan Studies and
began to dig out and publish historical and scholarly works. In 1998,

he arranged with the highly respectable China Book Corps (zhonghua shu ju) to publish an annual volume of *Chan Studies in China* (*zhongguo chan xue*), which targets scholars and advanced practitioners of Chan Buddhism. In 2000 he established the Hebei Buddhist Academy and began to recruit novice monks throughout the country. But the signature means of propagating Life Chan has been the Life Chan Summer Camp. Along with the "Life Chan Pronouncement" in the *Chan* magazine in the first issue of 1993 was an announcement that the Bailin Temple would hold the Life Chan Summer Camp for the young people who were interested in learning about Chan.

The first Life Chan Summer Camp was held in July 1993. The week-long camp included traditional Buddhist practices such as morning and evening chanting, sitting-still meditation, and walking meditation. It also had innovative activities appealing to intellectuals, such as lectures and discussion sessions with scholars and the more scholastic monks. In addition, it incorporated the modernized ritual of passing on the candlelight at an evening service, which has been popularized by Hsing Yun and his Foguangshan sect in Taiwan.

The first Life Chan Summer Camp was a great success. It attracted 150 young people from over 20 provinces, and two-thirds of them were college graduates or college students. That was unprecedented in mainland China because the vast majority of Buddhist believers have been less-educated, older people, mostly women. Most of the summer camp participants were readers of the *Chan* magazine who had not formally converted to Buddhism. However, on the fifth day of the week-long summer camp, over a hundred participants took a *guiyi* conversion rite (*Chan* 1993–4).

The Life Chan Summer Camp has become an annual event, with up to 500 participants in recent years, the maximum the temple could accommodate. It has also become known as the signature activity of the Bailin Temple, highly praised by the participants, top leaders of the Buddhist Association of China, overseas and domestic Buddhist clergy, and university scholars of Buddhist studies. The affirmation has come with generous financial support. The summer camp has been free of charge for the participants, and the funding has come from donations by Hong Kong Buddhist businesspeople. In fact, the summer camp has been the most effective means for Bailin Temple in attracting financial support for its physical expansion. Between 1993 and 2003, the Bailin Temple doubled in size by acquiring adjacent land. Several more buildings were erected, and each new one was finer and/or larger than the last. Most of the donors

were Buddhist entrepreneurs in Hong Kong or other overseas places.
What inspired these donors, in addition to the charismatic Jing Hui,
was the successful Life Chan Summer Camp. It gives them hope for
a Buddhist revival in China under Communist rule.

Political Support by the Authorities

Both the Sangha leadership and having a marketable brand of Buddhist ideas and practices have been important for Bailin Temple's
revitalization. But the most critical factor for its success has been the
political support of government officials. Without the permission of
the authorities, there would have been no reconstruction of the Bailin
Temple. After all, the old Bailin Temple had been largely destroyed
before the Communists took power, thus it fell outside of the range
of 'implementing the religious policy' after 1979. The post-1979 religious policy has been very much restricted to restoring temples,
churches, and mosques to the level immediately before the Cultural
Revolution or that of the late 1950s at best. The Bailin Temple was
not on the 1983 list of 'major temples' designated for restoration as
religious venues, which includes only two Buddhist temples in Hebei—
Linji in Zhengding and Puning in Chengde. That list was suggested
by the Buddhist Association of China, approved by the State Religious
Affairs Bureau, and decreed by the State Council, which is the top
cabinet of the Chinese government. In spite of the lack of status,
the Bailin Temple nonetheless was granted permission for restoration—indeed, not only permitted, but also actively encouraged and
supported by the authorities on all levels.

The Provincial Government

Before coming to Hebei, Jing Hui had no meaningful connection
with Hebei Province. He was not born there and had never lived
there. It is also important to note that there had been very few
Buddhist believers in Hebei in the 1980s. Catholicism and Islam
have been much more prominent with large and active communities,
and Protestantism has been growing fast.[6] However, for reasons not

---

[6] It has been well-known that about a quarter or more of Chinese Catholics
have been in Hebei Province. This means that there were about a million Catholics
in Hebei in the late 1980s, according to the officially published national statistics.

publicly articulated, the provincial government wanted to develop Buddhism. According to articles in the *Chan* magazine and our interviews with Jing Hui, it was the Hebei Religious Affairs Bureau (RAB) and the United Front Department (UFD) that initiated the contact with Jing Hui, inviting him to Hebei to establish the Hebei Buddhist Association. The first meeting of Buddhists in Hebei, organized by the Hebei RAB in anticipation of Jing Hui's arrival, was held on the second day of his arrival in the provincial capital of Shijiazhuang City.

What motivated the Hebei RAB and UFD to recruit an outside monk to establish the Hebei Buddhist Association? One reason might be that there had been strong demand by Buddhist believers in Hebei. But we have not found any evidence of this at this time. Or perhaps the Hebei RAB hoped to have a strong provincial Buddhist association in order to curb troubles caused by Buddhist believers. Articles in the *Chan* magazine indicate that there were some unspecified 'troubles' among Buddhists in Xingtai and other prefectures. Another possible reason might be that the underground Catholics and Protestants had been a constant headache for the Hebei RAB and UFD, so much so that the officials wished to use Buddhism to counterbalance the growing Catholicism and Protestantism. After Jing Hui's arrival in Hebei, one of his first assigned tasks was to organize the Buddhist association for the Prefecture of Baoding, which happens to be the very center of underground Catholics in China (Madsen 1998, 2003). Upon probing during an interview with us, however, Jing Hui responded by saying that he did not know and did not hear about such an intention of the authorities to use Buddhism to counterbalance Catholicism. Nonetheless, generally speaking, the Chinese authorities put more trust in Buddhists than Christians, and some officials have expressed their wish to see more and better development of Buddhism than Christianity, for Buddhism is considered a native or fully assimilated religion, whereas Christianity remains to be perceived as somewhat foreign. Finally, another likely reason for the provincial government's support of Bailin Temple is a pragmatic consideration for diplomacy. With the quite frequent visits of certain

---

There have been several Hui Muslim autonomous counties in Hebei. The Hebei Religious Affairs Bureau reports 580,000 Muslims and 350,000 Protestants in 2003 (see http://www.hebmzt.gov.cn/HBreligion/index.jsp, downloaded on December 21, 2004). We have not found specific statistics or estimates of religious believers in Hebei in the 1980s.

Japanese and other overseas pilgrims to the Buddhist holy sites in Hebei, it was an embarrassment for the Hebei authorities, especially those in charge of religious affairs, that there was no corresponding Buddhist association to receive the international Buddhist guests properly, who were considered to be among the friendly international forces for China. Nevertheless, based on our research up to now, we do not have clear evidence about the initial motivation of the Hebei RAB and UFD for recruiting Jing Hui to develop Buddhism in Hebei Province. Further research is necessary to clarify this matter.

No matter what was the motivation, however, the Hebei government has provided firm and persistent support for Jing Hui in his efforts to develop Buddhism in Hebei. The Hebei RAB actively and insistently recruited Jing Hui, covered the expenses of his initial activities in Hebei, and directed the local county government to 'return' the site of the Bailin Temple to the newly established Hebei Buddhist Association. Since then, the Hebei RAB has sent representatives to every major activity of the Bailin Temple, including every ceremony of ground-breaking and dedication of the buildings, every Life Chan Summer Camp, and other major gatherings. Furthermore, provincial support has gone up in rank. In addition to the Hebei RAB and UFD officials, several top-level officials of the Hebei Province have visited the Bailin Temple either as congratulatory representatives at major events or on special visits. The list of the provincial dignitaries includes provincial vice governors, the provincial governor, and the provincial CCP secretary. Their presence at the gatherings and their special visits have conveyed an unambiguous message of political support for Jing Hui and the Bailin Temple. Jing Hui told us in November 2004:

> Because the Life Chan Summer Camp is a cross-provincial activity, according to the state's regulations, each year we must send in advance an application to the provincial bureaus and departments in charge of religious affairs. Only after the application is approved can we proceed.... During the past twelve years, once or twice we considered not holding the summer camp. We reported [our intention] to the government. But the provincial RAB and UFD disagreed, asking us not to stop for any reason. They told us that we must continue to do it, for the summer camp is a bright spot in Hebei's Buddhist culture. It is also a bright spot in our province's religious affairs. They said that if you discontinue, the effect would not be good, for other people may think that it is we who did not allow you to do it. Therefore,

you have to do it. Whatever difficulties there are we can work together to solve them. [Therefore,] we decided to continue to do it by shoring up our courage, facing the reality, and overcoming difficulties.

Governmental support also means governmental supervision and pressure. The Hebei Provincial bureaus obviously liked the Summer Camp so much that the Bailin Temple could not stop doing it.

The County Government

Similarly important for the success of Bailin Temple is the support by the local government of Zhaoxian County. This is evident when we consider other unsuccessful efforts of Jing Hui. On top of the list of tasks handed to Jing Hui was to restore the Linji Temple, a much more famous temple designated for restoration by the State Council in 1983. Linji is in the jurisdiction of Zhengding County, which is in the same Shijiazhuang Prefecture as Zhaoxian County. The officials of Zhengding County have not been cooperative, so that the Linji restoration effort has made little progress. The head of the Zhengding County RAB was not in favor of developing Buddhism. Coincidentally, according to Jing Hui, he was a person of Hui ethnicity. The Hui is one of ten ethnic groups that believe in Islam. Another initial effort of Jing Hui in Hebei was to establish the Buddhist association in Baoding Prefecture and revitalize Buddhism there. That has not been successful either. Several Baoding Municipal and Prefecture bureaus have blocked the effort to return and restore a Buddhist temple—the Great Compassion Hall (*da ci ge*)—for religious services. One of the arguments was that the Great Compassion Hall was not a functional temple in the 1950s and 1960s, so that it was not within the scope of 'implementing the religious policy' meant to return the pre-Cultural Revolution religious properties to religious organizations.

In contrast, the Zhaoxian County government has given the Bailin Temple unequivocal support. First of all, in order to 'return' the site to the Hebei Buddhist Association, it had to relocate the Zhaoxian Normal School and the county Education Bureau that had occupied that site. Relocating important educational institutions to give way for building a Buddhist temple could have caused opposition by intellectuals as well as communist ideologues. The Bailin Temple had become defunct long before, thus not as justifiable for restoration as those temples that were closed down during the 'Cultural Revolution.'

After a brief round of talks, however, the Zhaoxian government generously granted about seven acres (40 *mu*) of land around the dilapidated stupa to the newly established Hebei Buddhist Association. Less than ten years later, another piece of land of similar size was added to the Bailin Temple compound. Meanwhile, the Zhaoxian County top-level officials have been present at all major events of the Bailin Temple.

Why does the county government support the construction and expansion of the Bailin Temple? The published speeches given by the county CCP secretary and county governor at major events of the temple clearly show that the major consideration has been economic. The local officials perceive the Bailin Temple as a potential opportunity for the county's economic development. They hope that the temple will attract domestic and international visitors and tourists, some of whom might become interested in bringing the goods and produce of Zhaoxian to other parts of the country and other parts of the world, and some of them might then also be lured to invest in Zhaoxian. The standard passage in the official speeches is about the economic strengths of Zhaoxian. For example, at the opening ceremony of the first Life Chan Summer Camp in 1993, the county governor said:

> The restored Bailin Temple is a golden bridge of exchanges between Chinese and foreign Buddhists. Zhaoxian has a long history, outstanding people, and abounding land. The folk ethos is simple and kind. . . . The Zhaoxian economy has made impressive gains in recent years, with advanced agricultural methods and rich products. It is our nation's distinguished base for commercial crops and high quality wheat. The superior quality of the Zhaozhou snowflake pear is well-known both in China and the world. The county and town industries have reached the primary level, with over five hundred products that are quite competitive. In order to speed up the pace of reforms and opening-up, the county government has established a four-square-kilometer economic development zone and has created a series of favorable policies to encourage investments by foreign businesspeople. We sincerely welcome Chinese and foreign businesses and individuals to come to Zhaoxian to invest in commerce and establish enterprises. Our unique advantages and the good investment environment have attracted many businesspeople to invest here. We genuinely hope Buddhist friends will get to know Zhaoxian and will spread good words about Zhaoxian, so that we can better develop this piece of sacred land. (*Chan* 1993–4)

Given that most of the participants of the Life Chan Summer Camp were young people and college students, the governor's pitch might seem to be out of place. However, the listeners of this speech, thus the intended audience of it, were not limited to the summer camp participants, but also the summer camp's sponsors and the temple's patrons, many of whom were overseas Chinese businesspeople.

The economic motivation of the county government becomes even more apparent in the Bailin Square Project. Beginning in 2001, a 33,000 square-meter (eight acre) commercial plaza has been developed across from the Bailin Temple. It was designated as one of the major economic development projects of Shijiazhuang Prefecture and Zhaoxian County. It claims to be the country's largest wholesale center for material goods used in Buddhism, such as statues, incenses, construction materials, music instruments, clothes, and other artifacts. The plaza is also intended to be a center for tourist goods and crafts, and to be a tourist spot along with the Bailin Temple and the famous Zhaozhou Bridge. How much economic benefits for the county have been generated by the temple-related projects remains to be studied.

The Central Government

The most important support for the Bailin Temple, however, comes from officials of the central government. Without the open encouragement of the highest authorities, the Bailin Temple would have been unable to hold the large-scale, high-profile, cross-provincial activity of the Life Chan Summer Camp. Without tacit backing by the highest authorities, Bailin Temple would have been unable to sustain criticisms from inside the Buddhist community and from Communist ideologues. At the interview in November 2004, Jing Hui said:

> Consistent support by the government is the fundamental assurance and guarantee for the expansion of our activities. This is because the Life Chan Summer Camp is a very sensitive activity. Many college students have participated in it. Some people raised criticisms, saying that Buddhism was competing with the Communist Party for the next generation. This view was brought to the Central United Front Department and the State Religious Affairs Bureau. In response, they [the officials] did some explanations, saying that the young people and college students we had were those who had been believers of Buddhism. Some college students came occasionally [without previous Buddhist faith], but they came not really to convert to Buddhism. They came because they were interested in Buddhism, and their study was related to Buddhism. It was helpful for their academic study to hear lectures

by some experts. Such explanations we cannot make. It must be done by the government [officials]. The State Religious Affairs Bureau, the Hebei Religious Affairs Bureau, and the United Front Department did a lot of work. They have indeed given us powerful support. They have given us the green-light. Their support is the fundamental assurance and guarantee.

The support of the central government manifests itself in publishing positive news reports in the *China Religions* magazine, the official publication of the State Religious Affairs Bureau, and other state media. They have also arranged to have China Central Television make a special news report about the Bailin Temple. But the most effective support is through the visits of high-ranking officials. On 15 April 1999, the Chairman of the Chinese People's Political Consultative Conference and Politburo member, Li Ruihuan, visited Bailin Temple. On 1 April 2000, Vice Premier Qian Qishen came. On 5 November 2001, President Jiang Zemin, accompanied by top military and party officials, made a visit. During the process of rebuilding the Bailin Temple, there have been various difficulties and obstacles. This is not really surprising in China today as the religious policy remains restrictive in many ways. But the visits of top officials changed things. Jing Hui told us:

> Things gradually began to turn better after the dedication of the Hall of the Universal Illuminating Light in 1992. The really important moment was after completing the Guanyin Hall in 1995, when the Provincial Party Secretary made a visit. From then on it has really turned better. . . . On 5 November 2001, President Jiang Zemin came to visit us. The situation turned unprecedentedly better. His visit itself was a very great support to us. It was not only helpful for us here, but also helpful for the whole Buddhist community.

Overjoyed by President Jiang's visit, Jing Hui published several pieces of poems in the *Chan* magazine to celebrate this unusual occasion. He explained in an interview with a Malaysia Buddhist magazine in 2002:

> President Jiang's descending upon our temple delighted all of our clergymen and laymen, even the whole Buddhist community [of the country]. It shows that leaders of the central government affirm Buddhist endeavors, Buddhist activities, and the Buddhist status in today's China. Therefore we were all delighted. This would bring a new momentum for our Bailin Temple's endeavors to spread the dharma and benefit the people. It was also an encouragement and impeller. President Jiang Zemin stayed at the Bailin Temple for over an hour, touring through all the buildings. During the tour, he spoke affirmatively about our

activities in the past few years. He thought that what we had done—
developing Buddhist culture, temple management, and contribution to
society—had great significance and very positive influence for the rule
of morality promoted by the state at the present.[7]

After Jiang's visit, other high-rank officials have continued to come
to visit the Bailin Temple. The latest one was Politburo member Li
Changchun on 11 November 2004.

Why does the central government support the Bailin Temple? The
last sentence of the above quote of Jing Hui suggests that the authorities might be interested in the positive moral functions of Buddhism.
Market transition has been accompanied by the moral and political
corruption of government officials, and social anomie among people
of all walks of life. In response, the CCP has periodically carried
out political campaigns and ideological propaganda to renew political
and ethical principles among its members and all citizens. However,
these efforts have failed to stop moral decadence. Some elite scholars and government officials have begun to consider the possibility
of using religions to supplement the political and ideological efforts.
However, this line of thinking—religions may make moral contributions to society—is contradictory to orthodox Marxism-Leninism-
Maoism. Dogmatic ideologues have criticized and resisted the change.
The more pragmatic leaders have also been cautious in calling for
contributions by religious groups. They share with the ideologues the
concern that strong religious groups could result in political challenges to CCP's rule. Jiang's visit to the Bailin Temple was indeed
a bold move in this regard. It indicates that this brand of Buddhism has gained some level of trust from the highest authorities.

However, the most important reasons to support the Bailin Temple
are political. One concerns the outside world: Bailin Temple is used
as a showcase of China's freedom of religion. The other concerns
managing religious affairs: Bailin Temple is used as a model of religious accommodation to the socialist society under CCP rule.

China has been constantly criticized by Western countries for its
bad human rights record, including its restriction of religious freedom. To answer Western criticisms, the Chinese government has
published the White Paper about Freedom of Religious Beliefs in

---

[7] See the WebPage of the Bailin Temple: http://bailinsi.fjnet.com/NEW-
CHANNE/blch/BOLINTALK26.HTM. Downloaded on December 28, 2004.

1997 and several other white papers about the human rights situation in China. It has also invited foreign delegations of religious leaders to visit religious sites in China. The Bailin Temple in the 1990s became an excellent showcase for the purpose of international public relations. In the most recent visit by the Politburo member Li Changchun, he made this remark: "We should more often arrange for foreigners to come here to see, to let them know, the real status of religion in China."[8] Jing Hui understands very well this intention of the central government, and he tries to use it for his own purposes of reviving Buddhism in China. He told us:

> The government wants to make us a window for external propaganda regarding religion. But propaganda about religion should play down the political ideology, only by doing so can it be effective for external propaganda, can it have positive effects. . . . Policy should leave enough space for religion. Zhao Qizheng [Director of the International Communication Office of the CPC Central Committee] and Li Changchun [Politburo member] both said that we had this space. Regarding religious affairs work for international and domestic purposes, I have over 20 years of experience, or it can be said that I have over 50 years of experience, borne with the new China. I have seen much and have done much, so that I am very clear about how far we can go, about the proper extent of observing the religious policies, about what to tell them [foreigners], and about what we want to get them to do.

Asian countries have been less confrontational in criticizing China's human rights situation, although they may also hold unfavorable views regarding it. Some Asian religious leaders try to promote their particular religion in China by making frequent pilgrim visits to the temples. In fact, without the frequent visits of Japanese Buddhists in the 1980s, the Bailin Temple would have remained a site of ancient relics at most. Jing Hui admits:

> In history, our country's Buddhism had a very great impact on the four countries of Vietnam, North Korea, South Korea, and Japan. Up to now they still come often to China to visit the original temple sites. After the Cultural Revolution, Chinese Buddhism has been restored and has developed quite fast. This is inseparable from the push by people of these countries. In Hebei, the most eminent sites are the

---

[8] See the WebPage of the Bailin Temple: http://bailinsi.fjnet.com/NEW-CHANNE/WSBL/FMQX/041111/lcclf.htm Downloaded on December 28, 2004.

Linji and Bailin Temples. Without the help of the Japanese, it would have taken another decade or more to begin the restoration (*Chan* 2000–2).

Not only do the Japanese continue to make frequent visits to the Bailin Temple, now European and American delegations have also been brought there.

The other important reason the central government supports the Bailin Temple is for domestic purposes. Since 1979, the Chinese government has allowed five religions to operate under the 'patriotic' associations. In spite of various pragmatic measures regarding the economy, culture, and social life, however, the reform-era CCP has not given up its Marxist-Leninist-Maoist ideology. Throughout the last two decades, restrictions on religious organizations have actually increased instead of being relaxed (Potter 2003; Kindopp and Hamrin 2004). However, restrictive regulations and heavy handed suppression have not been effective in curtailing religious revivals, but have driven some believers into the underground or into finding creative ways to go around the regulations (Yang *forthcoming*).

In the mid-1990s, an alternative strategy was adopted. Instead of confrontation and containment, the authorities now wish to co-op religious organizations. President Jiang Zemin called for officials to "actively guide the religions to accommodate the socialist society." Since then, concerted efforts have been made to encourage religious leaders to develop new theologies suitable for the socialist system under CCP rule. For example, the State RAB and Central UFD have pressed Protestants to undertake a campaign of 'theological construction.' Bishop Ding Guangxun has since advocated a theology of love, so that non-Christians would not feel excluded from Christian salvation. However, resistance by Christian clergy and lay leaders has been strong, for they believe the theology of love contradicts the belief in 'salvation by faith through grace.' Given this situation, it is indeed delightful for the CCP leaders to find that Jing Hui's Life Chan appeals to Buddhist believers. They hope that other Buddhist leaders would come in line, and wish that other religions would model themselves on the Bailin Temple's approach. For example, on 23 August 2004, a group of 66 Catholic leaders participating in a national seminar led by Bishop Ma Yinglin was brought to the Bailin Temple.

The Bailin Temple has not only developed a highly marketable brand of Buddhism, the Life Chan, its Sangha has also frequently expressed patriotism. At major gathering events, the first item of the ritual procedure has always been playing the national anthem, a clear symbol of patriotism. The Bailin monks have also learned to repeat 'love the country and love the religion,' with 'love the country' ahead of 'love the religion.' In the long speech given at the Third Conference of the Board of Directors of Hebei Buddhist Association on 29 November 2001, Jing Hui made repeated calls for patriotism:

> First and foremost [among the tasks of the Buddhist Association] is to love the country. The second is to do religious work. No matter what Buddhist organization on what level, whether you are at the county level or the municipal level, you must have a clear goal. First, it is to lead the mass of believers to love the country. Second it is to guide the masses of believers to have a proper religious life and perform corresponding religious activities. . . . The fundamental responsibility of the Buddhist association is to lead the mass of believers to walk on the way of love for the country and the religion, maintaining the orthodox beliefs and the orthodox acts. . . . Everyone must understand the rich contents of 'love the country.' Love the country is not abstract and empty talk. It has concrete contents. At the present time, to love the country is to passionately love our present socialist motherland. We live in the land of the People's Republic of China, so two fundamental principles are unshakeable. The first is to follow the Chinese Communist Party's leadership. The second is to support the socialist system. These two principles are the core of love the country. There is no ambiguity about it (*Chan* 2002–1).

In addition to frequently making patriotic statements, Jing Hui insists that the Life Chan is very compatible with the CCP's idealism. He states:

> It is totally possible to make Buddhism accommodate socialist society. The Buddha told us, the most fundamental principle of spreading the dharma is 'the proper theory for the right moment.' The proper theory for the right moment requires us to combine the Buddhist dharma with the particular social reality and mental reality, to serve the fundamental goal of purifying human hearts, and solemnifing the nation (*Chan* 2002–2).

Jing Hui even equates the ideal Communist Society to the 'Pure Land' in Buddhism, saying that it is the best social system that humans have ever come up with.

> If we really live according to those ideal goals, our country will have a very promising future. Communism is in accordance with the fundamental spirit of Buddhism. Because of this, we hope that Buddhist

thought, Buddhist culture, and Buddhist moral spirit can contribute to the construction of socialist material and spiritual civilization. Our future society, to use our Buddhist terminology, should be a pure land in the world. This is our ideal. To construct the pure land in the world, everyone of us must have high moral standards and conscience, put oneself under the cultivation ideal of Buddhist 'do no evil, do all good, and cleanse one's own mind,' and regulate one's words and acts by the rules of the five precepts and the ten goodnesses. If we can all do this, then we can say that we can realize the construction of a socialist spiritual civilization (*Chan* 1999–1).

These words are certainly music to the ears of the CCP leaders who are in pressing need for affirmation of its ideological goals and for popular support for its leadership.

Conclusion

Bailin Temple has been thriving. The major factors for its success include the able leadership of the well-connected and well-positioned Venerable Jing Hui, his articulation and promotion of a marketable brand of Buddhism—the Life Chan—with innovative slogans and practices, the financial support of wealthy overseas and domestic donors, and most importantly, the political support of government officials.

The political support of the authorities for Buddhist development may not be totally surprising in reform-era China. In spite of the fact that the Chinese Communist Party insistently claims to adhere to the ideology of Marxism-Leninism-Maoism, in fact pragmatism has dominated the process of its policy-making in most social spheres, including religious affairs. Before the reforms started in 1979, driven by the radical ideology, the CCP prohibited all religions in Chinese society. But the eradication measures from 1966 to 1979 failed. Religious believers persevered in the underground, and the number of Christians even multiplied during that period. With the publication in 1982 of "The Basic Viewpoint and Policy on the Religious Affairs during the Socialist Period of Our Country" (Document No. 19) the CCP acknowledges that religion will not wither away any time soon and that religious affairs must be handled with great care. It instructs CCP and government officials to rally religious believers for the central task of economic construction. Out of pragmatic considerations, religion has been tolerated. Buddhism, Daoism, Islam, Protestantism, and Catholicism under the government-sanctioned 'patriotic' associations have been allowed to operate as long as the believers love the country, support CCP rule, and observe the social- ist laws. Since the mid-1990s, the policy of passive toleration has been replaced by 'actively guiding religions to adapt to the socialist society,' which in reality means that religious believers must follow the Party line. All five religions have been pressed by the authori- ties to revise or reconstruct their respective theologies to make the adaptation.

The Venerable Jing Hui and his Bailin Temple have followed the Party line closely. He not only provides frequent lip-service to the CCP leaders, defers to them, and honors them on many occasions, but he also offers a new brand of Buddhism that seems to be quite compatible with Communist ideology. Or, at least he appears to speak in earnest about the compatibility of Life Chan Buddhism and Communism.

While winning the political support of the authorities, Jing Hui has also tried hard to maintain his legitimacy in orthodox Buddhism. In this regard, inheriting the ancient Bailin Temple that was emi- nent for a distinctive tradition of Zhaozhou Chan is very helpful. This religious capital has been indispensable for Jing Hui. Meanwhile, Jing Hui has repeatedly emphasized his discipleship status under the Venerable Xu Yun, who was probably the most revered monk among the Buddhist Sangha and laity in modern China. The aura of Jing Hui comes in part from his lineage claim as a loyal disciple of the charismatic Xu Yun. Interestingly, Xu Yun was known to be a tradi- tionalist monk, very unlike reformist Tai Xu who advocated 'Buddhism in the World.' Nonetheless, Jing Hui has managed to claim the heritage of both Xu Yun's traditionalist charisma and Tai Xu's reformist teaching.

To explain the success of the Bailin Buddhist Temple in today's China, it is necessary to go beyond institutional factors as well as individuals' tactics. In the sociological literature of religious growth and decline, the dominant supply-side model argues that in an unreg- ulated religious market, strict and competitive groups tend to grow (see Finke and Stark 1992; Finke and Iannaccone 1993; Iannaccone 1994; Finke 1997; Stark and Finke 2000). However, the thriving Bailin Temple is not strict, for it has offered the Summer Camp free of charge to the participants. Nor is its doctrine in high tension with the surrounding culture. To the contrary, Jing Hui has proclaimed a brand of Buddhism that clearly accommodates the ruling Chinese

Communist Party and its Communist ideology. The Life Chan emphasizes living harmoniously with other people, rather than challenging others. This low tension, not very strict temple has been thriving under Communism.

The key to understanding Bailin's success lies in the political context. The religious economy in China is highly regulated. To explain the religious dynamics in Communist-ruled China under heavy regulation, it is necessary to distinguish three parallel markets (Yang *forthcoming*). State-sanctioned religious groups and activities comprise the 'red market.' Underground religious groups and activities comprise the 'black market.' Legally ambiguous groups and activities comprise the 'gray market.' The group dynamics in the three markets are different. The Bailin temple has been thriving in the red market, in which the most important factor for success is winning the trust and support of government officials. Indeed, political submission to the government and theological accomodation to the ruling ideology are preconditions for a group's legal existence. The factors leading to Bailin's successes are likely to be relevant for other religious groups in the red market. But these factors probably are not effective for religious groups in the black or gray markets.

As a temple in a highly regulated economy, the success of the Bailin Temple has clear limitations. While the Life Chan doctrine pleases the authorities, some other Buddhists may regard it as a compromise and consider it unacceptable. In the limited time of this study, we have not found open criticisms of the Bailin Temple doctrine and practices by other Buddhist monks or lay believers. In the interview with us, however, Jing Hui did mention in passing that there were criticisms of the Bailin activities by other Buddhists as well as by people outside the Buddhist community, but that the criticisms were muted after President Jiang Zemin's visit in 2001. Therefore, the apparent blooming of the Bailin Temple is not a result of fair competition in a free market. In fact, there has been a shortage of supply in the highly regulated religious economy in Communist-ruled China (Yang 2004). As demand exceeds supply, religious seekers often fill most of the temples and churches that have managed to stay open.

Another limitation of the Bailin Temple's success is that it is not a local congregation. Although the local county government has supported the temple's expansion, we were told that not many local residents were regular participants in the temple. Most of the participants of the signature activity—the Life Chan Summer Camp—come from afar, often from other provinces. Most of the major donors have been overseas Chinese Buddhist businesspeople. How long the Bailin Temple can maintain the continuous support of these distant devotees remains to be observed.

REFERENCES

Finke, Roger. 1997. "The Consequences of Religious Competition: Supply-side Explanations for Religious Change." Pp. 45–64 in *Rational Choice Theory and Religion*, edited by Lawrence A. Young. New York: Routledge.

Finke, Roger and Laurence R. Iannaccone. 1993. "Supply-Side Explanations for Religious Change." *Annals* 527: 27–39.

Finke, Roger and Rodney Stark. 1992. *The Churching of America, 1776–1990*. New Brunswick, NJ: Rutgers University Press.

Iannaccone, Laurence R. 1994. "Why Strict Churches Are Strong." *American Journal of Sociology* 99: 1180–1211.

Kindopp, Jason and Carol Lee Hamrin, eds. 2004. *God and Caesar in China*. Washington, DC: Brookings Institution Press.

Madsen, Richard. 1998. *China's Catholics*. Berkeley: University of California Press.

———. 2003. "Catholic Revival During the Reform Era." *China Quarterly* 174: 468–87.

Overmyer, Daniel L., ed. 2003. *Religion in China Today*. Cambridge: Cambridge University Press.

Potter, Pitman B. 2003. "Belief in Control: Regulation of Religion in China." *China Quarterly* 174: 317–37.

Stark, Rodney and Roger Finke. 2000. *Acts of Faith*. Berkeley: University of California Press.

Welch, Holmes. 1967. *The Practice of Chinese Buddhism 1910–1950*. Cambridge, MA: Harvard University Press.

———. 1968. *The Buddhist Revival in China*. Cambridge, MA: Harvard University Press.

Yang, Fenggang. *Forthcoming*. "The Red, Black, and Gray Markets of Religion in China." *Sociology Quarterly*.

———. 2004. "Religion in Socialist China: Demand-Side Dynamics in a Shortage Economy." Paper presented at the Annual Meeting of the Society for the Scientific Study of Religion, Kansas City, Missouri.

CHAPTER FOUR

OF TEMPLES AND TOURISTS:
THE EFFECTS OF THE TOURIST POLITICAL ECONOMY
ON A MINORITY BUDDHIST COMMUNITY IN
SOUTHWEST CHINA

Thomas Borchert

Early in my fieldwork into the monastic educational practices of the
Theravāda monks of Sipsongpanna in Southwest China, I was sitting and chatting with one of the senior monks of Wat Pājie, the
central temple of Sipsongpanna. I had finished teaching English to
the novice monks, something I did everyday as a part of my fieldwork,
and had stopped in at the temple's office where Dubi Kham Bian
was sipping tea.[1] This monk was not one that I knew well. He served
as the temple's accountant and thus did not have much contact with
the novice monks who attended the temple's Dhamma School, one
of the main projects of the temple, and the reason that I was there.
Although he lived at Wat Pājie and worked as its accountant, he was
also the abbot of a small temple on the border with Burma. Un-
beknown to me at the time, he was quite an important monk at the
temple. In terms of years in robes (a principal marker of status in
Theravāda Buddhism), Du Kham Bian was among the most senior
monks at Wat Pājie, and was regularly involved in the major decisions of the temple.

As we were chatting, a Han Chinese tourguide came into the office,
and rather abruptly said to Dubi Kham Bian, "Eh, Is the abbot
here?" When Dubi Kham Bian replied in the negative, she asked about
one of the vice-abbots. They too were gone, out on errands or
officiating at ceremonies around the Autonomous Prefecture. The tourguide looked nonplussed. "Well, I have a bunch of tourists out there
who want to be blessed." She was referring to a regularly reenacted

---

[1] With the exception of Wat Pājie, temple names and peoples names have either
been altered or are obscured.

scene at the temple: A monk would chant a protective blessing (*paritta*) from the Mangala Sutta, pouring water as he finished his recitation. He would use this sanctified water to sprinkle the recipients of the blessing, and then give them thread bracelets, which are held by the monk while he is chanting.[2] This ceremony, which takes place in the worship hall of the temple (*wihān*), on a throne set up specifically for this purpose, is usually presided over by the abbot of the temple. Barring his absence, one of the vice-abbots usually performs the ceremony, though in fact, any fully-ordained monk may perform it. It is a little ritual greatly enjoyed by visitors to the temple, both Han Chinese tourists and Dai-lue followers of Theravāda Buddhism. In response to the tourguide's most recent comment, Dubi Kham Bian noncommittally said, "Hmm."

"Well," the tourguide said, getting snippier by the second, "what about you?" Pause. "Can you do it?" There was another pause, until Dubi Kham Bian sighed and said yes. He didn't get up however, until she said, "Well come on, let's go!" Finally he stood, rewrapped his robe, as is appropriate for a monk going into public space, and calmly walked behind the tourguide to the *wihān* where the tourists were waiting.

This little bit of foot dragging by Dubi Kham Bian immediately raised a number of questions in my mind. Why did he seem to be reluctant to perform the *paritta* ritual for the tourists? Why did he finally agree to it? Was it his duty as a monk, or was there some sort of deal: had Wat Pājie bought relative independence in exchange for servicing Chinese tourists? These led to larger questions: What is the impact of tourism upon the way monks and novices view themselves and are able to practice Buddhism, both at Wat Pājie, and in the wider Sipsongpanna monastic community? Does the tourist-industrial complex of Sipsongpanna serve to break down traditional culture, as a kind of secularization mechanism? Or does it have rel-

---

[2] This ritual seems to be a modification of the type of traditional blessing that ends with white threads tied around the wrists of the recipient. These threads, which are of home-spun cotton and are charged with the power of the monk from chanting the text, protect the wearer until they fall off his or her wrists. In the rite at Wat Pājie, this has become somewhat routinized. The threads are no longer undyed cotton, but multi-colored, machine-spun nylon threads imported from Thailand, and tied into bracelets by novices. Wat Pājie is the only temple in Sipsongpanna where I have seen this take place, though I have also observed it at some temples in Bangkok.

atively little impact, a thin veneer, as it were, over the deep cultural forms of this Tai community?

The obvious answer would seem to be to focus on tourism's destructive aspects. In a recent discussion of economics and national tourism in China, the authors comment on the damage caused to local cultures. They note that due to the massive, but chaotic increase in tourist infrastructure, integration into the market system has been accompanied by a number of negative consequences for local and ethnic communities. Thus, tourism presents something of a Faustian bargain for these communities: While it offers them opportunities to earn cash, they must sell off their heritage to do so, and the long term costs of doing so are rarely equal to the short term gains (Ghimire and Li 2001: 103).

Although I have little doubt that these authors are correct that the development of a tourist political economy has often not benefited locals to any great degree, in this chapter, I would like to look at the productive aspects of tourism. In other words, integration into the national (or provincial) economy by the development of tourist infrastructure is not simply destructive of local economies; it changes the conditions of cultural production as well. Indeed, in examining the effects of tourism within a religious ethnic minority of Yunnan Province, I want to suggest that instead of cultural breakdown, we see that in some ways at least, the practice of the religious specialists in this community is actually strengthened. In order to demonstrate this, however, it will first be necessary to develop a broader understanding of ethnicity and tourist development in China.

The Problem of Tourist Development in China

At the heart of my questions about the micro-interaction between a monk and a Han Chinese tourguide at a Theravāda Buddhist temple in China's Yunnan Province is a concern to understand the effects that development has upon the identity and cultural forms, and in particular the religious practices, of local people. In the contemporary People's Republic of China, this means coming to understand the relationship between a constellation of concepts and actors: development and modernization, tourism, ethnicity (or minority nationality), the state, and religion. While it is beyond the scope of this chapter to deal with these concepts with any degree of depth, it is possible at least to sketch out an outline of the issues at stake. While all of these concepts interact with each other in a variety of ways, I will begin with the concept of ethnicity because it provides a useful way to talk about the relations of all of these concepts.

Ethnicity in China is inherently about the Chinese nation, national belonging, and its status as a civilization. China, as is well-known by now, is a multiethnic state whose 55 national minorities comprise some 10% of the population and occupy perhaps 60% of the land-mass, particularly the border regions (Mackerras 2003: 1; Blum 2002).[3] Many of these minority groups reside in 'autonomous' communities, which range in size from a province down to a village. This 'auton-omy' (*zizhi*), which is ideally meant to allow a minority group to develop and modernize naturally and according to its own struc-tures, is generally quite limited. In point of fact the intervention of the Chinese state in the lives of many minorities is quite heavy. Rhetorically, at least, these interventions are meant to be benign, "civilizing projects" (Harrell 1995) which are intended to raise the civilizational status of the minorities up to that of the Han majority and Chinese modernity in general. Not surprisingly, much of the lit-erature on China's ethnic minorities has focused on the interactions of two, relatively homogenous agents: the minority group and the Chinese state (or the Han Chinese). This has meant that the litera-ture, which is often undergirded with questions about what defines a particular minority, has been driven by questions of cultural inte-grity, assimilation, and resistance to China (see, e.g., Heberer 1989; Mackerras 1994; Gladney 1991; in somewhat different ways, Litzinger 2000).

China's minorities are not simply the recipients of Chinese moder-nity, however. Although they have often not had much control over processes of national imaginings, China's national minorities have had a fundamental role in the constitution of the modern Chinese national identity. Indeed, the representation of national minorities as "exoticized, even eroticized" has been "essential to the construction of the Han Chinese majority, the very formulation of the Chinese

---

[3] 'National minority' is a translation of the term *shaoshu minzu*. There are a vari-ety of possible translations for the term *minzu*, such as 'nationality' or 'ethnic group,' though all are somewhat unsatisfactory. Because of the fact that it comes out of a particular nexus of power/knowledge, it has become not uncommon for scholars to leave the term untranslated (Oakes 1998: 232). However, for ease of understanding, I shall refer to *minzu* as nationality and *shaoshu minzu* as national minorities.

'nation' itself" (Gladney 1994: 94). As Louisa Schein has shown, however, the representations of the minority Other are not simply representations of multicultural difference, but are radically asymmetrical, most often along axes of class, gender, education, and region. Thus, in the logic of "internal orientalism," the Han majority are most often represented as male, urban, educated professionals, while minorities are usually represented as female, rural, and uneducated (Schein 2000: 101).[4] Not surprisingly, while the cultural production of these representations occur at all levels of society, from villages up to the state (and its media groups), it is those produced by the state that see the broadest distribution and most frequent reproduction. Nonetheless, Schein recognizes that both the majority and the minority groups are made up of a variety of fractions that have different opportunities to effect change upon the production and dissemination of these representations. By focusing on cultural production by different fractions, she allows us to see that minority identity is not simply about assimilation to or resisting China.

This is an important intervention, because discussions that focus on assimilation and/or resistance tend to emphasize the difference between the majority and the minority. Nonetheless, it is important to remember that national minorities are citizens of the People's Republic and most of their options for life choices are those that are produced in the Chinese public and private spheres. Dru Gladney (1998: 109) has talked about this in dialogical terms:

> Ethnic identity in China . . . is not merely the result of state definition, and . . . it cannot be reduced to circumstantial maneuvering for utilitarian goals by certain groups. Rather, I propose that it is best understood as a dialogical interaction of shared traditions of descent within sociopolitical contexts, constantly negotiated in each political-economic setting.

Susan McCarthy has taken this broad perspective in analyzing ethnicity-based social activism by various national minority groups in Yunnan. Rather than focusing on ethnic identity, she has discussed this activism in terms of citizenship. The Chinese state has provided

---

[4] I have often found that there is also a discourse of race, particularly in terms of skin color, included as another axis of differentiation. Thus, for example, I have heard Dai-lue women referred to as "backwards, fat and black" (*luohou, pang,* and *hei*). Note, however, the degrees of hierarchy. If Dai-lue refer to themselves this way in reference to the Han majority, they themselves are on top of this binary when it comes to some of the other 'less civilized' minority groups of Sipsongpanna.

certain opportunities and frameworks for national minorities to participate in Chinese modernity, and minority citizens can use these opportunities—"putting some teeth into the party-state's promises of autonomy" (McCarthy 2000: 108)—to expand their rights. In other words, ethnic mobilization in Yunnan is not necessarily about being separatist and should not be seen as a threat to the nation-state, but is instead an attempt to participate in the Chinese national community under the terms provided by the Chinese state.

This also directs our attention to the degree to which being a minority in China is relational and does not have to be an all-encompassing aspect of identity. In studying the minorities of China comparatively, Shih Chih-yu, a Taiwanese political scientist, has emphasized the point that China's minorities do not think about being minorities at all times; nor do they think of China at all times. Indeed, in my own fieldwork among the Dai-lue, I found this to be the case. When I directed conversations toward issues of politics and relations with the Chinese state, my informants were certainly able and often willing to discuss these subjects. Sometimes they also brought up these issues on their own, but I was in just as many conversations with people in which the Chinese state and politics did not come up naturally. To address this issue, Shih suggests that we need to think of China and Chinese nationalism only to the degree that it affects behavior and attitudes. This leads him to suggest that we think of China less in geographical terms, as an idea in space, but rather in temporal terms, as an idea in time. "China is no more than 'moments' for people who are busy with their own lives: China means something to ethnic minorities only at the moments when local people are dealing with the government or the Party" (Shih 2002: 8).

Domestic ethnic tourism is a major site where the interests of the state (both the local and national forms) and local ethnic groups meet (though they do not fully converge), and where the paradoxes of being ethnic within China are most clearly highlighted. Over the last ten years, the Chinese state has encouraged domestic tourism as a major source of consumption for its growing middle class (Ghimire and Li 2001). Indeed several years ago, the national government instituted a week-long holiday around International Labor Day, precisely so that its middle class would consume through tourism. This has benefited provinces such as Yunnan or Guizhou, which have many minorities, but are very much peripheral to the rest of the country. The governments of these places have sought to use tourism, and in particular ethnic tourism, to bring in cash that would otherwise not enter their local economies. Tourism in China's border regions, therefore, serves several different agendas. For the national state, it keeps money flowing, encourages development, and provides the middle class with consumption opportunities. For local governments in the peripheries, it provides opportunities for wealth transfer from China's centers. For the middle class, it provides them with consumption opportunities, as well as the chance to feel more modern (because they view backward minorities).

The situation for national minorities (collectively and individually) is more complicated. For most of China's rural population, majority or minority, participation in the economic boom of the last twenty years has been difficult at best. The ethnic "tourism political economy" (Oakes 1998) provides minority peoples that are not near regional economic centers opportunities for participation in Chinese modernity (i.e., the chance to earn some cash) that are simply not otherwise available. Yet at the same time, it leaves them in something of a catch-22 position. National minorities are understood to be the bearers of tradition and culture, and what they are selling in order to participate in Chinese modernity is their authenticity, in essence their backwardness. However, the degree to which they lose their tradition (whether through assimilation or through selling it in the tourist political economy), national minorities also lose part of what defines their place within the Chinese "nation-scape" (McCarthy 2000). One effort to address this difficulty is to produce multiple forms of minority culture in the same place: one (a thin version) for the tourists and the other (a thick version) for the locals (Davis 1999).

The practice of religion can be understood within these frameworks of tourism and ethnicity. While there are many Chinese who participate in religious activities, it is necessary in this context to differentiate religious activities of national minorities and those of the majority. For example, religious practices are often an important part of the tradition of which minorities are meant to be bearers, hence the religious activities of minorities are understood within the national culture to have a different social meaning. Unlike those who come to a religious community as adults, for whom interest in religion can be read as a sign of their modernity (modern subjects choosing to participate in world religions), in the post-Cultural Revolution era religious practices for China's minorities are generally understood as a return home to their tradition. The Chinese state has concerns around religions practiced by minorities different from those practiced by the majority. To the degree to which these minority groups' practices do not threaten the sovereignty of the Chinese state (as is perceived to be the case in Tibet and among some Muslim groups), the Chinese state has relatively little interest in minority religious practices. Where it does have an interest is in those minority religious activities that have viewable components. These provide the state with opportunities for development of the tourist political economy of minority regions. In sum, then, I am arguing that at least for minority regions, we need to see religion as existing within other frameworks of control and negotiation within Chinese society.[5]

Before applying this understanding of ethnicity, tourism, and religion in China to what Dubi Kham Bian was doing with the Chinese tourists, it is necessary to provide the context of his religious community and more specifically why tourism is an important part of it. I shall begin with a discussion of Sipsongpanna, the location of Wat Pājie, and its relationship to both China and Southeast Asia.

The 'Exotic' Tais of Southwest China

Sipsongpanna is an autonomous prefecture of the Dai-lue people (*Xishuangbanna Daizu Zizhizhou*).[6] This relatively small region, home to

---

[5] Although I am speaking of the Chinese state in rather monolithic terms here, I want to stress that the Party-State has many different factions based on a variety of factors, and it is always a danger to globalize the Chinese condition from one region. This is particularly true with problems around religions, where the experience of religious practitioners, minority or majority, vary greatly with regard to state response.

[6] In general, I use Dai-lue names and terms where relevant, rather than using the Chinese transliterations of these terms. Thus, I refer to Sipsongpanna, rather than Xishuangbanna. One exception to this is the capital city of Sipsongpanna, which I refer to as Jing Hong to avoid confusion. The *pinyin* is pretty close to a transliteration from Dai-lue. The name of the people that I am writing about here is somewhat more complicated. The Dai-lue are part of the Tai ethno-linguistic grouping, which stretches from Yunnan down to Southern Thailand. I use a "d" rather than a "t" here because in the local language (of the same name), the first sound is closer to the sounded dental, rather than the aspirated one. 'Lue' refers to their particular subset of the Tai grouping. In Chinese, the Dai-lue are referred to as the *Daizu*, or the Dai group. As Hsieh (1995) has pointed out, conceptually the term *Daizu* includes more than simply the Dai-lue of Sipsongpanna. There are three other Tai groups of Yunnan which through processes of "ethnogenesis" (Gladney 1991) have come to see themselves as related, but historically have had little contact with one another. On any given day, most Dai-lue people in Sipsongpanna simply refer to themselves as *Dai*; for reasons of the geopolitical shift described

approximately 1,000,000 people, is situated in the Southwestern Province of Yunnan, on the Mekong River as it leaves China and enters Burma and Laos. Historically—meaning pre-1953—it was a small, semi-independent kingdom sandwiched between the Chinese and Burmese empires. Overrun by both periodically, it was able to maintain a fairly high degree of independence because of its distance from regional capitals, and the difficulty of travel in this part of the world. Even in the 1950s, it took Chinese ethnologists over a month to get from the provincial capital of Kunming to Sipsongpanna on horseback (there are now over twenty 737s a day making the 400 km trip in about 50 minutes).

Charles Patterson Giersch (1998) has suggested that we think of Sipsongpanna as a "middle ground." By this he means that Sipsongpanna was a region of high contact and interaction, where no one group could achieve complete, long-term control. Even as the Dai-lue of Sipsongpanna (as well as the Dai of Dehong, another autonomous prefecture to the north) were not strong enough to resist the invaders fully, Chinese imperial armies were unable to resist the scourges of malaria endemic to the region. On the contrary, during much of the Ming and Qing periods, the imperial state was happy to accept tribute and bestow relative autonomy (and a *tusi* designation) upon the traditional king of Sipsongpanna, the *cao phaendin* (lord of the earth). This situation as a middle ground, and long term ties with both the Chinese empire and the Theravāda states to the south, is reflected in the traditional comment (quoted to me by both Han Chinese and Dai-lue residents of Sipsongpanna) that *haw bin paw, mon bin mae* (China is our father and Burma our mother). Nonetheless, Dai-lue culture is largely from Southeast Asia.

This is especially true in the realm of religion. Unlike the rest of China, where Mahāyāna Buddhism of either the East Asian or Tibetan variety is the norm, the Dai-lue of Sipsongpanna practice the same Theravāda Buddhism prevalent throughout mainland Southeast Asia and Sri Lanka. The local spirit cults are also similar to what we see to the south (Tambiah 1970; Terweil 1975). While this region seems not to have been the site of a galactic polity along the lines of Ayutthaya, Bangkok, or Pagan, Theravāda Buddhism

---

above (see again Hsieh 1995), "Lue" is of less relevance for most people. Nonetheless, I choose to use the term Dai-lue because it highlights the fact that these people continue to have important contacts with people both to the north (with China) and the south (with other Tai groups of Southeast Asia).

was basically an established religion (Hill 1998; Natchā 1998). Indeed, a variety of people, both Dai-lue and Han Chinese, have told me that prior to the changes in society around the Cultural Revolution, any young man who did not ordain at least as a novice would be unable to get married.

All of this changed in 1953 when the People's Liberation Army set up a garrison in Jing Hong, the capital of Sipsongpanna, establishing the region as an autonomous prefecture within a few years. China's sovereignty over this region had grown increasingly tight in the twentieth century. In 1896, an Anglo-French treaty deeded the region to the Chinese empire, mapping a part of four "geo-bodies" that had up to this point remained unmapped. Throughout much of the twentieth century, crown princes of Sipsongpanna lived in the provincial capital of Kunming as a sign of the good relationship between the Dai-lue and Han Chinese (though we might also call these princes hostages). Indeed, the last such prince was *cao phaendin* for only a very brief period and has not lived in Sipsongpanna since the 1950s. He is now a retired professor of Dai languages and culture at the Yunnan Nationalities Institute in Kunming. In the decades after 1953, the underpinnings of Dai-lue society were dismantled: The traditional 'feudal' (*fengjian*) social system was abolished, in large part by co-opting the traditional aristocracy into the Communist Party; the region went through no fewer than five different periods of land reform (McCarthy 2001); and starting in the late 1950s, the Buddhist Sangha was actively harassed before being abolished during the early days of the Cultural Revolution.[7] Indeed, by the end of the Mao era, Sipsongpanna had changed quite radically. If it was not quite a full participant in Chinese modernity, nonetheless, it was also barely a figment of its traditional self.

This remains an important aspect of the contemporary moment, for it clearly changes the position of Theravāda Buddhism in society. In the early 1980s, when the reforms of Deng Xiaoping finally made it to this corner of the People's Republic, the Dai-lue returned to their religious practice with an enthusiasm often described as a 'fever' (Tan 1995; Hansen 1999). Despite this enthusiasm, it took almost a decade for the demographics of the Sangha to return to

---

[7] Although the Sangha is the community of Buddhists, both lay and monastic, in daily usage it often refers only to those who have ordained. I follow this latter usage here.

their pre-1960 level. In part, this was simply due to the costs of re-construction. It took villages some time to rebuild temples, and it was often difficult to locate enough knowledgeable monks to take leader-ship roles in temples. Indeed, particularly in the 1980s, a number of monks from Thailand and the Shan States in particular served as abbots when suitable local candidates could not be found.[8] By the early 1990s, there were about 500 temples, between 500–600 monks and about 5,000–6,000 novices. These numbers are comparable to those of the late 1950s, and have indeed grown by 15% or so since then. At the same time, however, the overall Dai population has doubled since the 1950s.[9] Clearly, ordination no longer holds the same place it once did. Boys who have not been ordained can get married easily, and there are alternatives to the traditional education of boys in temple settings, namely the Chinese public school system. This is especially true for boys from the urban centers of Sipsongpanna where the schools are relatively strong and farming land is scarce.[10] For boys from rural areas, ordination remains a more common (and indeed preferred) option.[11]

---

[8] The Chinese government's response to these foreign monks is instructive. While it is aware of the phenomenon and has given its assent to it, my impression is that either it is not aware of the extent of cross-border networks or that it turns a blind eye to the movement of monks across borders. The Sangha of Sipsongpanna is careful not to bring the matter to the local state's attention. Thus, when the gov-ernment does start to get nervous about the numbers of foreign monks (which has happened from time to time over the last few decades), the Sangha hierarchy has acted to get these monks to return to their native countries. This assuages the fears of the government. For a useful discussion of premodern monastic networks in con-temporary Sipsongpanna (see Davis 2003).

[9] There are two notes to point out here. First, because temporary ordination is common in Sipsongpanna, the numbers of ordained are always in flux, and it is difficult to get an accurate count of the monastic population. Second, I suspect that the demographic figures from the 1950s are problematic. The official census from the early 1950s puts the Dai-lue population at roughly 150,000 (cited in Tan 1995; McCarthy 2001), but I would not be surprised by an undercount. The infrastruc-ture available in the 1950s to make an accurate count of the population in this particular region was inadequate. In the urban areas, such as around Jing Hong, this was not a problem, but it really took several decades for the Chinese struc-tures to penetrate adequately into the countryside.

[10] Girls have never been eligible to become novices, and there is (as yet at least) no female renunciant movement in Sipsongpanna comparable to those seen in other parts of Southeast Asia. Perhaps as a result, girls participate in the Chinese public schools at much higher rates than boys (see Hansen 2001).

[11] Parents of novices from villages in or near Jing Hong have told me that they largely opposed their son's desire to take the novice ordination. Their opposition was due to fears that it would hurt their son's performance in the Chinese public schools. None of the parents I spoke with outside of Jing Hong expressed ever feel-ing such opposition, which is in line with the findings of Mette Hansen (1999).

Beyond the demographic patterns of ordination, the changed context of monasticism is indexed by the refounding of Wat Pājie and the position it has since taken in Sipsongpanna. Wat Pājie is unique in Sipsongpanna as the only temple that is not directly attached to a village. It was refounded in 1990 at the behest of local villagers (Davis 2003), with some funding from the local government, and has since become the administrative center of the Sangha. It is the location of the local office of the Buddhist Association, the quasi-governmental organization that serves as the link between the government and Buddhists. The abbot of Wat Pājie is the director of the regional Buddhist Association, and is also recognized as the head of the Sangha by Dai-lue villagers and monks. What is interesting about this, however, is that it does not really have an analogue in pre-1953 Sipsong-panna. The *cao phaendin* certainly had one or two temples that were his, and there are temples around the autonomous prefecture which are called *mahāracathān* (royal temple), but there was no temple that one could point to as being *the* head of the Sangha.

Equally important, in 1994, the monks of the temple opened a Dhamma School (Dai: *hongheyn pha-pariyatti-dham*; Chinese: *foxueyuan*) to provide proper training for novices. While such schools are relatively common in other parts of the Theravāda Buddhist world, this was the first such school in Sipsongpanna, and it has served to help stabilize, and indeed foster, the development of the Sangha. Elsewhere, I have argued that its purpose is to provide not just a Buddhist education, but also a modern education in Chinese and computers, as well as an education in Dai-lue culture. In other words, they are not simply training Dai-lue men to be monks; rather, they are training monks to be Dai-lue men, who can also participate in Chinese modernity (Borchert 2004). Through this project Wat Pājie is producing (or trying to, at any rate) a cohort of men that we might classify as Gramscian "organic intellectuals" (McCarthy 2001: 190): Dai-lue men who are monks and capable of competing (or at least participating) in the Chinese political economy. In this sense, Wat Pājie is perhaps the central location for the development of a non-separatist Dai-lue nationalism. Ironically, at the same time, Wat Pājie is fundamentally implicated in the tourist political economy.

Sipsongpanna was an early entrant into the field of Chinese tourist destinations, for both foreign and domestic tourists. It was open to foreign tourists by the mid-1980s, and its Southeast Asian aspects made it a welcome change of pace for foreign tourists in China. For

Chinese tourists, it was also a bit of Southeast Asia during a period when it was all but impossible for Chinese citizens to leave the country for reasons of tourism. It was also perceived to be a place suffused with the exotic and the erotic, indexed by soft-focus photos of Dai-lue women bathing (publicly) in rivers and the whiff of bacchanalia surrounding the Dai-lue New Year, known in China as *Poshui Jie*, the Water Splashing Festival. When an airport opened up in the early 1990s, the tourist economy of the region exploded; at its peak, twenty 737s a day filled with Chinese tourists came down to the capital of Jing Hong. Not surprisingly, by some estimates, the number of domestic to international tourists in the region is something like 100 to 1.[12] While it seems that the late 1990s may have seen a peak in the number of domestic tourists, as well as a major glut in the development of the infrastructure to cater to these tourists, it remains true that with the tropical hardwoods already largely forested out and the price of rubber (another major export) quite low, tourism remains the most important 'industry' in the region.

Buddhism, and Wat Pājie in particular, are important parts of this industry. Much of the sales pitch to Chinese tourists is that they will get to see minority cultures, and in particular Dai-lue culture. Theravāda Buddhism is an essential part of this culture, and in fact provides a nice counterpart to the implied raciness of throwing water. Bucolic temples are filled with cute little boys worshipping the Buddha, providing a bit of spiritual authenticity that is both different from Chinese Buddhism (because it's Theravāda, with its meat-eating monks), yet still familiar (because it's Buddhism). The sight of these young religious actors might also provide Han Chinese tourists, many of whom will claim to "have no religion" (though they might be interested), the opportunity to feel modern. To facilitate tourists seeing these ethnic minority cultures, the provincial government, the prefectural government, and locals (both Han and national minority) have developed several 'minority culture parks.' These parks, which are modeled after the Splendid China theme park in Shenzhen (Anagnost 1997) and the nationalities park in Kunming (Blum 2001), have a variety of styles. Some of these are Disneyfied versions of

---

[12] This estimate was provided by Monica Cable, who has conducted field research on tourism in Meng Kham, to the south of Jing Hong (personal communication, March 2004). Ghimire and Zhou (2001) estimate that nationally about 90% of the tourists in China are domestic.

minority cultures, others are more troubling, and involve the transformation of a set of 'natural' villages into a park for tourists. Two
of these parks either contain or are attached to Buddhist temples,
and thus, these temples become the Dai-lue Buddhist experience for
most tourists.

In actuality, there are probably only about ten temples (out of
more than 500) that are regularly seen by tourists. Three of these
are in Jing Hong: Wat Pājie, which is attached to the 'Dai Minority
Culture Park' and two other small village temples that are nearby.
The 'Dai Culture Park' in Meng Kham has five temples within it,
though one of these, Wat Mengkham, receives many more visitors
than the others. Finally, there are two temples outside of the immediate vicinity of Jing Hong which are famous for their reliquaries.
One of these in particular, at Wat Baodī, has become a major tourist
stop. Because of its location in Jing Hong, and its proximity to a
national minority park, Wat Pājie probably receives more visitors
than any other park. Indeed, even during the off-season, Wat Pājie
is never fully empty of tourists. While the discussion below will talk
about the effects that tourism has had on Buddhist practice more
broadly, my data come principally from Wat Pājie and Wat Baodī,
and the most significant changes have occurred at these temples.

Buddhism Developed Through Tourism

If, as I noted above, tourism is one of the most important industries within Sipsongpanna, one might expect its effects to be pervasive
on cultural practices (cf., Davis 1999). While it can be difficult to
differentiate the effects of tourism specifically, nonetheless, I would
suggest that we see three major shifts within the Sangha that are
especially produced through the tourist political economy.

Political Cover in Sangha-State Relations

Although most scholars understand that the context of religious practice in China is much more complicated than we see in the popular
press, nonetheless it remains quite common to see the Chinese state
and religious actors in opposition to one another. This is reasonable,
insofar as the CCP still proscribes cadres from public participation
in religious activities. Nonetheless, despite what we might call a structural opposition between the party-state and religious actors, on the

ground there is often much negotiation between these two sets of actors. That this negotiation exists does not necessarily mean that religious actors ultimately get what they want, but it means there is a possibility for it. This negotiation arises out of two things: first, there is a legal framework of freedom of religious belief, buttressed by the relaxing of social freedoms in exchange for political allegiance that is the hallmark of the Reform Era (Potter 2003). Second, there is the fact that religion can be a big business, with a great deal of cash coming in, and the government wants its cut. I have actually seen this type of negotiation taking place over whether people need to pay entrance fees to get into Wat Pājie.

We can see these factors present in the celebration of the Water Splashing Festival. The Dai-lue New Year, *Song Khān*, has become an officially sanctioned three-day affair. While historically its celebration varied with the lunar calendar, it has come to be celebrated on 13–15 April every year by fiat of the government. According to Donald Swearer (1995: 37–38), the holiday throughout Southeast Asia derives more from Brahmanical and local traditions than it does from Buddhist ones, and there are some well-known legends about its origins in Sipsongpanna, which has long been known in China for this holiday. Zhou Enlai even took part in the late 1950s, and pictures of him participating in the festivities are not uncommon in Sipsongpanna (Blum 2001). As a consequence, it has been largely developed as an extravaganza for tourists, sanitized and spectacularized by the government for tourist consumption (cf., Davis 1999: ch. 2).[13]

It has often been noted that this holiday has lost its religious aspects (Davis 1999). Nonetheless, over the last decade, the second day of the three day festival in Jing Hong has come to be focused in large part around Wat Pājie. On this day, the monks process around the city, followed by a number of Dai-lue villagers. They are preceded by the temple's most precious Buddha image (donated to the temple by a famous Southeast Asian monk), which is placed in a truck and driven around the city. After the procession returns to the temple— at which point it has picked up a huge number of Chinese tourists— the Buddha image is placed back in its normal spot in the middle of a garden next the *vihāra*, the worship hall. Once there, folks crowd

---

[13] One of the years that I was present for *poshui jie*, there was a car-jumping motorcycle performance in the city's stadium.

in around the image, and a short ceremony takes place. The year that I observed this, 2002, the people in the temple garden were probably about evenly split between Dai-lue worshippers and Chinese tourists (with a healthy smattering of journalists with cameras). The key moment of this ceremony was when the abbot of the temple and the head of the autonomous prefecture, who is Dai-lue, poured water over the Buddha image. This was followed by two of the vice-abbots doing the same thing along with the mayor of Jing Hong and several other local politicians. After the Buddha was washed by these dignitaries, they processed out of the temple and into the park and down into a small pavilion, where they released some fish into the artificial lake in the middle of the park (where for a few *kuai*, one can reenact the dragonboat races across the Mekhong River, one of the highlights of Water Splashing Festival's first day).

I would like to suggest that what we see here is an alignment of the interests of the Sangha and the local state around the practice of Buddhism. The local government is deeply interested in developing its tourist infrastructure because it brings money into the autonomous prefecture; the monks are interested in perpetuating and developing their religious institution.[14] While these two interests are not precisely the same, they seem to have met a happy medium in Sipsongpanna. The reason for this has to do with the economics of Buddhism. Several of the monks have commented to me that the long-term viability of Buddhism in Sipsongpanna is closely aligned with the the long-term viability of the Dai-lue ethnicity. That is to say, that as long as the Dai-lue understand themselves to be Dai-lue, a Tai group separate from the Chinese, Buddhism will be supported. Accordingly, the monks believe it is necessary for them to preserve and develop Dai-lue culture in ways that are accessible to the Dai-lue people. It also, however, depends upon the Dai-lue people having enough surplus to support monks who can do relatively little work to support themselves.[15] Tourism is an important way to produce this surplus,

---

[14] Not all tourist developments bring in significant amount of money, of course. Nonetheless, there seems to be a widespread view that tourist development is a panacea for cash-strapped local governments and economies (see Ghimire and Li 2001: 98–102).

[15] Monks in Theravāda Buddhism are generally not supposed to take part in agricultural labor. I have found in Sipsongpanna that monks and novices in village temples generally do small amounts of labor to support themselves. One temple, for example, owns a grove of rubber trees, and the novices harvest the sap to sell to defray the costs of the temple.

and a number of monks are quite open to the development of tourist infrastructure, as long as they can have a hand in its development.[16]

What we see in the performance of the washing of the Buddha is a strategic alliance. Historically, Theravāda Sanghas and the state (local and otherwise) have had a symbiotic existence, and we see a symbiosis here too. Yet the legitimacy gained by the local government in supporting the Sangha in its washing of the Buddha image is probably not the same as that which the *cao phaendin* would have received prior to 1953. While the ceremony takes place at a temple, the government's position is that this is a cultural moment, a local custom that needs to be supported by the local authority, and through which the local government gains cultural, not supernatural, capital. It is a statement of cultural solidarity, not religious unity. It is not irrelevant that it happens at the moment of greatest tourist penetration into Sipsongpanna.

Another example will help clarify what I mean: I observed during the course of my fieldwork a crisis for the monks of Wat Pājie which they seemed unable to resolve. This occurred at Wat Baodī, one of the other temples on the principle tourist circuits (cf. Li 2003). Sometime in the late summer 2001, a group of Han Chinese men set themselves up, with the apparent support of the local villagers, first as Theravāda monks, then after they had been unmasked as false, as Mahāyāna monks. They did this in order to tell the fortunes of tourists. They charged exorbitant sums for the privilege of receiving these fortunes—about $100. While this was illegal, the greater problem in the eyes of the monks of Wat Pājie was the fact that it was a corruption of Theravāda Buddhism by Dai-lue villagers. During a meeting at Wat Pājie of the monks and villagers from that village, the monks articulated over and over again the need to maintain the purity of Buddhism in Sipsongpanna, for both practical and religious reasons.

Although these men were shown to be false monks, they nevertheless stayed in the tourist village by Wat Baodī for probably another half a year. Because the local villagers supported these 'confidence monks', the monks of Wat Pājie were unable to root them out. These men were finally, however, arrested and expelled from the autonomous

---

[16] Jing Li (2003) discusses the efforts of one monk, who is the abbot of a temple in Meng Kham, to develop tourism in the regions temples. Making sure that the development maintains "authenticity" is of great importance to him.

prefecture by the police. When I asked why this might be the case, I was told by both monks and a local government official (also Dai-lue) that it was because the government had finally acted. They had done so because they had received complaints from tourists. The officials could ignore the requests of the monks, but not the complaints of the tourists.

What this shows, though, is that even if their visions of Buddhism do not directly line up, the local state does view a properly working Buddhism as worth caring for. That is to say, Buddhism is an important asset within Sipsongpanna, one that needs to be maintained. "Cultures of all types—ethnic, national, regional, and the like—that are able to translate their qualities into marketable commodities and spectacles find themselves maintained, experienced and globalized" (Picard and Wood 1997: viii). Of course, this maintenance by the local authorities comes at a cost. The local state sets the rules as to what constitutes legitimate temple activities and what does not. When the folk festivals, pop concerts, and social justice issue conferences at Wat Pājie became too large, the government did not directly tell them these could no longer take place, but it was also communicated that these things needed to be reduced in size. That is to say, tourism does buy the monks from Wat Pājie some cover, but it is not limitless, and it needs constant 'cover maintenance' and *guanxi* management in order to be effective.

Corruption and Distortion

One of the questions I asked above in response to Dubi Kham Bian's experience with the Chinese tourguide was whether or not tourism, and the tourism political economy, served to secularize the monks of Sipsongpanna. In this context, secularization, a decreased participation in religious activities of various sorts, would probably be the result of increased participation (and incorporation) into the Chinese national political economy (through public education and other media). As a whole, we do not see large-scale processes of secularization. The temple is no longer *the* center of village life in the way it was prior to the 1950s, and the Sangha is smaller as a percentage of the general population. Nonetheless, we continue to see regular participation in Buddhist activities by large numbers of Dai-lue, and large numbers of boys continue to ordain as novices for a period of time.

What we also see, however, is a degree of corruption and distortion in the Sangha, largely as a result of tourist development. I suggested above that the Sangha is ready and willing to participate in the development of the tourism infrastructure, even if the monks would like to maintain some control over this development. Yet, clearly, there are a number of things over which they do not have control. We have already seen two different examples of ways that the development of tourism has been problematic for even an enthusiastic Sangha. I noted above that the false monks at Wat Baodī were supported by the villagers ("Because," one of the Wat Pājie monks told me, "they are clearly getting money."). It is highly unlikely that situation would have developed were there not a large number of wealthy tourists coming through the area. While it is a dramatic case, it is clearly a situation in which Buddhism is taking part in the fleecing of tourists.

We also see a significant distortion in the lives of monks simply around the need to attend to tourists. I began this chapter with one such distortion at Wat Pājie. This kind of thing is quite common at the ten or so temples that are on the tourist circuit. Wat Man Jiang, a small temple near the entrance to the Dai Minority Park, has a small bench in front of the front door with a bowl and sign stating in Chinese and English that it costs 1 *yuan* to enter the temple.[17] This bench is normally staffed by novices of the temple (except when they are in school; then it is staffed by older laymen). Similarly, there are gift shops at several temples in Sipsongpanna, in which tourists (and nontourists) can purchase Buddhist paraphernalia. Resident monks generally staff these. At the gift shop at Wat Pājie, much of this paraphernalia is actually from Chinese Mahāyāna temples, and thus clearly intended for Chinese visitors. My point is not that there is anything inherently wrong with these activities, but rather that these are not what monks and novices have historically done. The need to direct staff into tending to tourists means that they have less time for other activities, such as study, meditation, or caring for the laity.[18]

---

[17] Dai-lue do not have to pay to enter these places. After I had been teaching at Wat Pājie for a while, I discovered that I no longer had to pay when I used the front gate of the Dai Minority Park to get in and out of the area. They recognized me as a teacher at the school at Wat Pājie.

[18] Birnbaum (2003) makes a similar point about monks in Mahāyāna temples throughout China

Reinforcing Dai-lue Identity

Despite this distortion and loss of labor to attend to the needs of tourists, I want to suggest that the most significant impact that tourism has had, at least among the monks of Wat Pājie, has been to reinforce their "dai-ness," and indeed even to radicalize it. This does not happen solely because of tourism, but tourism plays an important role in this process.

Tourism within a place like Sipsongpanna relies upon an 'economy of authenticity'. That is to say, although Chinese tourists may be coming to Sipsongpanna because of its reputation as being erotically exotic, for this reputation to hold up over the tourists have to view their experience this to some degree as authentic. Authenticity is of course an extremely elastic term and does not mean the same thing for all tourists or groups of tourists (Davis 1999). This economy of authenticity relies on perceptions of essences. To gain the authentic, the tourist must have a vision of what the 'essence' of a group is. They do not have to be right, they simply have to believe in it. For the Dai-lue, and particularly for Dai-lue men, being Theravāda Buddhist is a fundamental part of who they are perceived to be. In the state's classification, and thus in the popular national culture, the Sipsongpanna *Daizu* are believers of Theravāda Buddhism. Chinese tourists coming to Sipsongpanna do not expect all Dai-lue men to be monks, but they do expect to see Theravāda Buddhism. This produces a market for the selling of Theravāda Buddhism, which we see at a certain number of temples throughout the autonomous prefecture. It also helps maintain the choice for ordination as a natural one for Dai-lue men.

Of course, tourist visions of being a monk and the lived experiences of being a monk are different things. When Chinese tourists come to Wat Pājie, they see a bunch of men and boys wearing orange robes in a tropical setting. They seem to find the boys cute, or at least picture-worthy, given the numbers of pictures they try to take. As evidenced by their giggles and laughter, they find the temple itself, with a monk giving them a blessed thread, and the 10 *yuan* fortune-telling amusing. And undoubtedly, they also find themselves feeling superior when faced with their co-nationals' relatively poor Mandarin Chinese whenever they need to ask a question.

The monks and novices, of course, see different things. They see Chinese tourists walking around their temple grounds and acting inappropriately. They have to avoid tourists trying to touch them on their heads, and they often seem to avoid the tourists with cameras (or at least the Chinese ones). They are always having to tell the tourists to take off their shoes before they go into the worship hall, despite the large sign in Chinese and English making this request. This problem is not limited to Wat Pājie. In village temples, where the worship hall has a platform for monks, attendant monks and novices often have to tell the tourists that they are not allowed to walk on these platforms. The monks at Wat Pājie find the loudness of the tourists annoying. This does not mean that the temple is silent. Novices in particular are often quite boisterous, but it is also their home, and being respectful has different demands. Nonetheless, the monks and novices are also not in a position to remove these tourists from the temple grounds. Despite the annoyances, they rely on tourists. They rely on their money; the monks continued good relations with the local government depend upon their participation in the tourist political economy; and the local villagers, who support the temple, depend upon the tourists.

Indeed what we see here are examples of Shih Chih-yu's notion of 'China' moments, produced very much in the encounter between Han Chinese tourists and monks. The monks of Wat Pājie regularly interact with a variety of officials from the local government, even officials from the Public Security Bureau. Some of these interactions are vertical, i.e., the official telling the monks they have to do something. Others are more horizontal: Negotiations about some matter or other in which the power differential is less stark.[19] With tourists, however, the monks are in something of a bind. They are not under the control of the tourists, but neither can they kick them out. Nonetheless, they are constantly faced with being the object of a

---

[19] We see both examples in a small interaction over one of the temple's vehicles. This was a truck, donated to the temple by a monk from Burma. Because the truck entered China through the gray market, it did not (and does not) have proper license plates. One day, I was told by one of the monks, the old prefectural head, who was himself Dai-lue, saw this illegal truck and blew a gasket. He reamed out the monks and told them they had to get rid of the truck. Then he told the PSB about the matter. When the monks talked to the PSB, they were told not to worry about it. The PSB knew where the truck had come from, and they knew the monks were not causing trouble. Ironically, it was the Dai-lue official with whom the monks faced their relative powerlessness in 'China', and Han officials with whom they had a negotiating experience.

somewhat rude and ignorant touristic gaze. While none of the day-to-day interactions that I observed, such as the subtle interactions over the taking of pictures, were in and of themselves difficult to endure, over time the realization of difference builds up. These 'China' moments become regular reminders that they are different from the Han Chinese tourists, not so much because they wear different clothing and shave their heads, but rather because they are at the opposite end of a camera lens. The monks and novices are the ones who are less powerful, less modern, perhaps even less Chinese. It is clear, and perhaps not very surprising, how tourism helps magnify within the monks a sense of being different, and a heightened sense of being both Dai-lue and being a monk. However, what is perhaps more interesting here is the way that this partici-pates in a radicalized Dai-lue identity. For this to make sense, we need to have a better sense of what else happens at Wat Pājie.

I noted above that in addition to being the largest temple in Sipsongpanna and the location of the Buddhist Association in the region, Wat Pājie is also something of a Dai-lue cultural preserva-tion center. This is done in part through preserving texts and fos-tering the survival and development of the Dai-lue language. This is also done through the efforts of Wat Pājie's Buddhist Studies School, where the pedagogical efforts are not simply for an innocent production of religious specialists, but are rather for the training of religious specialists who are grounded in a particular national minor-ity identity. We see this, for example in an alphabet book, produced by the temple, which is filled with lessons about the necessity to pro-tect and love the Dai-lue people, the Dai-lue language, and Buddhism. These lessons, and the subnationalism they represent, are not aimed at the support of a separatist movement; most of the Dai-lue that I talked to, monk and lay, were at worst resigned to their colonized situation, and at best happy to see themselves as Chinese citizens. What it does, however, is inculcate the novice monks into an ethos that is pro-Dai. They become well educated in their own culture, and they care about it. This ensures the long-term survival of Buddhism.

That this nonseparatist Dai nationalism is being produced in a context of regular 'China' moments is important. The monks and novices are constantly reminded not only of their difference, but of their relative inability to control the spaces of their temple as well. They are also learning about (and attempting to preserve) their culture. The lack of control and the emphasis on their own culture reinforce one another in the promotion of a modern ethnic identity. While it has not yet taken an overtly political turn, that is not an impossible direction for it to take.

Conclusions

I never again saw Dubi Kham Bian performing the blessing in the worship hall, whether for tourists or Dai-lue villagers. Nonetheless, it is important not to read too much into this fact. Perhaps it was simply personal preference. As I noted at the beginning, the abbot of Wat Pājie did this more than anyone else, and he truly seemed to enjoy it. Indeed, Dubi Kham Bian's reluctance to perform the protective rite for the tourists may have had nothing to do with tourists themselves. After all, while very friendly, I found over the course of my fieldwork that he was also rather shy. Perhaps he simply did not enjoy performing this service. The abbot on the other hand, who was and is extremely gregarious, seems to have found performing this rite publicly, whether for Han or Dai-lue, to be an enjoyable act. In other words, the small scene I watched between Dubi Kham Bian and the Han Chinese tourguide might or might not have been a 'China moment,' to follow Shih Chih-yu's formulation.

Whatever the case for Dubi Kham Bian, tourism has had clear effects within the Sangha of Sipsongpanna. This chapter has suggested that the development of the tourist political economy in Sipsongpanna has been productive for the redevelopment of Theravāda Buddhism in Sipsongpanna, particularly at Wat Pājie, the central temple of the region. It has been so by providing political cover and strategically aligning the interests of the senior monks of the Sangha and the local government. It has been so by radicalizing the religiopolitical identity of the monks of Sipsongpanna, producing a context in which they think of themselves as the guardians of both their religious and national minority communities. There have been other consequences of tourist development which have been less positive, notably the need to shift attention away from traditional roles to taking care of tourists and the possible corruption brought on by the relatively greater wealth possessed by tourists. Indeed, although the monks understand that tourism is not all-negative and has not destroyed their culture, I believe they would also prefer it not to be present.

Although I have focused on tourism, it should also be clear that tourism and its effects upon the political economy of the practice of religion need to be understood as a subset of the policies of the party-state of the People's Republic. Although there is a degree of entrepreneurial spirit in the tourist economy of Sipsongpanna, much of the tourist infrastructure is produced and directed by the local state, not by individual investors. Thus, the effects of tourism upon religion, and culture more broadly, need to be seen as part and parcel with the projects of the Chinese state to modernize and civilize its ethnic minorities. In this way, although the effects that I have described may be limited to the small number of temples regularly visited by tourists in Sipsongpanna, they belong in the broader narratives of Buddhism, religion, and modernization in modern China.

REFERENCES

Anagnost, Ann. 1997. *National Past-Times*. Raleigh, NC: Duke University Press.
Birnbaum, Raoul. 2003. "Buddhist China at the Century's Turn." Pp. 122–44 in *Religion in China Today*, edited by Daniel L. Overmeyer. Cambridge: Cambridge University Press.
Blum, Susan. 2001. *Portraits of "Primitives."* Lanham, MD: Rowman and Littlefield Publishers.
Borchert, Thomas. 2004. "Theravāda Training in the Chinese National Sangha." Paper presented at the Annual Meeting of the American Academy of Religion, San Antonio, TX.
Davis, Sara. 1999. *Singers of Sipsongpanna*. Ph.D. dissertation, University of Pennsylvania.
———. 2003. "Premodern Flows in Postmodern China: Globalization and the Sipsongpanna Tais." *Modern China* 29: 176–203.
Ghimire, Krishna B. and Zhou Li. 2001. "The Economic Role of National Tourism in China." In *The Native Tourist*, edited by Krishna B. Ghimire. London: Earthscan Publications.
Gladney, Dru. 1991. *Muslim Chinese*. Cambridge, MA: Harvard University Press.
———. 1994. "Representing Nationality in China: Refiguring Majority/Minority Identities." *Journal of Asian Studies* 53: 92–123.
———. 1998. "Clashed Civilizations? Muslim and Chinese Identities in the PRC." Pp. 106–134 in *Making Majorities*, edited by Dru Gladney. Stanford, CA: Stanford University Press.
Hansen, Mette Halskov. 1999. *Lessons in Being Chinese*. Seattle: University of Washington Press.
———. 2001. "Ethnic Minority Girls on Chinese School Benches: Gender Perspectives on Minority Education." Pp. 243–80 in *Education, Culture and Identity in Twentieth-Century China*, edited by Glen Peterson, Ruth Hayhoe, and Yongling Lu. Ann Arbor: University of Michigan Press
Harrell, Stevan. 1995. "Introduction: Civilizing Projects and the Reaction to Them." Pp. 3–36 in *Cultural Encounters on China's Ethnic Frontier*, edited by Stevan Harrell. Seattle: University of Washington Press.
Heberer, Thomas. 1989. *China and its National Minorities: Autonomy or Assimilation?* Armonk, NY: M. E. Sharpe.

Hill, Ann Maxwell. 1998. *Merchants and Migrants*. New Haven, CT: Yale University Southeast Asia Studies.

Hsieh, Shih-chung. 1995. "On the Dynamics of Tai/Dailue Ethnicity: An Ethno-historical Analysis." Pp. 301–328 in *Cultural Encounters on China's Ethnic Frontier*, edited by Stevan Harrell. Seattle: University of Washington Press.

Li, Jing. 2003. "Making the Dai Temple Its Own: Ethnic Tourism, Theravada Buddhism, and Upholding Dai Culture in Contemporary Xishuang Banna, China." Paper presented at the Annual Meeting for the Association of Asian Studies, New York City.

Litzinger, Ralph A. 2000. *Other Chinas*. Raleigh, NC: Duke University Press.

Mackerras, Colin. 1994. *China's Ethnic Minorities*. Hong Kong: Oxford University Press.

———. 2003. *China's Ethnic Minorities and Globalisation*. London: Routledge.

McCarthy, Susan. 2000. "Ethno-Religious Mobilisation and Citizenship Discourse in the People's Republic of China." *Asian Ethnicity* 1: 107–16.

———. 2001. *Whose Autonomy is it Anyway? Minority Cultural Politics and National Identity in the PRC*. Ph.D. dissertation, University of California, Berkeley.

Natchā Laohasirinadh. 1998. *Sipsongpanna*. Bangkok: Thailand Research Fund.

Oakes, Tim. 1998. *Tourism and Modernity in China*. London: Routledge.

Picard, Michael and Robert E. Wood. 1997. *Tourism, Ethnicity and the State in Asian and Pacific Societies*. Honolulu: University of Hawaii Press.

Potter, Pitman B. 2003. "Belief in Control: Regulation of Religion in China." Pp. 11–31 in *Religion in China Today*, edited by Daniel Overmeyer. Cambridge: Cambridge University Press.

Schein, Louisa. 2000. *Minority Rules: The Miao and the Feminine in China's Cultural Politics*. Raleigh, NC: Duke University Press.

Shih, Chih-yu. 2002. *Negotiating Ethnicity in China*. London: Routledge.

Swearer, Donald K. 1995. *The Buddhist World of Southeast Asia*. Albany: State University of New York Press.

Tambiah, Stanley J. 1970. *Buddhism and the Spirit Cults of Northeastern Thailand*. Cambridge: Cambridge University Press.

Tan, Leshan. 1995. *Theravada Buddhism and Village Economy*. Ph.D. dissertation, Cornell University.

Terwiel, B. J. 1975. *Monks and Magic*. Lund, Sweden: Scandanavian Institute of Asian Studies.

CHAPTER FIVE

THE CHANGING ECONOMY OF TEMPLE DAOISM IN SHANGHAI

Der-Ruey Yang

The rapid resurgence of all sorts of religious practices in China since the mid-1980s has attracted a great deal of attention and curiosity from all over the world. The expanding scale of economic transactions involving religious activities has especially become an eye-catcher for students of Chinese religions. Anthropological works by Anagnost (1987, 1994), Siu (1989, 1990), Gates (1996), Jing (1996), and Yang (2000) are among the most prominent ones in this field. These works well documented various forms and aspects of ritual-instigated economic activities and insightfully analyzed their wide-ranging ramifications for the politics, interpersonal relationships, and general economy in contemporary China. Regrettably, however, systematic studies of the economy of religious professional and institutions, i.e., the ways in which these professional agents actively function to produce and reproduce religions for their own survival and development, are still scant in the existing literature. To fill this vacancy, I did fieldwork from July 1998 to May 2004 on 100 or so young Daoist priests to observe the process in which they learn to discern the structure and change of the local religious economy, to recognize their assets, to envision their niche in the changing economic landscape, and to adjust themselves accordingly.

Based on the data collected through this fieldwork, I suggest viewing the material side of Daoism in Shanghai as a service industry or an economic sector, which I term the 'Daoist economy' in what follows. Temple Daoist priests, relevant governmental bodies, occupational associations, and the free-lance Daoist priests and shamans who constitute what Yang (*forthcoming*) defined as the gray and black markets are all crucial constituents of this economic sector.[1] Yet, it would be

---

[1] Yang (*forthcoming*) defines the gray market as "religions with an ambiguous legal/illegal status" and the black market as "officially banned religions." Accordingly,

wrong to apply the model of a market economy (cf., Warner 1993, 1997; Neitz and Mueser 1997; Stark and Finke 2000) to understand the dynamics of the Daoist economy because it is actually a "hybrid" of four rival economic patterns—socialist public-supply economy, market economy, gift economy, and tributary economy—with their idiosyncratic logics and ethics (cf., Dalton 1969; Sahlins 1972; Yang 2000). Therefore, the key dynamics of the Daoist economy concern not so much about improving 'product-range' or 'marketing strategy' in order to win the patronage of more 'customers,' than about shrewdly maneuvring among diverse economic patterns and selectively integrating them into a distinctive, viable niche. As such, the adjustment process through which temple Daoist priests adapt to the denationalized Daoist economy since the early 1990s cannot be simply understood as a series of instrumental improvements. It is also a process of learning and creating through which they gradually updated their perception about social exchange, relationships, Daoism, and the priesthood—which amounts to the invention of a concise version of 'this-worldly' temple Daoism.

Background: Daoism and Daoist Professionals in Shanghai

Daoism is the religious reinterpretation or representation of the ancient traditions of nature worship and divination in China, although it has been widely alleged to be the legacy of the classical Daoist philosophy (or 'philosophical Daoism') founded by *Laozi* and *Zhuangzi* before the third century B.C.E. Religious Daoism first appeared as two millenarian movements—*Taiping Dao* and *Tianshi Dao*—in the late second century C.E. Afterward, Daoism gradually evolved into a massive and obscure jumble of theological, philosophical, scientific, skilful, and liturgical traditions championed by innumerable sects and orders. Except for a similar pantheon headed by *San Qing Si Yu* (the Three Pure Ones and the Four Emperors) and a commonly shared cosmological vocabulary featuring *Yin, Yang, Wuxing* (Five Elements), *Bagua* (Eight Trigrams) and so on, there are not many similarities

---

the practices of free-lance Daoist priests that are neither recognized nor banned by the authority can be properly categorized as belonging to the gray market. Contrarily, although the government somehow tolerates the activities of shamans in practice, the latter are nevertheless prohibited by law. Hence, shamans' practices can be categorized as somewhat between the gray and the black markets.

or organizational links among the countless Daoist sects. However, since the thirteenth century, Daoist sectarianism has been simplified into the dichotomy of the *Zhengyi* tradition and the *Quanzhen* tradition, although each of them still consists of many sects and orders. These two traditions are most obviously differentiated by the rule of celibacy and vegetarianism—the *Quanzhen* tradition requires celibacy and vegetarian diet while the *Zhengyi* tradition does not (Qing 1996).

The *Zhengyi* form of Daoism and a variety of Daoism-related cults have been the mainstream religious practices in the Yangtze River Delta ever since the late fourth century C.E. (Chen 1993). Although having been challenged by Buddhism, *Quanzhen* Daoism, and Christianity, the prominent status of *Zhengyi* Daoism in Shanghai has never really been endangered until the establishment of the PRC regime in 1949. Since the 'socialist reformation' movement launched by the government in 1954, Daoism and related cults began to be prosecuted as *fengjian mixin* (feudal superstitions). Daoist priests were forced to leave temples and *huansu* (return to the secular world). Hence, the practice of Daoist ritual and the transmission of Daoism were virtually stopped. Then, Daoist temples and temple-owned estate properties were confiscated by the state or appropriated by neighboring residents. Consequently, at the end of the 'Cultural Revolution' (1966–76), Daoism seemed to have been completely extinguished. However, the Reform and Open Door brought about by Deng Xiaoping caused a turn of events. Soon after the government's announcement about religious liberalization was released at the end of 1978, Daoist practices rapidly resumed in the countryside. Veteran Daoist priests who had been forced to 'return to the secular world' began to provide ritual services again, while Daoist devotees set out to rebuild/refurbish old temples or to construct new temples. Later, the government rehabilitated some symbolic figures of Daoism and gradually released some illegally confiscated or occupied temple properties. Finally, responding to the call of the Religious Affairs Bureau (RAB),[2] a number of 'self-governing' organizations of Daoist priests were established in many parts of China; the founding of the Shanghai Daoist Association (SDA) in April 1985 is one example.

---

[2] This office has been renamed as the Ethnic and Religious Affairs Bureau since 2003, but I will still abbreviate its name as RAB below.

However, the SDA has never become an all-encompassing association for the professional practitioners of Daoism in Shanghai. At least two groups of Daoist professionals have been excluded from the association—*sanju daoshi* (literally 'dispersed dwelling Daoist priests,' meaning 'free-lance Daoist priests') and shamans. Therefore, Daoist priests in Shanghai became divided into two categories—temple priests and free-lance Daoist priests, the former refers to the members of SDA who work in temples, while the latter denotes those non-members who work as freelancers. Despite a variety of differences between these two types of Daoist priests, they all follow the liturgical tradition of *Zhengyi* Daoism and provide their clients with similar rituals. As for shamans, they are purposefully excluded from the association because their practices are not considered as proper Daoism. Normally being addressed as *xianren* (immortal) or *daxian* (great immortal) instead of *Daoshi* (Daoist priest), shamans establish themselves not by providing Daoist ritual services but by helping clients with all sorts of 'superstitious tricks' such as spirit mediumship, divination, healing magic, and trivial magic for various purposes. Based on their heterodox practices, they have made great contribution toward Daoism by recruiting devoted temple worshippers, creating demand for Daoist rituals, organizing donations for temple buildings, and by many other ways.

It is into the historical and institutional context outlined above that the younger generation temple Daoist priests were brought up. The most pressing legacy that Daoism inherited from the three decades of oppression is the lack of qualified younger priests. At the end of the 1970s, there were no qualified Daoist priests in Shanghai who were trained after 1949—this implies that even the youngest ones were older than 52 years in 1985. Therefore, the SDA quickly founded a novice training school in late March of 1986. A group of 33 young men, aged 18 to the early 20s, and mostly from Jiangsu Province, became the first class students of the *Daoxueban* (Daoist Knowledge Course). Later in 1992, this course was further formalized and renamed as *Daojiaoxueyuan* (College of Daoism).[3] The curriculum of the Daoist College is not based on the monastic tradition of Daoism but on the standard curriculum for junior colleges fixed by the Ministry of Education. Accordingly, the occupational training

---

[3] I will address this organization simply as the Daoist College in the following discussion regardless of the difference between *Daoxueban* and *Daojiaoxueyuan*.

given by the Daoist College takes three years, which consists of two years of classroom pedagogy and a one year internship. The Daoist College has already finished training three classes of students whose study periods are 1986–89, 1992–95, and 1995–98, respectively; a fourth class enrolled in September 2004. The graduates were then deployed to staff the one dozen or so affiliate temples of the SDA. Currently, almost all these one hundred or so graduates are still working in those temples. The long process in which these young *gangbaning*[4] learn to survive in Shanghai's Daoist economy is what this chapter discusses.

Starting Point: Socialist Public-Supply Economy

Certainly, the first thing young Daoist priests have to learn is their place in the current economic landscape, which requires them to focus on *lingdao* (leaders)—a category of people who have the most decisive power over their positions.

This category consists mainly of local agents of the Party-State and people who possess access to the political process, such as the staff of the RAB, the United Front Department (UFD) of the CCP Shanghai Committee, Representatives of the People's Assembly, Members of the Political Council of Shanghai, and so forth. In a looser sense, it also includes the *ganbu* (cadre) of the SDA, i.e., the priests who possess offices in the association. *Lingdao* are extremely significant because they authoritatively decide the fortune of young priests by controlling their promotion.[5]

The legitimacy of *lingdao*'s authority is derived from the founding history of the SDA. In the wreckage of the Cultural Revolution, there was virtually no other way to acquire initial funding except through

---

[4] *Gangbaning* (or *jiangbeiren* in mandarin), literally means 'people from the north of the Yangtze River,' has long been a despised term in Shanghai. Originally, it was a neutral term for the poor migrants who took refuge in Shanghai from the North Jiangsu and Anhui Provinces because of warfare and natural disasters during the early part of the twentieth century. Later, this term was heavily charged with negative connotations such as illiteracy, ignorance, violence, poverty, madness, being unsanitary, and so on. Local people in Shanghai use this term as an adjective to describe all sorts of improper behavior. For a more detailed discussion about the history and current use of this term in Shanghai, see Honig (1989; 1992).

[5] Although promotion, degradation, and other personnel issues are supposed to be decided by the SDA through 'democratic' procedures, the decision-making process is actually dominated by the bureaucrats of the RAB, UFD, and SDA.

government endowment. So, the state did not just approve but also funded the establishment of the SDA. The SDA obtained its first property—the Baiyunguan temple, which was built at the end of nineteenth century and had been occupied by factories and neighboring households since the 1960s—from the government in 1985. Afterward, the state 'returned' more and more confiscated or appropriated estate properties like the Baiyunguan temple to the SDA.[6] Consequently, the SDA expanded steadily from genuinely zero in early 1985 to the present 12 middle- to small-sized temples in and around Shanghai. Apart from being used as the grounds for temples, some of the estate properties acquired from the state are rented out, swapped, or liquidated. The revenue thus produced still constitutes the main resource of the SDA's investment today. Hence, the most critical material basis of the SDA—and thus that of the young priests it employs—is 'granted' by the state.

Furthermore, the legitimacy of the bureaucrats' authority is reinforced by the chartered monopoly granted by the state. This monopoly is guaranteed by two principles of the current law of religious activities: first, only the SDA can own Daoist temples in Shanghai; second, people are not allowed to conduct any public religious activity involving Daoism except in Daoist temples. By implication, the SDA is entitled to claim ownership over any Daoist temple located in Shanghai, whether it is created by the local community (such as a village council or township) or by a group of devotees. Theoretically speaking, any temple that is not owned by or affiliated to the SDA could be given to SDA unconditionally or be confiscated and demolished.[7] Meanwhile, any public religious activity held outside legal Daoist temples is banned by law. This means that no one is allowed to

---

[6] It should be noted that the official terminology 'return' is misleading since the present beneficiary, SDA, is completely different from the original property holders. In fact, most of the original property holders have already vanished in various ways, and their offspring have no effective means to prove their heritage (cf. Anagnost 1994).

[7] At least three cases that I met during my fieldwork period can prove the validity of this rule. All three temples were revived by local devotees during the late 1980s to the early 1990s as they all existed there long before 1949. First, the estate property of the West Qijia Temple, in which the direct descendants of previous temple keepers still reside, was appropriated by the government and transferred to the SDA. Second, the buildings of Dragon King's Temple in Huamu town were simply demolished, and the land was confiscated by the government. Finally, the building and the land of the King Chen's Temple in Zhangqiao town was transferred from a village committee to the SDA without any repayment.

perform public Daoist rituals on clients' behalf apart from temple priests who are members of the SDA.

Therefore, as the representatives of the most prominent donor and patron, bureaucrats enjoy authority over the young priests employed by the SDA. This authority is not just symbolic but is actualized as a system of strict regulations controlling the time, space, styles, and relevant conduct of all sorts of rituals performed by temple priests. These priests are prohibited from performing any ritual before 7 a.m. or after 6 p.m. Besides, their ritual activity cannot go beyond the boundary of the temple compound. Moreover, they can neither install individual incense burners in front of specific gods nor light up real candles beside the altar because the security law prohibits setting any flammable item in an interior space.[8] Finally, the SDA bans any ritual containing 'superstitious,' violent, unsanitary elements and those that may "contradict the state's jurisdiction and public security."

These rules serve to prevent the temple priests from providing what the people really like and to make the services they can offer rigidly standardized. Thanks to these regulations, many rituals that used to be very popular in Shanghai before 1949 have been eliminated.[9] For example, one of the most characteristic elements of popular Daoism—the ritual procession around the boundary of a temple's symbolic jurisdiction with various kinds of amusing or cliff-hanging jugglers during temple festivals (Feuchtwang 2001; Sangren 1987: 61–92; Dean 1993)—is completely banned. On the other hand, the 'products' (ritual services) sold in every local temple are so standardized as to lack the flexibility to suit the needs of individual clients. The entire style is exactly identical to that of state-owned industries in general.

Furthermore, the state instituted a surveillance framework for auditing the financial and personnel affairs of the SDA in the name of "preventing corruption." Accordingly, the SDA set up a stereotypical socialist redistribution system based on six principles: (1) charges for

---

[8] The absurdity of this rule can be illustrated by the fact that every kitchen in Shanghai—including those in temples—contains something flammable. Despite its ridiculousness, this rule is compliantly observed in all the temples—except on ritual occasions.

[9] For example, rituals such as Jin Dao Duan Suo (cutting off the rope with a golden knife), He Yuan Fan Jie (reconciling feud and switching the judicial judgment), and Yi Xing Huan Dou (replacing an inauspicious constellation with an auspicious one) were abolished.

ritual services of all the temples are standardized in a common pric-
ing list; (2) all the income earned through ritual service belongs to
the temple rather than to individual priests; (3) the temple must hand
over all its earnings to the SDA headquarters; (4) the SDA headquarters allocates the total revenue contributed by all the temples
back to each temple administration and each individual priest; (5)
the budget allocation among temples is decided by the temple size
(the larger temples get more); (6) the salary and other welfare distributions among priests are decided by job title (people with the
same job title get the same salary and same welfare).

This socialist re-distribution system is succinctly described by young
priests as *daguofan* (a big pot of rice)—"Daoist priests share the temple's big rice-pot, temples share the SDA's big rice-pot." All the
earnings are pooled together and then redistributed by the SDA
headquarters to temple units and individual priests regardless of the
actual contribution one temple or individual priest has made to the
pooled revenue. So, the diligent will not be rewarded while the lax
will not be punished, or, in the young priests' mock saying: "No
matter whether you do things well or badly, no matter whether you
do or don't do your job, it's all the same." Therefore, there is no
point to work hard. The only sensible way to advance one's material
welfare is to raise one's job title through networking. Since the promotion of individual priests is controlled by the *lingdao*, priests have
to flatter them to an amazing extent. As a result, *lingdao* are actually enthroned as *tu huangdi* (earthy emperor) who do not hesitate at
all to abuse their overwhelming authority in many 'creative' ways.

In summary, the *lingdao* embody the state-established economic
order upon which these young priests' living depends. This order
can best be named a 'socialist public-supply economy' since it is at
once 'socialist' in terms of the internal redistribution system of the
SDA and is 'public-supply' in terms of the style in which the SDA
deals with the clients. The morality it claims to embody is egalitarianism and unselfish devotion for common causes, but in reality this
economy encourages hierarchical exploitation, sloth, and apathy.

Breaking the Big Rice-pot

The way of life of temple priests as structured by the socialist public-supply economy was disturbed by the economic reforms of the
state since the early 1990s. From 1990 onward, direct fiscal trans-

fer from the state to the SDA has been significantly decreased. Being rejected from the state's big rice-pot, the SDA has had to live up to the slogan that has prevailed throughout China since the 1980s—"every unit to take up its own financial responsibility."

Unfortunately, this was also the period when SDA was terribly thirsty for funds. On the one hand, the second and the third class students were enrolled in 1992 and 1995 respectively. The training cost, living expenses, allowances, and all sorts of welfare payments for students seriously increased the burden of the SDA. On the other hand, the first class of graduates desperately needed more income to support their new families since they got married and began to have babies just a few years before. The situation was made even worse by the fact that the majority of their wives (who remained in the countryside with the babies) could not find jobs due to the emerging economic recession that swept across rural China during this period. Hence, the SDA reformed the established socialist public-supply economy in order to increase its total earnings. The 'theory' on which the SDA's reform was based is identical to the rationale for the state to reject the SDA from accessing its resource: "Breaking up the big rice-pot" would "stimulate the motivation" of the people and so would bring about efficiency.

The SDA started to break up its own big rice-pot during 1993 to 1995, when the first class of graduates of the Daoist College began to be promoted to leading posts. The main idea was, first, to eliminate the 'unconditional reliance' of temple priests on the SDA; secondly, to increase the financial autonomy of the temple unit. While the SDA is still the nominal owner of all the estate property and the legal employer of all the priests, the centralized redistribution system of the SDA was divided into relatively independent units—the SDA secretary office and affiliate temples. Every temple unit must contribute a certain percentage of its annual revenue to the SDA.[10] Having paid the duty, the temple unit can then allocate the surplus (after deducting money for temple maintenance and managerial cost) to its staff. Relating to this reform, the SDA gradually stopped its

---

[10] Apart from a small amount that would be spent on the maintenance and personnel of the secretary office itself, these contributions would be redistributed by the SDA to pay the basic salary and other welfare of all the priests, to subsidize the extremely poor temples, and to build up funds for future investment projects. The percentage of each temple's contribution is decided by the General Council of the SDA annually.

expenditure on general welfare, especially the *fuli fenfang* (welfare housing distribution system). Temple units were to take on the responsibility to manage the housing for their staff. This project—generally named as *fanggai* (housing reform)—is one of the main topics of the entire reform.

The SDA expected that this institutional reform would "stimulate the motivation" of temple priests by linking a priest's bonus directly to the performance of the temple unit to which he belonged. Meanwhile, increasing the autonomy of temple units would grant temple managers greater authority to discipline their slack colleagues. It was presumed that working hard could, by itself, bring about prosperity.

The second wave of reform was proposed by the incumbent leading priests (mainly the first class of graduates) during mid-1998, when I was conducting fieldwork in Shanghai. The main idea was to break up the big rice-pot of each temple unit further and to institute a more exact distribution mechanism to link an individual priest's performance to the bonus he gets. The rationale was still relying on 'mobilizing motivation': Rewarding hard-working and skilful priests while punishing the lazy and unskilled ones. The inventiveness of the new project lies solely in its strict measures toward 'free rider' practices inside each temple and its inclination to increase the authority of temple managers. Further, to strengthen the effect of this reform, the revenue allocated through the merit-oriented bonus system would be increased, while the budget for the general welfare system would be cut—especially the budget for financing housing reform.

As expected, this proposal won whole-hearted support from most of the temple leaders and those who are confident about their ritual skills. They relentlessly argued for the efficaciousness of a competitive allocation mechanism for improving efficiency by taking the flexible personnel management of free-lance Daoist troupes as their reference. In contrast, the priests who belong to the lower strata in the administrative hierarchy, and those without good ritual skills, furiously challenged the fairness of the proposal and denounced it as a downright betrayal of the idea of monastic brotherhood that had been expounded by the SDA and the Daoist College. Consequently, the controversy gradually escalated from rumors to open quarrels, and finally ended up with an unprecedented strike of junior priests.[11] Later, I was told that the proposal was deferred for-

---

[11] The strike was conducted in a very peaceful way. Before the strike, some

ever—ostensibly. Nevertheless, most of the younger graduates, including those who organized the strike, do not really believe their opposition could retard the trend toward *shichanghua* (marketization).[12] "There is no future for the big rice-pot anymore," they bemoaned to me.

The strike itself is a trivial event, but it nevertheless represents the profound moral crisis of the new economic order. Although the argument that 'breaking the big rice-pot' and 'marketization' would bring about efficiency has been widely accepted by most of the priests as true, whether junior or senior, this does not imply that they would agree to ascribe economic efficiency and materialistic drive with a higher moral value than equality, moderation, and benevolence. In fact, many leading priests I interviewed in 1998 to 2000 confessed to me privately that they themselves were ambivalent or even anxious about the moral value of the new economic order, although they were convinced that marketization is indispensable for the survival of temple Daoism. Responding to this, the SDA organized a series of lectures under the 'guidance' of RAB to persuade young priests to replace the 'backward ascetic morality' of traditional Daoism with the 'modern entrepreneur spirit' and to replace the 'outmoded mandarin approach' with 'advanced business management.' The cast of speakers ranged from prominent government officials, CCP cadres, and academy-based scholars specializing in current economic affairs. It is hoped that younger temple leaders can learn to justify the change of their role from the guardian of a hierarchical cosmic order to the efficient interest-maximizer seeking this-worldly success.

However, for most of the young priests, the lectures were not at all impressive except for the two given by senior Daoist priests—Chairman Chen and Master Gao.

Chairman Chen, a *fashi* (master of magic) of the *Zhengyi* tradition, has been the chairman of the SDA for more than ten years and the

---

second- and third-class graduates demanded that the leaders of the SDA (most of whom are first-class graduates) organize a question-and-answer session to settle controversies focusing on the current distribution of housing welfare and the SDA's relevant policy within a week's time. Their request was rejected. As a result, they stopped serving their routine duties and stayed quietly in their dormitory until the deputy head of the SDA came to respond to their questions.

[12] In fact, this term can be better translated as 'commercialization' as it implies 'running things according to the rules of market.' However, since the Chinese term *shichang* is normally translated as 'market,' I innovate the word 'marketization' to translate it in order to catch its original savor.

chairman of the nation-wide Daoist Association of China for two years. The lecture he gave was about the modern interpretation of ancient Daoist philosophical ideas. According to Xiao Liu, a young Daoist priest:

> Chairman Chen said that Lao Jun[13] taught us: "The supreme goodness is like water" (Laozi 1995: ch. 8). Water is changing all the time. You can pour it into any space and make it into any shape, but water is always water. So, we Daoist priests should release ourselves from any prejudices and adapt ourselves to the current environment smoothly just like water. . . . Later, he quoted one widely known sentence in the *Daodejing*—"Humans follow the earth, the earth follows the heaven, the heaven follows Dao, and the Dao follows *ziran*"[14] (Laozi 1995: ch. 25). What is *ziran*? he said, it's acclimatizing oneself to the changing environment incessantly.

In sharp contrast to the scholastic style of Chairman Chen's lecture, the speech given by Master Gao, an heir of the Quanzhen tradition and a renowned medical doctor based in Hangzhou, Zhejiang Province, was continuously mentioned by young Daoist priests as an amusing anecdote regarding marketization. As a role model of a 'successful Daoist entrepreneur,' he was expected to reveal some secrets about how to develop 'the tertiary industry' of Daoist temples. However, his speech concerned how modern Daoist priests should change their worldview rather than any practical advice. As was recounted by Xiao Cao, a young temple manager, Master Gao said:

> We modern Daoist priests shouldn't avoid talking about money. We should not feel embarrassed about doing things only for money. Also, he said it is wrong to imagine that people would respect us because we follow the traditional value—*An Pin Le Dao* (staying with poverty and enjoying the Way). Just the opposite, he said; we cannot win others' respect unless we can make ourselves wealthy, well educated, nice and clean dressed, . . . and so on. In short, we should turn ourselves into smart and civilized people first, then we could start to talk about reviving Daoism and those kinds of high-flying ideas. He encouraged us to address ourselves and each other as *laoban* (boss) instead of *tongzhi* (comrade) or *daozhang* (senior fellow Daoist).

---

[13] Lao Jun, also named as *Taishang Laojun*, is one of the godheads among Daoist pantheon. Li Er, the philosopher who authored the book Laozi (or Lao Tzu) in the sixth century B.C.E., is alleged to be one of the reincarnations of Lao Jun.

[14] The term *ziran* is normally translated as 'nature,' but I agree with David Jones's idea to translate it as 'self-soing' in this particular context, see Jones (1999) and Jones and Culliney (2000). Chairman Chen's teaching about the new morality for modern Daoist priests can be found in Chen (1996).

Mr. Cao's account was confirmed immediately by his colleague, laughingly. When I was in Shanghai during 1998 to 2000, it became a fashion among young priests to address each other as 'boss' as Gao Laoban ('Boss Gao,' the nickname they give to Master Gao) had taught them.

Apart from 'boss,' young priests also adopted some slogans from the other lectures of the series, such as "Daoism should adapt to the modern socialist society!" "Modern Chinese Daoist priests should catch the tide of socialist commodity economy to raise our level of material civilization!" "Daoist temples should develop 'the tertiary industry'!" and so forth.[15] These slogans and new forms of address literally changed the way these young priests speak. The old-fashioned socialist rhetoric that used to dominate the discourse in the SDA was quickly replaced by new clichés. Although it is hard to judge whether or not the rhetorical change has indeed changed their mentality, it certainly helps young temple leaders to ignore the widespread questioning of the moral value of the ongoing marketization and somehow to justify their pursuit of economic reform.

Turning Toward the Market Economy via Sanju Daoshi

Although the young temple leaders didn't get any practical knowhow for developing the 'tertiary industry' from the lecture series, their fellow priests—free-lance Daoist priests—provide them with a ready-made model about how to run Daoism like a business in a free market. In fact, the commercialized Daoism embodied by these free-lancing Daoist priests is probably more authentic than the quasi-socialist temple Daoism of the SDA in terms of Shanghai's grassroots society in the last few centuries. The market economy of those free-lancing Daoist priests can be roughly outlined as follows:

Basically, they earn their living mainly by *zuodaochang* (performing Daoist rituals) for clients. Yet, their status as Daoist priests is *not recognized* by the state as they are not members of the SDA, which implies that their practice is outside of the law, namely, neither legal nor illegal. As such, they are not allowed to perform any public,

---

[15] The term 'tertiary industry' normally refers to the industries involving service as opposed to extraction (the primary industry) or manufacture (the secondary industry). In this context, 'the tertiary industry' implies temple commerce and tourist services that are not directly related to their main task—ritual service.

communal rituals because, according to the rules established by the
RAB, these rituals can be performed only by SDA's members in its
affiliate temples. Therefore, they concentrate on the market of private rituals, i.e., perform rituals for individual clients in their household compounds.

The key reward they earn through *zuodaochang* is cash, although
the clients' household should also provide drinks, cigarettes, snacks,
and good meals during the ritual day according to local custom. The
cash payment not only reflects but also makes their relationship with
clients a one-off transaction. Although their business opportunities
are channelled through existing interpersonal networks, they do not
normally know their clients directly and, after the service is completed and payment cleared, will never meet them again. Likewise,
clients in general are not loyal to any specific troupe.

The services are very flexible in time, place, group size, product
range (ritual genre), and price so as to be able to suit the diverse
conditions of their clients. They can start at 6 a.m. and work until
midnight or start at 4 p.m. and get it all done before 9 p.m. They
can perform in a crowded unit of an apartment building or in a
large country house in the midst of open paddy fields. The size of
a free-lance Daoist troupe can vary from six to more than fourteen
persons, depending on the client's requirement and budget.[16] Moreover,
they do not hesitate to perform any 'superstitious' ritual as long as
they know how to do it. Finally, their service charge is not fixed.
Bargain, concession, and 'robbery' are necessary components of their
business.

Corresponding to this, they are also very flexible in matching contribution and reward among the members of their troupes. The *bantou* (the heads of free-lance Daoist troupes), are at once the property
owner, employer, and general manager of those troupes, and can
reward the skilful, diligent members with a lucrative salary and fire
immediately those who are unskilled or lax. An outstanding priest
can work simultaneously with many *bantou* to fill up his schedule and
reject those who cannot afford to employ him.

The features outlined above clearly show that the economic pattern
of free-lance Daoist priests is quite similar to the ideal 'fully competitive

---

[16] The ideal size for a troupe is alleged to be twelve persons: three orators (including one *gaogong fashi* [the head master of magic]), four chanters, and five musicians.

market' in some critical aspects. First, there is no monopoly or oligarchy in the supply side. There are more than sixty-six free-lance Daoist troupes working in Shanghai.[17] In addition, these troupes are all mobile. They can move to clients to provide their service on-site. So, geographical distance cannot really prevent clients from getting access to many suppliers. Second, the demand side is also multiple. There are probably more than 100,000 potential household clients in Shanghai. Third, there is no institutional mechanism (such as the SDA) standing between providers and clients that can manipulate the terms of transaction. Finally, the influence of ideological factors such as propaganda, image fabrication, consumer-loyalty, etc., is negligible in this market. Clients enjoy a considerable amount of freedom to choose one supplier among numerous options based on price calculation/quotes or other rationales.

Free-lance Daoist priests appear to be stereotypical 'marketeers' who work diligently for cash and are always ready to adjust themselves according to the mechanism of price. Their flexible approach makes them much more popular than temple priests, even though their floating service charge is generally higher than the standard price of the latter. As a result, despite the fact that free-lance Daoist priests outnumber temple priests by at least two-fold,[18] they still manage to have full schedules and to procure lucrative cash incomes.

As all the Daoist priests are heirs of the same Shanghai-style *Zhengyi* liturgy and know each other quite well, the contrast between temple priests and free-lancing priests becomes all the more remarkable:

---

[17] The exact number of practicing free-lance Daoist priests in Shanghai is unknown. According to Mr. Guo, a graduate of the Daoist College who is now the deputy general secretary of the SDA, this number was roughly 300 to 400 during the latter half of the 1980s. There is no more recent statistic available. Yet, he is convinced that the number has substantially increased since the early 1990s. On the other hand, according to some leaders of free-lance Daoist troupes, the average size of a troupe is six standing members—the minimum size for a troupe to handle most of the normal rituals, although standard rituals require twelve to fifteen persons. They prefer to hire temporary staff from other troupes whenever it is required because to keep more than six persons in one troupe may reduce the possible income of every member—somebody in the troupe would become idle when clients ask for humble rituals that require only six people. So, if we presume the total number of practicing free-lance Daoist priests is 400 and the average size of a troupe is six persons, then there may be at least sixty-six free-lance Daoist troupes in Shanghai. In fact, this number was generally considered to be too small by almost all the priests with whom I discussed this issue.

[18] The number of temple priests is less than 200, as contrasted to the 400 or more free-lance Daoist priests working in Shanghai.

Whereas temple priests are trained through the Daoist College's
schooling and end up being trapped in the poverty of socialist public-supply economy, free-lance Daoist priests are trained through a
moderately revised form of traditional apprenticeship that can result
in making a fortune through the free market of rituals.[19] Hence, it
seems to be a natural choice for temple priests to have ventured
into a market economy by following the suit of their 'master-brothers.' Expectably, the first step they took was to collaborate with free-
lance Daoist priests. Despite the prohibitions of RAB and SDA, the
joint ventures between individual temple priests and free-lance Daoist
troupes existed long before the early 1990s. However, these early
joint ventures were normally temporary, individual-based arrangements outside of temples, namely, free-lance Daoist troupes invited
individual temple priests to join their ritual service in clients' houses
when there was a temporary shortage of staff.[20] Since the mid-1990s,
temple priests extended the old model of cooperation in three aspects:
First, the joint venture has been broadened from individuals to include
the entire crew of a temple; second, joint ventures are introduced
into temple compounds; third, the cooperation is gradually being institutionalized and directly handled by young temple leaders themselves.

For example, Mr. Jin, a first-class graduate of the Daoist College
and the general manager of the poorest temple in Pudong district,
started half-openly to invite free-lance Daoist troupes to perform both
private and communal rituals in his temple since mid-1999. In
exchange, he asked those *bantou* to invite his colleagues whenever
they got some appointments in clients' houses. His offer is appealing for both free-lance Daoist priests and their clients because it can
save them from a lot of hassles—making a proper ritual space in
the crowded family house, arranging meals for priests and visitors,
pleading for the neighbors and local police to ignore their noise, and

---

[19] The vast majority of free-lance Daoist priests are native Shanghaines and are
related to traditional Daoist families in one way or another. They learn Daoist craft
through apprenticeship in senior masters' family schools. It should be noted that
it's quite common for the *fashi* candidates from the Daoist College to learn *fashi*'s
art in senior masters' family schools together with other apprentices who would
become free-lance Daoist priests in later days. This is the first reason why some
temple priests address free-lance Daoist priests as *shixiongdi* (master-brother) because
they are literally 'master-brother' in many cases.
[20] In some extreme cases, the temple priests involved may go so far as to quit
their temple jobs and turn themselves into professional free-lance Daoist priests.
However, the existence of these cases would not contradict my argument.

so on. Besides, to be able to offer clients the option of having their rituals performed in temples increases the competitive edge of a free-lance Daoist troupe because, as a *bantou* said, "rituals performed in temples always look nicer than those in someone's living room." Consequently, Mr. Jin's experiment produced good results. For one thing, his colleagues earn immediate cash reward without going through the legacy of the big rice-pot system—a complicated real-location mechanism that costs them a great deal of time and energy. Meanwhile, the accounts of the temple unit also profit from the increased room rent and the selling of entrance tickets, incense, can-dles, paper money, and dining services for temple visitors. Moreover, Mr. Jin's flexible approach successfully makes the temple more pop-ular than it was before. To hold either a family ritual or a com-munal festival in that temple has now become some sort of convention among his village neighbors.

Another example can be found in a distant temple situated along the coast—from where Mr. Jin got the inspiration for his new approach. According to senior Master Jiang, the *zhuchi* (the honorable leader of a temple), this temple began to invite individual free-lance Daoist priests to perform death rituals inside the temple since the mid-1980s. Originally, this practice was intended to fill a temporary shortage of staff in order to meet the desperate requests from loyal clients. Later, this practice was institutionalized and became a kind of public 'secret' around the neighborhood. Since the mid-1990s, the old practice was developed further. The manager of ritual affairs of the temple told me that he actually functions as a broker of a local ritual market during recent years—although he insisted that most of his work has nothing to do with 'real business' but is "just a kind of customer service . . . without any charge." His brokerage reveals the ambition of the temple to make itself the local transaction center of Daoist ritual services by incorporating local free-lancing Daoist troupes into its marketing network.

Apart from collaborating with free-lance Daoist priests, temple priests went even further to change their own practices by imitating the approaches of their 'master-brothers.' The most salient example of this trend is to liberalize the rate for ritual service, namely, to replace the standard price list that symbolizes the outmoded social-ist public-supply economy with floating rates. Young priests told me that they have dropped the standard price list since the big rice-pot of the entire SDA was broken up in the early 1990s. When I was there in 1999, the standard price list had already become a decoration or a basis for bargaining. Except in a few big temples downtown, all the other countryside temples have lowered their actual charge for ritual services. Numerous forms and levels of concessions have become a conventional tool for distant, badly equipped temples to compete with larger, well-equipped, and better-located temples.

In addition, temple priests began to differentiate the level of cash reward for individual priests. The bonus for *gaogong fashi* (presiding master of magic), *sigu* (head drummer), and *bingdi* (head flutist) gradually increased to two or three times more than that for average chanters and musicians. Meanwhile, since the profits received from the rituals performed in collaboration with free-lance Daoist priests are often distributed immediately without processing through the central treasury of the temple, the more skilful and diligent ones (who are invited to these rituals more often than others) can earn higher incomes quickly.

Finally, to satisfy the taste of clients, temple priests began to expand the range and style of their rituals. They persuaded senior priests to teach them more about the distinctive features of parochial ritual traditions. Their interest in collecting different variations of the standardized liturgy has become stronger and stronger. Some temples have begun to organize exclusive courses for "making out some shining spots" for the temple's ritual performance. Within this process, some 'feudal superstitions' such as *Shunxing Jie'e* (Resolving Bad Luck by Appeasing Baleful Stars) were tacitly reintroduced into temple rituals.

In conclusion, temple priests gradually assimilated their economic pattern to that of free-lance Daoist priests through collaborating with and imitating the latter. To expand their enterprise in the private ritual market, they increased their flexibility in space, group size, product range, and price in order to satisfy the diverse needs of clients. Moreover, they instituted a self-governed income distribution system in order to match cash reward and individual contribution, which is 'illegal' but tacitly tolerated by the SDA. By so doing, temple priests indeed developed the tertiary industry and "raised their level of material civilization." However, ironically enough, the actual way they accomplished this task involved not so much about adopting 'modern' ideas or perspectives than learning to be more authentic or traditional by copying the approach of free-lance Daoist priests—which is almost identical to what their predecessors did in Shanghai before 1949.

Gift and Tribute: Learning from Daxian

Despite all the effort to learn from the free-lance Daoist priests, the differences between the temple and free-lance priests are nevertheless obvious. First of all, the former have exclusive control over temples, which means the monopoly of communal rituals. Hence, they cannot and need not depend solely on the market of private rituals like those freelancers do. Secondly, apart from communal rituals, a great deal of the earning of temple priests actually comes from the temple space itself, such as room-rent, entrance tickets, and temple shops, instead of their ritual service. Thus, they have to pay for temple maintenance. Finally, since their business is attached to temples, they cannot avoid being fixed in specific locales. Therefore, temple priests tend to build up long-term instead of one-off relationships with neighboring clients. All these differences point to a significant reality: Temples bestow them with a distinctive structure of advantages and burdens, so the cost-benefit structure temple priests face can never be identical to that of freelancers. This implies it is neither feasible nor desirable for them to copy the market economy of free-lance Daoist priests. Temple priests have to seek for some other ways to maximize the economic potentials of temples as a sedentary industry. It is for this reason that the economic pattern of the other category of religious professionals in the local Daoist economy—*daxian* (shamans)—is relevant. Temple priests were inspired by the shamans' approach and have tried to imitate it.

The Economic Pattern of Shamans

Daxian, 'great immortal,' is the colloquial salutation for a shaman in suburban Shanghai. They may also be addressed as '*xiangtou*' (the head of temple worshippers) or, in some private occasions, '*wupo*' (women witch). Daoist priests generally refuse to recognize their practice as Daoism. Some aged priests assured me that they are the disciples of a mystic master who insisted on transmitting the *Xuanjuanren* (scripture-chanters) tradition—a longstanding heterodoxy in Pudong—until the late 1980s.[21]

---

[21] This statement can be partially confirmed by the fact that many shamans have an intimate relationship with the secret *Xuanjuanren* troupes who chant *Baojuan* (a specific expression for 'scriptures' of heterodox religions) in believers' households

The typical image of a shaman is of a middle-aged, illiterate or barely literate, while extremely eloquent, woman from a peasant family.[22] The vast majority of them are married (their husbands are normally peasants or manual laborers) and have grown children. According to their reports, the process through which they have become shamans is quite similar to that of the Cantonese women shamans documented by Potter (1974)—a personal trauma (e.g. the death of one or several close relatives) brings about serious illness, followed by strange visions in dreams or hallucinations that ask them to serve as gods' mediums, and finally, a felt need to conform to the divine will to save their own lives. Then, they become the apprentices of some established shamans for several months. Afterward, they set out to build up their own careers by forming intimate ties with some prominent figures among local devotees via the references of their masters.

Despite the great variation in their individual expertise, style, and image, the fundamental features of their economic pattern are more or less the same. First of all, their economy is an integrated system of a gift economy in the private/individual domain and a tributary economy in the public/communal domain. In the private domain, they provide individual devotees or families with magical or non-magical healing, spiritual protection, divination, psychological consultation, and so on. In the public domain, they take the initiative to organize communal religious activities.

In the private domain, they strictly follow the ethics of the characteristic Chinese gift economy. They do not require a cash reward for their services, although the clients have to pay for all the materials required for the operation—such as all the items for ritual sacrifice or the medicine for the patients' usage. In exchange, clients should present the shaman with lavish hospitality (in terms of local standards), banquets, and gifts in kind according to the stereotypical ethics governing Chinese gift exchange, such as *guanxi* (relatedness), *renqing* (human feeling), *mianzi* (face), and *bao* (repayment).[23] To con-

---

during mourning rites or religious festivals. In addition, I witnessed many times that many followers of shamans (mostly aged, illiterate peasant women) are taught to chant vernacular verses in the local dialect when they are folding paper money, praying to gods, and burning incense or paper money. For more detailed information about the *Baojuan* tradition and its complicated relations with heterodox religions, see Naquin (1985), Overmyer (1985), and Yu (1994).

[22] As far as I know, there is no male shaman currently working in Shanghai.

[23] In brief, *guanxi* (relatedness) refers to all sorts of interpersonal relationships—

duct this kind of exchange in the private domain is the key mechanism for shamans to accumulate moral credit (*renqing* or *mianzi*) over clients and to expand their network in the local community.

Once a shaman's network and the moral credits in her command have grown to a considerable scale, she can then begin to organize splendid communal tributes toward gods in local temples. In Shanghai, there is a conventional range of tributary activities that can serve as a scale for measuring the status of a shaman's career. According to the amount of funds each activity requires, the hierarchy starts with organizing communal rituals and goes up to the installation of gods' statues in existing temples, to temple refurbishment, and finally reaches the peak, to temple reconstruction.

The most prominent feature of the shamans' tributary economy in the public domain lies in the fact that, unlike the socialist public-supply economy, the market economy, or the gift economy, it is not based on reciprocity. In the tributary economy, offering tangible resources is not premised upon a symmetrical return of a specifiable value from a tangible agent. The putative recipients here are intangible beings (gods), and the expected return (divine blessing) is also intangible and noncalculable. In addition, the tributary economy is premised on an indisputable asymmetry between inferior donor and superior recipient, and the inequality is perceived as so enormous that the common ethics of gift exchange—*renqing, mianzi, guanxi*, and *bao*—are nullified in this context.

But, why would people like to be involved in a transaction that is neither reciprocal nor equal? It is because they seek merit and reputation. It is the idea of gaining *gongde* (merit) instead of reciprocity or '*guanxixue*' (the art of networking) that functions as the central dynamism of tributary economy (Yang 1994). *Gongde* refers to the honor one earns through contributing to the reproduction of a

---

kinship, friendship, neighborhood, or instrumental (business) relationship. *Renqing* (human feeling) mainly means the general moral obligation of a social person to conduct proper gift exchange with related others. *Mianzi* (face) mainly refers to the relative balance of moral credit or debit between two specific persons. *Bao* (repayment) refers to the act of repaying the *renqing* or *mianzi* owed to others. I should note that the glossary listed here is highly over-simplified. In fact, each one of these terms has many possible meanings depending on the context in which it is used. These concepts and the general features of Chinese gift economy have been well analysed by Yang (1957), Hwang (1987), King (1988, 1994), Yang (1994), Yan (1996), and Stafford (2000a, 2000b).

righteous political, social, or cultural order that is sanctioned by sage-
leaders and benefits the general public. This idea encourages humble people to share the glory and holiness of the moral order by
assuming the status of donors/co-producers. If the people are persuaded
by this idea, a "long-term cycle of exchange" (Parry and Bloch 1989)
will be established—treasures (e.g. paper money and food offerings)
are siphoned from the humble to Heaven (gods) in order to rein-
vigorate the cosmic order, while magical power (*ling*) and moral values (*gongde*) trickle down from Heaven to the humble. This principle
enables the people to *presume* that their tribute has been acknowledged and appreciated by gods although they can neither sense nor
ask for divine repayment.

However, in practice, *gongde* as an abstract idea always needs to
be realized through this-worldly reputation. That is, how much *gongde*
one has won is perceived to be easily measurable on the basis of
how much reputation one has earned. Consequently, the incentive
of secular reputation—*chutou loulian* (literally "to protrude one's head
and show one's face"; meaning 'to become a celebrity')—often replaces
(or hides behind) *gongde* discourse as the main appeal for the tributary
economy. As such, the tributary economy often appears to be a game
of reputation since the zeal to engage in the tributary economy is
motivated by the envy of fame (Feuchtwang 2001; Feuchtwang and
Wang 2001).[24]

In conclusion, the main referential framework for the shamans'
career is not market but family. Unlike free-lance priests, they don't
sell their ritual skills through the market. Instead, they construct
divine kinship networks among gods and human beings wherein they
function as the pivot. In the private domain, shamans create fictive
kinship with devotees through continuous gift exchange—not only
the normal service-gift exchange but also the peculiar soul/body
exchange conducted through divination, magical healing, and spiritual

---

[24] It should be acknowledged that my conception of tributary economy is far
different from the "tribute mode of production" proposed by Gates (1996). In Gates,
the "tribute mode of production" refers to a form of class-exploitation and the false-
consciousness it produced for justifying itself. My conception of tributary economy
mainly concerns a specific cultural model for the exchange between tangible resources
and moral value, general order, and reputation. It is beyond any doubt that tributary economy is dominated by hegemonic ideologies, but I want to stress the strong
potential of tributary economy to empower subalterns by creating a space for them
to assert their right and morality.

consultation.[25] Then, through organizing communal religious activities, shamans stretch the imagined family ties to local deities. By claiming themselves as the adopted or sworn daughters of powerful gods and substantiating these claims through celebrating gods' birthdays and creating new statues for gods, they offer the humble devotees the chance to be related to sacred, mighty beings via themselves. Consequently, a devotee group centering on a shaman is perceived as a holy family consisting of gods as patriarchs, shamans as mother/matriarchs, and humble devotees as sons and daughters. The paradigmatic values in these holy families are *zhong* (faithfulness), *xiao* (filial piety), *ci* (benevolence), *he* (harmony)—exactly identical to those of the traditional Chinese family and the Chinese empire.

Imitating the Shamans' Approach

Temple priests are keenly aware of the fact that shamans start their career by offering free divination and magical healing to build up a relationship with followers. Unfortunately, young priests cannot follow suit because they have never learned relevant skills in the Daoist College as those skills have been strictly prohibited by the SDA and RAB on the ground that they are at once 'heterodoxies' and 'feudal superstitions.' However, they nevertheless find ways to set up gift exchanges with common folk as well as shamans by making good use of the scarce resource of the Daoist economy under their control—temples. The following three cases well illustrate this process.

Gods' Statues and Spirit Tablets

The first tactic of temple priests is to offer the usage of some temple space as an initial gift. More precisely, they offer shamans the right to install gods' statues in temples. As for common folk, they provide the right to store spirit tablets in temples.

As was mentioned before, to install gods' statues in temples is a crucial step for the career development of a shaman. If a shaman

---

[25] The confessions of clients in these sessions inevitably consist of highly confidential privacy. Responding to their privacy as gifts, a shaman should repay with her body/soul: she resigns her soul and makes her body the medium for clients to have contact with gods and ghosts. Moreover, it is widely alleged that, in some extreme cases, shamans may incur fatal damage to themselves by providing spirit-medium service. So, I suggest that divination, magical healing, and spiritual consultation can be seen as a particular range of in-depth exchange between shaman and clients.

manages to achieve this goal, her influence would be greatly enhanced because, first, followers tend to believe that she must have stronger magical power because she has attained such great merit and, secondly, the solidarity of her follower group will be greatly intensified as the statue would naturally function as the cult center for them. However, temple priests used to reject shamans' requests of this kind—not only because their temples normally don't have much extra space but also because they did not want the authenticity of their temples to be 'polluted' by heterodox gods. So, shamans were always at odd with temple priests over this issue during the previous decades. However, temple priests have gradually softened their stance during the recent years. Currently, the right to install gods' statues in temples is a key favor by which temple managers consolidate friendships with influential shamans who have brought about numerous ritual appointments and who have the potential to do so in the future.[26] Consequently, except for a few temples located in the downtown area, almost all the other temples in Shanghai are now packed with statues. Only a few of them can keep the main halls as they were before by putting aside all the statues offered by shamans in specially reserved side-rooms. The smaller temples have no choice but to let the whole lot of incoming statues—which range from life-size to less than a foot high—flood everywhere.

In addition, temple priests offer the common folk the space to house the *paiwei* (spirit tablets) of their deceased relatives or friends. In fact, to house spirit tablets is one of the traditional services widely offered by Daoist and Buddhist temples in China. As a kind of charity as well as business, it was said that the temples providing this service would incur great merit by taking care of the pitiful dead souls who might have no living descendants to worship them, or who were considered as potentially dangerous due to their tragic death (Ahern 1973; Wolf 1974; Harrell 1974; Nelson 1974; Naquin 1988; Feuchtwang 2001). According to custom, those who brought in spirit tablets should pay for this service upon their first visit and then regularly make some donation to the temple. This tradition was revived in

---

[26] On the other side of the coin, whenever a statue fails to attract visitors or ritual appointments due to the sponsor shaman having left the business for whatever reason, temple priests do not hesitate to remove it quietly to the storage room and make the space available for the incoming shaman.

Shanghai's Daoist temples since the late 1980s. Currently, almost every temple in the countryside prepares one or two side-rooms to house spirit tablets. According to some temple managers, this service has indeed turned some clients into regular temple worshippers.

Amulet

Since 1998, the second tactic of temple priests to fuse longer, deeper exchanges with common folk is to issue amulets. The key point is to make amulets a constant bond for channelling the magical power of temples to individual followers.

This project was directly handled by the SDA from the end of 1998 until early 1999. The amulet is a golden chip. On one side is inscribed the image of *Taishang Laojun* (the divinity of Laozi) or Heavenly Master Zhang or the God of Wealth, while the other side is inscribed with the old official seal of the City God's Temple. Interested buyers are asked to provide their name, birthday, and contact address when they place the order. Then, their personal name will be inscribed on an amulet they choose themselves. Afterward, during the days before *Chongyang* (the ninth day of the ninth lunar month), several senior Daoist masters stage a series of spectacular rituals to sanctify these golden chips in the City God's Temple. All the buyers are invited to witness the ritual and to collect their orders afterwards. Unsurprisingly, the last day of the ritual—the *Chongyang* Festival—is an opportunity for propaganda. Local television news covers the day's events. The whole project is unquestionably a big success. Summarizing the success of this project, Mr. Ye, a first-class graduate, said:

> The most significant advantage of this project is the idea of personalized service. Our clients like to buy the amulet with their names on it. Besides, we take down their contact details and contact them individually, either by phone or by well-printed mail. This pleases them very much. The other important advantage is it is a long-lasting service. We keep contact with our buyers long after the purchase. Before Chinese New Year, we send them greeting cards. When we have temple festivals, we send them invitation cards. Moreover, before the end of the year, we invite them to come back to our temple and renew the magic power of their amulet for free. . . . Personalized and continuous service makes the buyers feel that we do care about their personal well being. This feeling is much more powerful than any advertising tricks.

Divination

Being encouraged by the great success of amulet sales, temple priests began their attempt to bring back a key symbol of Daoism—divination, which is also the crucial mechanism for shamans to form in-depth exchange relationships with local folk. The first step toward this goal was the revival of *lingqian* (oracle sticks). The definition and rules of oracle sticks need not repeated here as they have already been well documented by other anthropologists (cf. Ahern 1981). Suffice it to say that oracle sticks used to be one of the most popular methods for divination in Daoist and Buddhist temples all over China, and this is now still a widespread service of Daoist and Buddhist temples in many Chinese communities outside of the Chinese mainland. It has been banned on the Chinese mainland as a quintessential 'superstition' from the early 1950s to the early 1980s. It was gradually revived during the recent two decades, except in metropolitan cities such as Shanghai because the RAB has not yet removed the old prohibition.

The lack of this service in Shanghai's temples disappoints many temple worshippers as well as tourists. Countless complaints and requests from the public regarding this issue pushed the City God's Temple of Shanghai to find some way to get around the RAB's prohibition. Consequently, young priests decided to change the name and process of this divination method into *muo fudai* (Lucky Envelope Draw) and to incorporate it into the charity fund-raising program of the year 2000 New Year Festival. Temple visitors were first invited to make voluntary donations to charity projects such as "helping the pupils in flood-inflicted areas" and the like, and then to pick up one *fudai* (lucky envelope) from a large wooden box placed in front of main altar.[27] Contained in the lucky envelope was one of the one hundred or so 'modernized' oracle poems that temple priests selected from some archaic collections of oracle poems and translated/revised into modern spoken Chinese.

As was anticipated, this invention attracted an enthusiastic response from the public. According to temple priests' estimation, since 2000, more than one hundred thousand lucky envelopes have been taken

---

[27] China suffered serious flooding of the Yangtze River and a few other main rivers during summer-autumn 1998. So, Chinese society was overwhelmed by donation appeals for the resumption of primary and middle education in the afflicted area.

by temple worshippers. From 2002 onward, it gradually became a routine service of Daoist temples in Shanghai. When I visited Shanghai in May 2004, I found that lucky envelopes had already become a 'free' service in quite a few temples. Currently, young Daoist priests in Shanghai are discussing how to develop further the existing divination service. Moreover, several young priests in rural temples have begun studying palmistry, calculating the eight characters, geomancy, and other fortune-telling skills that are traditionally categorized as *Daomen Wushu* (the Five Arts of Daoism)[28] in order to prepare themselves for meeting clients' requirements in the future.

In sum, temple priests have begun to assimilate the economic pattern of shamans in four ways. First, they try to build up long-term relationships with individual clients by involving themselves deeper and deeper into an escalating gift exchange with common folk. As the exchange escalates from 'offering a space in the temple' to 'providing an amulet to be worn by the client' to 'giving guidance to soothe client's anxiety,' temple priests manage to get closer to their clients.' As the terms and the tokens of exchange multiply, the ties between clients and temples become more and more sustainable. Second, just like the shamans, they start to mobilize the network built up through gift exchange to sponsor communal tributes that they organize themselves. Third, temple priests shape their conduct in accordance with the 'principle of merit,' which can be easily seen from their efforts to house unattended spirit tablets (to earn merit for temples) and to situate the 'lucky envelop draw' within the context of a charitable fund-raising activity (to create a chance for common folk to earn merit to increase their luck). Finally, they try to use people's desire for fame. The endeavor to make amulet sales a big event covered by television (for the buyers to 'show off their faces') and to decide the position of donors in the queue for picking up a 'lucky envelope' (which is under the gaze of the public) according to the amount of one's donation clearly reveal this intention.

---

[28] The five arts are *shan* (geomancy), *yi* (therapeutics), *ming* (fortune-telling), *bǔ* (divination), and *xiang* (palm-reading and other fortune-telling methods based on discerning one's visible, physical features).

Learn to be Immortal Magistrates:
Toward a Distinctive Synthesis

Despite all the attempts to assimilate their approach to the shamans'
economic pattern, the cases described above nevertheless reveal a
fundamental difference between the economy of temple Daoism and
of shamanism: The ultimate basis of the former is temples or, more
precisely, the gods in temples, whereas the latter is personal charisma.
Almost all the value of what temple priests offer to their clients comes
from temples and gods in temples—the space for housing gods' statues and spirit tablets, the amulets sanctified by the official seal of
City God's Temple and by the ritual conducted in front of the divine
gaze of temple gods, and the validity of lucky envelopes that is
premised upon the efficacy of temple gods. Therefore, it is fair to
say that the real partners of those exchanges organized by temple
priests are devotees and temples or temple gods, not temple priests
themselves. This implies that the economy of temple priests is con-
ditioned by the traditional role they are assigned by *Zhengyi* Daoism—
xianguan (immortal magistrate), the servants of gods' palace in the
secular world who mediate between the humble earthly creatures
and the almighty governors of the celestial court.[29] If they act out
this traditionally assigned role accurately, the exchange between devotees and temples or the tribute from devotees to temple gods would
be secure or, quite likely, be increased. The legend about Xiao Wang
illustrates this possibility.

Xiao Wang, a dutiful first-class graduate of the Daoist College,
was appointed as the *dangjia* (temple manager) of the most prominent temple in southeast Shanghai in the mid-1990s. In 1997, he
managed to refurbish the temple by raising funds from neighbors
and made the main hall of the temple become a pride of the locals.
Unexpectedly, Xiao Wang was not honored but publicly denounced
by the SDA shortly after the completion of the project due to an
unconfirmed allegation of corruption against him. He was dropped
from the post and downgraded to a minor musician. A few months

---

[29] It is a tradition for Daoist temples to be named as *gong* (palace)—especially
those belong to the *Zhengyi* tradition, although *miao* (temple), *guan* (observatory or
pavilion), and *tan* (shrine) are also quite widespread. Also, it is a tradition of the
Zhengyi Daoism to bestow the lowest-level *fashi* (master of magic) with the title
xian'guan through ordination.

later, all the accusations charged against him were proved false. Yet, the SDA did not formally purge Xiao Wang from the guilty verdict as the SDA hesitated to embarrass itself. Later, a dispute that occurred in a poor rural temple changed his life.

The old temple was reopened by some devotees and registered with the local government as a 'villagers' assembly hall' in the early 1990s. Later, a self-proclaimed shaman came to occupy this temple as her 'office.' She and her companions put everything of the temple including the donation box under their control.[30] Although local devotees detested her gang, they dared not fight against her because they were scared by the rumor about her intimate relationship with some powerful figures in local government.

However, the sweeping persecution toward *Falungong* since 1999 encouraged them to take action to expel the gang. So, they wrote a series of letters to report her to the police. For convenience, they simply fabricated her as a *Falungong* practitioner. Meanwhile, to avoid a similar situation happening again, they decided to re-register the compound as a Daoist temple instead of a villager assembly hall, which implies that they agreed to transfer the ownership of the whole property to the SDA. While transferring the property right, local devotees expressed their wish to the SDA that Xiao Wang be made the manager of this temple because he has made great contributions to local devotees. The splendid new temple buildings he managed to construct pleased the gods and won a great amount of merit for local devotees. Consequently, Xiao Wang was soon appointed as the manager of the temple. On his arrival, many devotees came to worship the gods with food offerings and cash donations. The whole scene looked not unlike a temple festival. Many aged devotees came and greeted him: "You are a good *cadre*!"

Meanwhile, someone in the RAB warned the occupying shaman to leave the temple immediately and stay away from it if she did not want to spend the rest of her life in prison. Shocked by this news, she returned home and died two weeks later. People said that she starved to death because she could not eat or drink anything during

---

[30] This woman, whose name is *Hongbing* (Red Guard), is a stereotypical "Maoist shaman" (Chao 1999). Her approach—the way she occupied the temple as her 'office,' the 'ruling bloc' she organized around her, her self-proclaimed relations to the gods, and her authoritarian attitude toward neighboring peasants—reminded everybody of Red Guards during the Cultural Revolution era.

the last two weeks of her life. They asserted this was the result of divine wrath that she incurred by appropriating temple property for her personal gain. Besides, they assured me that the appointment of Xiao Wang was warranted by gods and so was protected by *lingwei* (the valor of divinity). As would be true for anyone who has earned great merit, any *xiémo waidao* (the devious and heterodox) blocking his way would be devastated.

After that, the anecdotes concerning the temple's past made the temple become a symbol of local solidarity and divine protection. Thus, this temple became the first case in which the local township government subsidized the recurrent expense of a temple. "They [bureaucrats of the township] are devotees themselves. Of course they don't want this temple to be closed down because of bankruptcy . . . Besides, they cannot avoid the blame from locals if this temple does not survive," said Xiao Wang in his reasonably well-furnished office in 2004.

This story shows that the ideal role of temple priests in local people's minds is at once as a religious expert and as a 'cadre,' that is, a magistrate.[31] This misconception about temple priests can be seen as the legacy of socialism that makes all institutions in China appear to be part of the state. However, it should be noticed that the fusion of politics and religion has been a strong tradition in Daoism, especially in the *Zhengyi* tradition. As has been explicated by many anthropologists (Ahern 1981; Gates 1996; Feuchtwang 2001), the omnipresence of political symbols and the imperial metaphor has always been an outstanding feature of Daoism or Chinese folk religion in general. In fact, Feuchtwang's suggestion that what Chinese popular religions (including Daoism) collectively represented is a celestial empire that stands in a metaphorical relationship with secular Chinese regimes may not be an exaggeration. As an instance of this long-established cosmology, Daoist priests have been recognized as *xian'guan* (*immortal magistrates*) ordained by the celestial court to rule a locality— including the minor gods and ghosts lingering around. Although this

---

[31] Feuchtwang and Wang (2001) document similar cases that happened in Meifa, Fujian Province. All these cases show that the roles of 'righteous cadre' and 'religious leader' tend to be interchangeable in rural China. Moreover, local people tend to actively credit those who have assumed these two roles with some mystical attributes, which can be characterized either in Western term such as 'charisma' or in local terms such as 'the valour of divinity.'

idea has never been fully realized after the demise of the *Tianshidao* (Heavenly Master Daoism) at the end of the second century, it nevertheless persists in Daoist liturgy, especially that of the *Zhengyi* tradition. Therefore, it is virtually impossible for *Zhengyi* Daoist priests, especially temple priests, to avoid the image of 'bureaucrat' and the stamp of 'politics' in their careers. This is probably the reason why they are not expected to be 'marketeers' like free-lance Daoist priests or networking experts like shamans, but upright and authoritative good cadres like Xiao Wang. As the servants of gods in this world, temple priests are expected to accumulate merit by devotedly endeavoring to organize communal tribute to Heaven (e.g., by creating splendid temples for glorifying the gods). However, just like their counterpart in the secular world, the bureaucrats, they are expected to keep a proper distance from the local gift economy and from network politics to prevent the public assets dedicated to gods—temples—from being tarnished by factionalism in grass-roots society. Likewise, they are expected to be very cautious about their involvement in the commercial market in order to avoid the accusation of *fubai* (corruption) or *gongqi siyong* (appropriating public assets for private gains). If they perform their role correctly, they could be conceived as being protected by 'the valor of divinity', and the charisma thus procured could be so 'efficacious' as to make the local government feel obliged to support the temple, financially as well as politically.

The above case foreshadowed a new era of Shanghai's Daoist economy. Soon after the appointment of Xiao Wang, there emerged a dramatic conceptual change among the local bureaucrats in Shanghai and its satellite towns. Daoist temples began to be considered as a crucial means for revitalizing the economy of old, run-down neighborhoods instead of as a 'waste of resources' or a 'symbol of backwardness.' Moreover, some bureaucrats and businessmen in Shanghai's satellite towns went even further in reviving historically well-known Daoist temples situated in their communities as a way to boost the motivation of the local population for pursuing economic development. Consequently, in satellite towns such as Qingpu and Songjiang, local townships have taken the initiative to reconstruct the City God's temples of their region. To realize their '*yi miao xing shi*' (vitalizing the market by means of the temple) strategy for local development, they offered land, financial resources, and administrative support to the SDA, and invited the SDA to handle the construction project and then to run the newly refurbished or constructed temples. In

Shanghai city, the municipality offered the *Baiyunguan* temple with a government-owned estate located amid a run-down neighborhood in the southern downtown in order to 'revitalize' the area.[32] In addition, the municipality agreed to help the City God's Temple buy back the estate properties surrounding the temple, which have been occupied by a lot of shops and restaurants for decades, in order to revive the original design of the magnificent temple. Expectably, this terribly delayed decision was caused by the fact that the market surrounding the old temple had shown signs of decline during recent years. So, it was hoped that the expansion and refurbishment of the City God's Temple would boost up the surrounding market again.

Responding to the new tendency, young temple leaders began learning to broaden their thinking to match that of local 'cadres.' More precisely, they started to be trained to project the development of their temple as an integral part of the larger plan for the comprehensive socioeconomic development of a local community. Some temple leaders have gone even further to suggest that the role of Daoist temples should be changed to become museums for the general public to get access to the elegant living heritage of elite Daoism and Chinese culture in general. Consequently, "*yu difang gong-cun gongrong*" (forming a partnership with local community toward common prosperity) replaced 'marketization' and 'the art of networking' to become the trendiest activity among young temple leaders. The following speech made by Mr. Ji, the young general manager of the City God's Temple of Shanghai, in answering my questions about the reform measures he put into practice in his temple, outlines this wave of new economic thinking for temple Daoism in Shanghai.

> Currently, we are planning to abolish entrance tickets permanently. Moreover, we may try to completely eradicate the prefixed linkage between money and all sorts of Daoist merit we deliver to the devotees, such as rituals, protective charms, Daoist scriptures, and so on, in a few years time. Sooner or later, the notorious price list will be replaced by the principle of voluntary donation in our temple. Certainly, this new approach will incur a lot of doubt and opposition from our fellow Daoist priests, especially those who are in other temples. However, I keep on preaching the necessity of changing our approach as well

---

[32] This is not a free offer but a swap. The original site of Baiyunguan was confiscated by the municipality because it has decided to reconstruct the entire neighborhood around the old temple. However, the new location is larger than the old one and the municipality promised to provide the entire construction cost.

as our way of thinking. Honestly, the majority of Daoist temples in Shanghai do not have to worry about survival anymore. So, what we should strive for now is to make more and more people know the precious value of Daoism and so commit themselves to Daoism instead of making more profit. . . . To win a large flock of followers through promoting egalitarianism—I mean, to equalize the chance for the poor and the rich to get access to the blessing of Daoism and to create a partnership for the common prosperity of Daoism and the local community—is much more valuable than monetary income. For attaining this goal, abolishing admission tickets is but the first step. We should also commit ourselves to charity, to organizing temple festivals to stimulate the local economy, to provide a spiritual sanctuary for the extremely stressed urbanites, to create a space for modern Shanghainese to indulge temporally in the beauty of classical Chinese culture, and a lot of other things. The Daoist Ensemble of our temple is a good example of our endeavor to share the abundant cultural heritage of our religion and our temple with the general public.

Conclusion

As a provisional conclusion, I suggest that temple Daoist priests have gradually developed a distinctive synthesis of all the economic patterns they can learn from bureaucrats, free-lance priests, and shamans. As a group of educated professionals who are guaranteed, supervised, and supported by a quasi-official organization, they are bestowed with a monopoly to manage a strategic public space—temples, the authoritative centres of communal religious activity. Moreover, the value or power of these temples is enlarged by the symbolic assets they obtain from the religious tradition, which defines priests as immortal magistrates. The access to the state's power grants them the privilege of being identified as 'cadres' by the local people while restraining them from going too far in either the market economy or the local gift economy, as accusations of corruption or factionalism are always ready to be charged against these cadres. It is only through more than ten years of trial and error that they gradually clarified the limits and opportunities laid down by their structural position. Moreover, it is not until recently that they found out all of their assets and began to think about how to utilize these assets in an integrated way.

For the moment, some of the most sensitive and creative leaders among Daoists have proposed a new way of thinking to combine their assets to form a positive symbiosis between Daoism and the local community, which implies making Daoist temples a public good for (1) organizing communal religious rituals and festivals for gods and ghosts (tributary economy); (2) promoting egalitarianism and the national cultural tradition among the communal members (the heritage of the state's socialist public-supply economy); (3) boosting tourism and all kinds of commercial transactions in a neighboring market (market economy); and (4) delivering charitable welfare and religious merits to needy individuals (gift economy). Since the economic and political conditions of temples in Shanghai are diverse and there does not seem much chance for this inequality to be levelled in the foreseeable future, the prospect for the new thinking to be widely accepted as the new paradigm of Shanghai's temple Daoism is uncertain. However, it nevertheless epitomizes the great effort of contemporary Daoist priests to envision a sustainable, this-worldly temple Daoism.

References

Ahern, Emily Martin. 1973. *The Cult of the Dead in a Chinese Village*. Stanford, CA: Stanford University Press.
————. 1981. *Chinese Ritual and Politics*. Cambridge: Cambridge University Press.
Anagnost, Ann S. 1987. "Politics and Magic in Contemporary China." *Modern China* 13: 41–61.
————. 1994 "The Politics of Ritual Displacement." Pp. 221–54 in *Asian Visions of Authority*, edited by Charles F. Keyes, Laurel Kendall and Helen Hardacre. Honolulu: University of Hawaii Press.
Chao, Emily. 1999. "The Maoist Shaman and the Madman: Ritual Bricolage, Failed Ritual, and Failed Ritual Theory." *Cultural Athropology* 14: 505–34.
Chen, Lian-Sheng. 1996. *Daofongji* [*On Daoist Ethics*]. Shanghai: Shanghai Academy of Social Science Press.
Chen, Yiaoting. 1993. "Shanghai daojiao shi" ["The History of Daoism in Shanghai"]. Pp. 353–440 in *Shangha izongjiao shi [The History of Religions in Shanghai]*, edited by Ruan Renze and Gao Zhennong. Shanghai: Shanghai People's Press.
Dalton, George. 1969. "Theoretical Issues in Economic Anthropology," *Current Anthropology* 10: 63–102.
Dean, Kenneth. 1993. *Taoist Ritual and Popular Cults of Southeast China*. Princeton, NJ: Princeton University Press.
Feuchtwang, Stephan. 2001. *Popular Religion in China*. Richmond, Surrey: Curzon.
Feuchtwang, Stephan and Mingming Wang. 2001. *Grassroots Charisma*. London: Routledge.
Gates, Hill. 1996. *China's Motor*. Ithaca, NY: Cornell University Press.
Harrell, C. Stevan. 1974. "When a Ghost Becomes a God." Pp. 193–206 in *Religion and Ritual in Chinese Society*, edited by Authur P. Wolf. Stanford, CA: Stanford University Press.
Honig, Emily. 1989. "Pride and Prejudice: Subei People in Contemporary Shanghai." Pp. 138–55 in *Unofficial China*, edited by Perry Link, Richard Madsen and Paul G. Pickowicz. London: Westview Press.
————. 1992. *Creating Chinese Ethnicity*. New Haven, CN: Yale University Press.

Hwang, Kwang-Kuo. 1987. "Face and Favor: the Chinese Power Game." *American Journal of Sociology* 92: 944–74.

Jing, Jun. 1996. *The Temple of Memories*. Stanford, CA: Stanford University Press.

Jones, David E. 1999. "Tao's Metaphor: The Way of Water." *Asian Culture Quarterly* 27: 15–26.

Jones, David E. and John Culliney. 2000. "The Fractal Self and the Organization of Nature: The Daoist Sage and Chaos Theory." *Asian Culture Quarterly* 28: 59–70.

King, Ambrose Yeo-Chi. 1988a. "Mianzi yu zhongguoren xingwei zhi fenxi" ["An Analysis of the Relationship between 'Face' and Chinese Behavior"]. Pp. 75–104 in *Zhongguoren de xinli* [*The Psychology of Chinese People*], edited by Yang Guo-Shu. Taipei: Guiguan Press.

———. 1988b. "Renji guanxi zhong renqing zhi fenxi" ["An Analysis of *Renqing* in Interpersonal Relations"]. Pp. 319–45 in *Zhongguoren de xinli* [*The Psychology of Chinese People*], edited by Yang Guo-Shu. Taipei: Guiguan Press.

Lao Tzu. 1963. *Tao Te Jing*. Translated by D. C. Lau. Harmondsworth, Middlesex: Penguin Books.

Naquin, Susan. 1985. "The Transmission of White Lotus Sectarianism in Late Imperial China." Pp. 255–91 in *Popular Culture in Late Imperial China*, edited by David Johnson, Andrew Nathan, and Evelyn Rawski. Berkeley: University of California Press.

Neitz, Mary Jo and Peter R. Mueser. 1997. "Economic Man and the Sociology of Religion." Pp. 105–18 in *Rational Choice Theory and Religion*, edited by Lawrence A. Young. New York: Routledge.

Overmyer, Daniel L. 1985. "Values in Chinese Sectarian Literature." Pp. 219–54 in *Popular Culture in Late Imperial China*, edited by David Johnson, Andrew J. Nathan, and Evelyn S. Rawski. Berkeley: University of California Press.

Parry, Jonathan P. and Maurice Bloch. 1989. *Money and the Morality of Exchange*. Cambridge: Cambridge University Press.

Potter, Jack M. 1974. "Cantonese Shamanism." Pp. 207–31 in *Religion and Ritual in Chinese Society*, edited by Arthur Wolf. Stanford, CA: Stanford University Press.

Qing, Xitai. 1996. *Zhongguo daojiao shi* [*The History of Daoism in China*]. Chengdo: Sichuan People's Press.

Sahlins, Marshall. 1972. *Stone Age Economics*. Chicago: Aldine-Atherton.

Sangren, P. Steven. 1987. *History and Magical Power in a Chinese Community*. Stanford, CA: Stanford University Press.

Siu, Helen F. 1989. "Recycling Rituals: Politics and Popular Culture in Contemporary Rural China." Pp. 121–37 in *Unofficial China*, edited by Perry E. Link, Richard Madsen, and Paul Pickowicz. London: Westview Press.

———. 1990. "Recycling Tradition: Culture, History, and Political Economy in the Chrysanthemum Festivals of South China." *Comparative Study of Society and History* 32: 765–94.

Stafford, Charles. 2000a. "Chinese Patriliny and the Cycles of Yang and Laiwang." Pp. 37–54 in *Cultures of Relatedness*, edited by Janet Carsten. Cambridge: Cambridge University Press.

———. 2000b. "Deception, Corruption and the Chinese Ritual Economy." Working Paper 3, Asia Research Centre, London School of Economics.

Stark, Rodney and Roger Finke. 2000. *Acts of Faith*. Berkeley, CA: University of California Press.

Sutton, Donald S. 2003. *Steps of Perfection*. Cambridge, MA: Harvard University Press.

Warner, R. Stephen. 1993. "Work in Progress toward a New Paradigm for the Sociological Study of Religion in the United States." *American Journal of Sociology* 98: 1044–93.

———. 1997. "Convergence toward the New Paradigm: A Case of Induction." Pp. 87–101 in *Rational Choice Theory and Religion*, edited by Lawrence A. Young. New York: Routledge.

Wolf, Authur P. 1974. "Gods, Ghosts, and Ancestors." Pp. 132–82 in *Religion and Ritual in Chinese Society*, edited by Authur P. Wolf. Stanford, CA: Stanford University Press.

Yan, Yunxiang. 1996. *The Flow of Gifts*. Stanford, CA: Stanford University Press.

Yang, Fenggang. Forthcoming. "The Red, Black, and Gray Markets of Religion in China." *Sociology Quarterly*.

Yang, Lien-Sheng. 1957. "The Concept of '*pao*' as a Basis for Social Relations in China." Pp. 291–309 in *Chinese Thought and Institutions*, edited by John King Fairbank. Chicago: University of Chicago Press.

Yang, Mayfair. 1994. *Gifts, Favors, and Banquets*. Ithaca, NY: Cornell University Press.
———. 2000. "Putting Global Capitalism in its Place: Economic Hybridity, Bataille, and Ritual Expenditure." *Current Anthropology* 41: 477–509

Yu, Song-Qing. 1994. *Minjian mimi zongjiao jingjuan yanjio [A Study of the Scriptures of Heterodox Folk Religions]*. Taipei: Lianjing Chuban Shiyie Gongsi.

CHAPTER SIX

TEMPLES AND THE RELIGIOUS ECONOMY

Graeme Lang, Selina Chan, and Lars Ragvald

Temples attract more worshippers than any other public religious sites in China. A large and popular temple in Guangzhou, for example, has accommodated more than 60,000 worshippers during the course of a single worship day—the first day of the Lunar New Year—and some other temples are equally crowded and busy at such times. Although temples are subject to many state regulations, and are constrained by these regulations, they provide most of the god-worship activities that were available in premodern China. During the past twenty years, thousands of temples have been renovated or rebuilt, and hundreds of new temples have been constructed, attracting millions of citizens to these traditional forms of worship. Devoted to deities from Buddhism, Daoism, and Chinese 'popular' religion, these temples appear to be an important part of the emerging 'religious economy' in China. This chapter examines whether we can analyze these temples using a 'religious economy' model such as that outlined in the work of Rodney Stark and other theorists (Stark and Bainbridge 1987; Stark and Finke 2000).

When the religious economy model directs our attention to the producers of religious goods and services, it tells us that these producers try to address the needs of their intended constituencies, adapting their services as conditions change or as competition with other suppliers increases. It also tells us that the consumers of religious goods and services compare various suppliers and choose the ones that seem to give them the best return on their investment of time, energy, and resources, relative to their goals, needs, and current knowledge.

When the model focuses on the full range of suppliers and consumers, it tells us to expect that unless a monopoly is rigorously enforced by the state, there will be competition, variations in the ability to attract and hold adherents, periodic innovation, occasional copying, and a variety of strategies to market or promote religious goods. Some suppliers may have no ambition to succeed beyond a narrow niche in the religious market and may even isolate themselves from that market. Others try to gain as many adherents as possible and adopt strategies designed to achieve that goal in competition with other groups with similar ambitions.

If the religious economy paradigm is useful for studying competition among temples in a religious market in China, we would expect to see the following:

(1) People who are interested in temple worship can visit and compare temples, choosing to worship at those that most suit their needs.[1]
(2) Temples vary in their success or failure in attracting worshippers on the basis of these choices by worshippers.
(3) Temple managers adapt their services and the features of their temples to what they perceive to be local preferences about temple worship and occasionally add or enhance features that are not already well-developed in other nearby temples.
(4) The existence of more temples in a district will lead to more worship, other things being equal: that is, where there are a number of different temples for a variety of deities, with a variety of religious services, more people will visit temples than will do so in a district that has only one temple with a more limited range of deities or religious services, even if the total size of temple area is comparable in the two districts. (This is a key prediction of the religious economy model.)
(5) Revenue from worshippers is the major form of temple income, and is directly related to the success of a temple in meeting worshippers' needs. (Otherwise, the organization that manages a temple does not have to pay any attention to the religious 'market', since the organization gains its revenues from other sources, and we would not expect to see evidence that temples really 'compete' with each other.)

Of course, temple worship in a polytheistic culture is a nonexclusive form of religious activity, and temples cannot bind worshippers to a particular temple to the exclusion of worship at other temples. In

---

[1] Under some conditions, there might be no choices among local temples, for example, when a village maintains only one temple and there are no other easily accessible temples for that kind of worship. There are also small ethnoreligious enclaves that are able to support only one temple for that ethnic group and in which ethnic membership virtually requires worship in that particular setting and forbids visiting other religious sites, even if they are locally available and nonexclusive.

this sense, temple worship is unlike the kind of religious activity and religious adherence associated with the exclusivistic religions that have formed the main testing ground for the religious economy model in North America and Europe. However, this makes the religious economy model even *more* applicable to temple worship than to worship in exclusivistic religions. We pause to explain this point further.

Many urban and suburban settings in Asia provide a number of temples, shrines, and worship sites for a variety of deities, and in a polytheistic milieu, there is no enforced prohibition against worshippers making their own individual choices. Hence, in temple worship in which a number of temples are available, as in a secular economy in which a number of producers are available, worshippers can visit, compare, and choose which temples to revisit on the basis of their experiences at each temple. Although people in some rural areas are mainly committed to a particular temple cult (see, e.g., Dean 1993, 1998), no temples try to prevent them from visiting other temples or making such comparisons, because it would be impossible to do so. Where a number of temples are available, worshippers may alter their temple worship on the basis of relatively small differences in outcomes or in worship experiences.

In exclusivist religions, by contrast, it might require quite large differences in the specifically religious outcomes or benefits to motivate a change from one church or sect to another. This is because an individual has probably invested a great deal in the social relationships within a church or sect, and this is part of the reason for the individual's commitment to that group (i.e., the loss of this social capital becomes a part of the calculus of costs in leaving such a group). It is also notable that churches and sects usually require a considerable investment in learning texts and rituals.

In temple worship, there is little or no social network that entangles the individual within a particular temple sect, and there is little need to learn complex texts or rituals (hence, to relearn them when switching to another temple). Hence, switching is easier between temples than between churches and sects. Of course, this depends on the availability of a variety of temples within one's district.[2]

---

[2] Village religious festivals, however, are also social productions that utilize social capital and organizational expertise to achieve goals that include prestige maintenance and economic support or aggrandizement. Thus, religion is only one dimension of temple-related activity. A village temple and temple-related activity cannot be comprehended by using *only* an analysis of religious motivations (see Chau 2004 for further analysis of this feature of village temple festivals).

To summarize, temple worship in an environment where a number of temples are available might be more amenable to analysis using the religious economy paradigm than is worship in more exclusivist religious groups in which individuals must invest much more in the group as the cost of belonging.

There are other features of an active religious market that might or might not occur. These include: promotion or advertising by temples, to attract visitors; copying of the innovations of other temples which seem to be successful; 'market research' by temple managers to assess better the needs and interests of visitors and worshippers. We can document a local religious economy even if promotion or advertising, copying of other temples' successful innovations, and market research do not occur. But if evidence of such practices is observed, this greatly strengthens the case for using this model to understand the activities of those who build and operate temples. Of course, the competition among suppliers is not the only dynamic feature of religious or secular economies. For example, suppliers and consumers in both the religious and secular economies can be greatly affected by interventions from the state.[3] But here, our main focus is on the religious market.

We now turn to a consideration of temples as 'firms' in the religious market and then illustrate from some of our research on temples in China.

Temples as Firms

How would an economist view a temple? First, we observe that it offers religious goods and services from a building that can be described in terms of location, size, design, and the variety of services and goods that is available on-site. Hence a temple is like a retail outlet. A small temple in a neighborhood is comparable to a local

---

[3] In the religious economy as in the secular economy, state rulers might favor one enterprise over others for reasons of mutual benefit: hence that enterprise may prosper as long as the leaders remain in power. In the religious economy as in the secular economy, a firm's leaders can be penalized or imprisoned for violating rules or annoying the rulers. Some religious enterprises, like some secular enterprises, seek deregulation in order to facilitate their expansion into new niches or new services, but others might try to induce the state to grant a monopoly and suppress competitors. In both economies, a framework of enforceable rules operates in the background, largely invisible in normal times. All of these processes can occur in the interactions between the temple economy and the state.

specialty shop: It can survive with a trickle of local patrons and a few staff. A large temple with several buildings and many different god-statues in different parts of the complex, and with courtyards, gardens, ponds and so on, is like a shopping mall or a large 'religious supermarket'. The size of a temple, of course, is usually related to the size of its intended constituency: A large temple must draw visitors from a large area to attract enough patrons to pay for the costs of building and operating it.

How do shopping mall developers strategize about building and operating shopping malls to obtain the largest flow of visitors and revenue? The key to a successful mall is that it is well located in relation to prospective consumers and is bigger, grander, and more diverse, in terms of the goods and services offered, than any nearby malls. Location near major transportation routes is essential, since the success of the mall depends on people getting there without difficulty. Shopping mall developers often use a statistical model of the local market to assess the prospects for a new mall in a particular location. Called the 'retail gravity' model, it focuses on the relative sizes of existing malls, and their locations in relation to large concentrations of consumers. It predicts that a new mall can draw patrons away from existing stores and malls, if it is well located in relation to the population and is grander than its competitors. Location is the key factor.

Do we find, among temples, an important 'location factor'? Do temple-builders take account of this factor in placing their temples, or do well-located temples (whatever the reasons they were built on particular sites) do better than poorly located temples? Do temple builders or temple managers also alter and customize their temples as a result of competition among temples?

In our research in China between 1987 and 2004, we observed nearly all of the conditions and processes that would lead to the conclusion that the builders and managers of some temples participate actively and consciously in the religious economy and attempt to develop the features of their temples to increase their appeal to their intended constituencies in the religious market. We have observed market-oriented temple construction, strategic decision making about the promotion of a temple, copying of innovations from other temples, successes and failures among temples as a result of these decisions, and attempts to change the mix of religious goods, services, and promotion in response to the competition among temples and other sites for visitors. We have also observed worshippers visiting several temples and deciding which temples to patronize on the basis of their experiences at each temple.

Our research has been mainly devoted to the study of temples to one particular deity in two provinces, but we think that our conclusions may also be applicable for major temples in other provinces.

Wong Tai Sin (Huang Daxian) Temples in China

To illustrate the usefulness of the religious economy model for the study of temples and temple-based religion in China, we will use some results from our study of temples to the deity Wong Tai Sin (Huang Daxian)[4] in Guangdong and Zhejiang.

According to legends that have been incorporated into the literature of Daoism since the 4th century C.E., Wong Tai Sin was a hermit who attained immortality through Daoist self-cultivation in the Jinhua region of what is now Zhejiang province and was subsequently worshipped in that region for more than a thousand years. The last temple to Wong Tai Sin in Jinhua was destroyed only in the late 1950s, submerged under a reservoir. More than a thousand years after it had begun in Zhejiang, a new version of the sect appeared in Guangdong, in the 1890s, with a somewhat different character, amid a wave of plagues and political turmoil. The sect was established in Guangdong through spirit-writing about these events and their implications, with messages from the gods about the ongoing turmoil and troubles as well as about the ways in which the Guangdong believers should deal with these crises (Lang and Ragvald 1998).

During the Republican period after 1911, folk religion temples were suppressed in some areas, and the chaotic political and economic environment induced many religious practitioners to move to Hong Kong. The worship of this deity was transferred to Hong Kong early in the Republican era by the founder of the Guangzhou temple and eventually flourished in the colony (Lang and Ragvald 1993). By the 1960s, all of the Wong Tai Sin temples in Guangdong and Zhejiang had been destroyed, and no Wong Tai Sin temples apparently survived anywhere in the coastal provinces.

---

[4] *Wong Tai Sin* is the most common Hong Kong transliteration of the god's name, from Cantonese. *Huang Daxian* is the pinyin transliteration.

As it became possible to rebuild temples after the end of the Cultural Revolution, and especially with accelerating economic development in the 1980s and 1990s, many temples were rebuilt throughout mainland China, including a number of new Wong Tai Sin temples in both provinces. Lang and Ragvald have been studying these temples since the 1980s. During the course of our research on the main Hong Kong temple to the deity, we looked at the origins of the Hong Kong version of the sect in Guangdong and Zhejiang, the two provinces where the sect had been most active before 1949 (Lang and Ragvald 1993).

In the late 1980s, we began to notice and study the revival of the worship of this deity in a number of locations. At least nine new Wong Tai Sin temples and one major shrine were built in Guangdong and Zhejiang between the late 1980s and 1999. Lang and Ragvald (between 1987 and 2001) and Lang and Selina Chan (from 2000 to 2004) visited all of these temples repeatedly, conducting interviews with worshippers, priests, officials, and temple managers. From this research, we can begin to describe the reasons why these temples were built, the reasons why some of them have been much more successful than others, and the ways in which some of them have been modified to try to increase their appeal or profitability.

First, we should classify these temples and clarify the focus of this analysis. The temples range in size from a small peasant temple, not much bigger than a hut, in a rural village, to midsize rural temples, to grand god-palaces in rural, suburban, and urban locations (see Table 1). The smallest temples can survive on the patronage of a trickle of local clients and employ at most only a temple-keeper and a fortune-teller. The largest of these temples employs more than eighty staff members, and must attract a substantial number of worshippers from a wide area around the temple to pay the temple's operating costs.

In this chapter, we will discuss mainly the large temples (Temples E, F, G, and H, in Table 1), since they are most concerned with strategic decision making, have absorbed the largest investments, provide the most graphic illustrations of success and failure, and produce the largest variety and intensity of innovations in their attempts to succeed in the religious market. However, the smaller temples sometimes preserve forms of religious belief and behavior that are lost or hidden in the larger temples, as we will note in the last part of the chapter, and they occupy distinctive niches in the religious economy.

Table 1. *New Wong Tai Sin (Huang Daxian) Temples in Guangdong and Zhejiang, China, 1989–2004*

	Date, Location	Size	Founders or Initiators	Patrons	Success/Failure
A	1989: Xinhui, Guangdong	Midsize, rural	Wealthy Hong Kong-based believer (from Xinhui)	Local people from the city, villages	Moderate success: appears to attract enough visitors to cover costs and generate some revenues for local charity and education
B	1990: Rengang village, Guangdong	Small village temple	Villagers	Villagers	Moderate support from villagers, but insufficient for aggrandizement of the temple
C	1991: Jinhuashan, Zhejiang	Midsize, rural, tourist temple	Jinhua government and businesspeople	Tourists, mainly from China	Moderate success; the site is near the famous Double-Dragon Cave, the main tourist attraction on the mountain
D	1993: Jinhuashan (near site of Qing-era temple), Zhejiang	Mid-size village temple	Villagers	Villagers, a few local tourists	Few visitors, but enough to sustain the temple-keeper and fortune-teller
E	1995: Lanxi, near Jinhua, Zhejiang	Very large, suburban	Villagers initially; taken over and expanded by the city government	Villagers, local urbanites, tourists	Notable failure, relative to the size of the temple, the cost of the land and buildings, and the expectations of the founders
F	1996: Jinhuashan (near top of mountain), Zhejiang	Very large, rural	City government, in league with local business sponsors	Tourists, some local urbanites, villagers	Marginal; below the expectations of the founders
G	1998: Jinhuashan (on hilltop above temple D) Zhejiang	Midsize, rural	Hong Kong-based Taiwanese entrepreneur	Villagers, local and regional tourists, Taiwanese groups	Successful enough (financial backing from the wealthy founder continues)
H	1999: Guangzhou, Guangdong	Very large, urban	Fangcun government, then Hong Kong-based entrepreneur	Guangzhou, Pearl River Delta	Most successful of all the temples; some decline after the first year, then growth

Competition, Innovation, and Promotion

In this section, we will discuss the motives and calculations that are involved in building the large temples, attempts to increase the flow of visitors later through innovations within a temple, and various kinds of promotion and marketing in the surrounding communities. We will conclude with an analysis of the reasons why some of these temples were much more successful than others within the local religious market.

Temples are designed for the worship of gods, but they are also frequently designed and located to appeal to potential visitors and patrons. Some temples that have been renovated since the 1980s sit on the same site and occupy some of the same buildings as in the imperial period before 1911. (Many were built during the Qing, and a few were built during the Ming or earlier.) We will not discuss these temples here. Instead, we focus on new temples that have been built since the 1980s. One reason is that the people who initiated these projects can still be interviewed, or if not, their intentions can still be recovered from existing documents or from conversations with current managers of those temples. Hence, we can reconstruct the logic of building the temples in those locations at that time. Whereas we have been visiting most of these temples since shortly after they were built, we have also been able to follow some of the changes in the mix of religious features and activities as the managers have attempted to make them more appealing. This is much more difficult to do for temples that were built during the Ming and Qing periods.

Temples as Investments

Why were these temples built? Many of the new temples in China were intended to promote economic development by attracting tourists from among overseas Chinese in Hong Kong, Taiwan, and Southeast Asia. In our sample of temples, we have found that this motivation was expressed by agents who were involved in the planning or construction of six of the eight temples (Temples C—H in Table 1). All of these temples were built at or near the sites of earlier, now destroyed temples to this deity that had existed in Jinhua, in what is now Zhejiang province, for most of the past thousand years, and in Guangdong since the 1890s. The builders of these temples believed that worshippers of this deity, particularly those from Hong Kong, would be interested in making pilgrimages to new temples built on these historic sites. In the case of Jinhua, the Daoist legends about the hermit saint later known as Wong Tai Sin claimed that he had lived and become immortal in Jinhua in the 4th century C.E. Hence, local entrepreneurs believed that this local history of the saint gave the area a deep pool of religious capital which could be exploited to attract tourists.

The largest of those temples were very costly, and local government-affiliated units borrowed millions or tens of millions of renminbi for these projects from local banks, in some cases with contributions from local business groups. The local governments and businesses expected to achieve long-term net gains from these projects through construction, temple revenues from visitors, and spending by tourists in the districts surrounding the temples. In some cases, they also hoped that overseas Chinese would come for the temple, but stay to invest and create jobs in the region.

This kind of motivation was especially common among local officials during the 1990s, when many towns and counties in China were searching for ways to stimulate economic development using whatever local resources they could exploit to attract investment and generate revenue. The central government in the 1990s under Deng Xiaoping and Jiang Zemin was politically repressive yet was simultaneously supporting and encouraging the coastal provinces to be creative in their economic development efforts, using their own resources. Rebuilding a temple to a famous Daoist immortal and promoting the deified person's historical connection to the district was an obvi-ous way to try to generate tourist income. But this was only one of the motivations of the various parties who collaborated in the build-ing of these temples.

Some local groups that supported these projects also wished to revive local cultural history and use these revived historical sites as a basis for local cultural self-assertion (see also Jing 1996). This was espe-cially true for some local intellectuals and retired cadres, who found a role for themselves in the genesis and promotion of these projects by researching and documenting this cultural history. For example, in the town of Lanxi, a group of local intellectuals met regularly, starting in the late 1980s, to exchange ideas and findings from their investigations into the historical accounts of the Daoist saint immor-talized as Wong Tai Sin after one of them discovered the connection between this deity—during his earthly life—and a suburban village next to their town. Their historical research and articles were eventually used by local officials to justify the construction of a major temple to the deity near the village (Temple E in Table 1).

Other local people wanted to revive worship of a reputedly efficacious deity and saw an opportunity to do so under the slogan of economic development. That is, they had essentially religious motives, but were able to use the language of economic development to propose and support the reconstruction of temples, since this kind of language fit more easily into the mainstream discourse of the contemporary Chinese political system in the 1990s.

We do not think it necessary to claim that all of the motives for building temples are religious. Indeed, in the history of other civilizations, churches, mosques, temples, and shrines have apparently been built with a variety of secular motives in addition to the religious reasons for building them, and the anticipation of revenue and desire for local economic and cultural aggrandizement appear to be common motives.[5]

In any case, the developers of these temples were not motivated only or even mainly by piety. Nor did they ignore the likely longer-term returns on their investments in these temples. The construction of these temples was intended as a strategic investment in local economic development. But to make such temples successful, and produce returns on the huge expenses involved in building the biggest of these temples, they had to be designed, located, and promoted to draw visitors and generate revenue.

Location

To draw worshippers, a temple must offer attractive goods and services, and be accessible. A remote temple in the mountains that requires a long and tiresome journey can attract worshippers only if there are some extraordinary rewards from visiting it. The site

---

[5] We could offer many examples. All major pilgrimage sites are also sites of business and enterprise. In Europe during the Middle Ages, the deliberate use of relics to attract pilgrims for economic reasons was common. The Muslim pilgrimage to Mecca was also an occasion for business transactions and for profit (Peters 1994), and the resistance to Muhammad's revelations by his tribe, the Quraish, was evidently motivated in part by the fear that his determined monotheism would undercut the economic returns from the pre-Islamic pilgrimages to Mecca that were already a well-established tradition by the 7th century C.E.

might be prominent in the historical and cultural literature of the society because famous religious specialists lived there, or it might be the setting for extraordinary events in the religious history of the region, such as miracles or revelations. Or the site might be famous because of its extraordinary beauty—on top of a mountain, for example, overlooking ravines and gorges, surrounded by mists. Such sites, which have been the destinations of Asian pilgrims for millennia, can prosper without a 'convenient location'. The Shaolin temple in Henan is a good example of a temple that draws a steady stream of visitors (most of them arriving in tour buses) because of its historic significance and its uniqueness as a famous center for martial-arts training. Some Buddhist and Daoist monasteries in the mountains are able to attract visitors for similar reasons.

But for new temples, which do not already have such a reputation, location is very important. To be successful, a large and costly temple should be sited near a large population of potential visitors, and access to the site should be convenient for people who might wish to visit. In our study, the four large Wong Tai Sin temples differed greatly on this important factor.

Temple E, near Lanxi in Zhejiang, was built in 1995 in a suburban location near a small town and cannot be reached by such scheduled public transportation as buses, trains, or subways. The builders hoped to draw tourists from the region and overseas on the basis of the temple's main claim to fame: The nearby village was, according to legend, the birthplace of the Daoist who eventually achieved immortality and became Wong Tai Sin. But there is little in Lanxi besides this temple to attract tourists. It is quite inconvenient for outsiders to reach the site, and it has no extraordinary features except a large bronze statue of the deity. It was doomed to failure, and indeed, it has been a great disappointment to the local government, which supported its construction and acquired the land for the temple from the village. (Below, we outline some of the innovations adopted by the managers to try to increase the flow of visitors in the face of this failure.)

Temple F, also in Jinhua, was built for the same reasons near the top of the mountain in 1996. It was a very large and very expensive project. The local government had to build a road up the mountain to allow visitors to reach the site and had to compensate the villagers for the land. But as with Temple E, there is no extraordinary historical or cultural feature at the site sufficient to draw a stream of visitors, and a casual or curious visitor must make a long, tedious, and some-what dangerous journey by taxi or car on a narrow, winding road up the mountain. For these reasons, this temple has failed to attract enough visitors to pay off the debts that were incurred in building it or even to cover the full costs of running the temple. Local officials considered building a cable-car line from the base of the mountain up to the site of the temple to produce a greater flow of visitors and revenue, but gave it up as too costly. Eventually, the temple was sold to a private Zhejiang firm involved in construction, tourism, and other industries, and that company now covers the deficits in running the temple and contemplates how to try to make it a suc-cess in the future.

Temple G is somewhat better located. Built in 1998, it is in a rural area near a village, but at the base of Jinhua Mountain rather than near the summit. The roads in the area are well paved, except for the dirt road to the village and the site of the temple, which runs about 800 meters from the main road. The temple overlooks a reser-voir, and the location is quite scenic. It is also not far from Jinhua City, which is much larger than Lanxi. The location, however, would not be very appealing to visitors if the site had not been improved greatly to provide a more satisfying experience than the urban temples in the area, and if transportation to the site had not been upgraded. The builder, a Hong Kong-based Taiwanese entrepreneur, paved the dirt road from the main road, installed a large parking lot for buses next to the temple, added a public park with various attrac-tions next to the temple, and engaged in a program of promotion that greatly enhanced the visibility of the temple. These measures have made this temple, alone among the Jinhua Wong Tai Sin tem-ples, a relatively successful enterprise.

The best located of all the temples, however, is Temple H, which opened in 1999. It is in a suburb of Guangzhou, with more than six million people living within five kilometers of the temple. Many of these Guangzhou residents are aware of this deity since many of them watch Hong Kong television (Zhu and Ke 2001), and broad-casts during the Lunar New Year period always devote some atten-tion to the huge crowds at the Hong Kong Wong Tai Sin temple during the first day of the New Year. In addition, there is a new subway in Guangzhou that runs to the district in which the temple is located and has a stop about 300 meters from the temple; thus it is quite convenient for residents to get to the temple from many parts of Guangzhou. The temple also has some religious capital to increase its appeal, since it is on the site of the first major temple to this deity in Guangdong, built in the 1890s and destroyed in the 1930s.

The local government initiated the project, bought the land from the local peasants, started construction, but then ran out of money. Eventually, they persuaded a Hong Kong-based entrepreneur who was active in construction projects in that part of Guangzhou to take over the project and complete the construction with his own funds. He realized the potential of the site and built the temple on a grander scale than was the original intention of the local government. In planning the project, he spent months visiting temples all over China to look for good ideas and useful designs. The resulting temple, which opened in 1999, has been highly successful, attracting visitors from all over the city (arriving by bus and subway), and from other towns in the nearby Pearl River Delta (arriving mostly on tour buses). This temple has also been promoted in the region as part of the builder's larger marketing strategies, and this promotion is one of the reasons for its great success. We now turn to a discussion and some examples of the marketing and promotion of a major temple.

Promotion and Innovation

The temple that was most desperately in need of innovation to increase its appeal to visitors was the Lanxi temple (Temple E). We visited this temple repeatedly between 1996 and 2003 and noted very few visitors in the years after it was opened in 1995. The temple managers had hired a number of Daoist priestesses from Hangzhou, along with a priest, but the few visitors did not provide enough revenue to support the enterprise, and the priestesses claimed that they had not been paid for months. They became so disaffected with the poor management and the trickle of worshippers that they all left the temple after a year of service. The residents of the village next to the temple also mostly stopped worshipping at the temple; instead, they installed a statue of the deity in their own village temple to bring the worship activities more fully under their own control. Once the priestesses left and the villagers had their own impressive new statue of the deity in their own temple, they had little incentive to visit the large main temple just outside the village, even though it required only five minutes walk for a visit. The temple managers first tried to rescue the temple first by subleasing it to the priest, hoping that he would find a way to make it more attractive. However this priest, who possessed a motorcycle and a cell-phone, was more interested in providing religious services to fee-paying clients outside the temple and spent most of his time elsewhere. The experiment in leasing the temple to him was not a success.

Noting, however, that a group of the village women were particularly devout and that they were patronizing a local spirit-medium who claimed to be able to speak with the voice and words of Wong Tai Sin, the managers decided to try to get these women back to the temple. As a concession, they allowed this spirit-medium to use an office inside the temple as a base for her consultations with worshippers, as we discovered during a recent visit. They also installed statues of three Buddhist deities, since the temple managers were aware that some worshippers in the area were devotees of these deities. This 'supermarket of deities' approach is typical in many popular-religion temples in this region. But we were able to confirm that in this case, the deities were added explicitly to increase the temple's drawing power in the local religious market. These innovations made the temple marginally more attractive, but have not been sufficient to attract more than a small number of new worshippers.

Other temple managers have been much more successful in promoting their temples and in adding appealing features. As we noted above, Temple G, built by a Taiwanese entrepreneur in Jinhuashan, was located in a rural area, but the entrepreneur who built the temple also advertised it through pamphlets and posters distributed in nearby markets. In addition, she organized a program of special medical services for poor and elderly villagers in the county and used these services to increase the local profile and visibility of the temple in the district. She also upgraded the area around the temple as a public park, with gardens, walkways, craft shops, and activities for children. Finally, she installed a traditional orchestra in the temple to play Chinese instrumental music every day for visitors. As the temple gradually became more popular, a local bus company that operated occasional buses to the site added more frequent service with larger buses. With these aggressive measures in upgrading the appeal of the site, facilitating access to it by paving the road and installing the parking lot, and building goodwill in the district through charitable services and public events to commemorate these services, the builder has managed to turn an obscure rural site into a successful temple enterprise that attracts streams of worshippers and visitors from the city, especially on weekends.

At Temple H, the very successful Guangzhou temple, the builder also decided to use advertising to try to attract more visitors to the temple. Before the Lunar New Year in 2000, his company placed 30-second ads about the temple on Hong Kong television stations and print ads in two Guangzhou newspapers. The company also conducted a survey of worshippers at the temple to find out how they had learned about the temple. On the basis of the results of the survey, the temple managers changed the advertising campaign for the 2001 Lunar New Year period, placing newspaper ads only in the Guangzhou Daily. From their survey in 2000, they had discovered that most visitors to the temple had seen the ads in this newspaper; hence this was the most cost-effective way to reach potential worshippers.

As an example of how a newspaper ad is used to promote visits to a temple, we provide some details from the advertisement in the *Guangzhou Daily* published on January 24, 2001 (the first day of the Lunar New Year). The ad is titled "Wong Tai Sin Temple," and includes a picture of the site. Under the title are the following lines:

> During the Spring Festival, the temple is a good place to visit, with many things to see and many things to do; lion dancers welcome the New Year, and the God of Wealth welcomes guests. There are many good things here to bring you wealth [sic!]. New scenery has been added, such as millions-of-years-old oddly-shaped stones, a pool where you can free fish and turtles [to accumulate merit], a God of Wealth Hall, a Confucius Holy Hall, a Guan Gung Hall and a Guan Yin Hall [Guan Gung is a famous deified historical figure; Guan Yin is the popular Chinese-Buddhist Goddess of Mercy] . . . all in a special park-like design. . . . There is free incense available with purchase of a ticket for entry to the temple [for those don't want to buy incense], and visitors purchasing the entry ticket can get a coupon for a second free entry later.

The ad concludes with information on hours of operation and detailed instructions on how to get to the temple by bus or subway. The ad does not say anything about religious doctrines, organized worship or ceremonies, the presence of Daoist priests, or involvement of the temple in charitable services. None of these things are as important, from the point of view of the temple managers, as the themes listed in the ad.

The advertisement also shows that the temple managers marketed the temple according to the standards of modern business advertising. They stressed utility (getting wealthy), the variety of 'goods' available (the chance to worship a number of well-known deities, in addition to the principal deity, Wong Tai Sin), aesthetic enjoyment (interesting scenes, a pleasant environment), and convenience (easy to reach by public transportation). Advertisements for a new shopping mall could be analyzed by using precisely the same categories. The long business experience of the Hong Kong-based builder of the temple in a capitalist environment clearly shaped the way the temple was marketed.

Like the Taiwanese entrepreneur who made Temple G such a success despite a rural location, the builder of the Guangzhou temple added further attractions to the site, including unusual animal-shaped stones from Guangxi, gardens and trees, and most recently, a stage on a plaza immediately behind the temple for cultural performances for visitors on special occasions. He had observed a smaller version of such a stage at a temple in Shanghai during his travels to see how temples were built elsewhere, and decided to install one at his temple, but he built it on a larger scale, with his own modifications to increase its usability for community events. The builder also commissioned a company in Foshan to produce ceramic versions of the characters in the Dao De Jing, the Daoist canon, and when the Foshan company finally perfected the technology to do this after a year of experimentation, he installed the complete Dao De Jing in ceramic characters on a wall next to the main temple. Finally, he had inherited the remaining pieces of the original temple, built in 1899 and destroyed in the 1930s, and after storing these pieces for several years, he installed them in an attractive garden next to the performance stage, where the relics were displayed as part of a demonstration of the temple's significance and cultural capital.

To summarize: large new temples are not passive operations in which temple-keepers sit in a building and wait for visitors. The managers of the most successful of these temples actively promote them in the surrounding districts with advertising (newspapers and television ads, pamphlets, and posters) and programs of activities that are at least partly designed to increase the visibility and reputation of the temple in the community. They also add features to the temple that are designed to attract more visitors, usually after comparing the features of other big temples, and they change their own temple's mix of activities and features according to their perceptions of what is most likely to be appealing, within the constraints set by the government.

Of course, government constraints limit some of these activities. The Guangzhou temple might be one of the few that has been allowed to advertise its services in a newspaper, and promotional activities must be done carefully and with the compliance of local officials. Compliance and good will are facilitated when a temple provides substantial funds for local charitable and other activities, as at the most successful of these enterprises (Temples G and H).

Research on Visitors to a Large and Successful Temple

All of these examples and our analysis refer to the supply-side activities of the temple builders or temple managers. Ideally, we should also study the activities, interests, and choices of the consumers. It is possible, with a suitable approach or the right introductions, to talk to temple-keepers, temple builders, temple managers, and temple staff. It is more difficult to talk to visitors and worshippers, beyond casual conversations at these temples, and it has been nearly impossible to conduct any kind of random survey of temple worshippers among the population in the districts surrounding these temples. However, it is possible to do useful research on religious consumers and temple visitors at some of these locations. To illustrate, we provide data from a survey at one of these temples.

Since there are no membership lists for temples, it is not possible to sample worshippers on the basis of lists. It is also not feasible to sample worshippers through random sampling of the population, by telephone surveys or in-person interviews, at least in mainland China. However, it is possible to study worshippers arriving at a temple. We have done such research at the Guangzhou temple, and the data allow us to begin to answer some important questions.

Our method was to talk to worshippers inside or just outside the temple compound, as they arrived but before they began their worship activities. We conducted this kind of research during the Spring Festival at the Guangzhou temple in 2001, on the first day of the New Year. On that day, we estimated, on the basis of periodic timed counts of worshippers ascending the steps to the main platform in front of the temple, that about 60,000 people visited the temple. Our research assistants—two university students—worked from 9:30 a.m. to about noon, interviewing 131 people and producing data on 198 visitors (Many people arrived in small groups, with friends or family members, so it was possible to interview one person in some groups and obtain data on the other members of the group.) The interviews were conducted in Cantonese or in Mandarin, depending on the preference of the interviewee.

These data do not come from a random sample, since some worshippers would not agree to be interviewed, and willingness to be interviewed was probably related to other important characteristics of these individuals. However, we managed to get interviews with people in every age category of adults, and the data also allow us to draw some conclusions about the frequency of temple visits and the residential locations of worshippers. To illustrate how such research can be used to answer important questions, we outline some of the results in this chapter.

Our first question was about residence (for mainland Chinese, the location of the household registration or *hukou*). We knew that the builders of the temple had hoped to draw Hong Kong worshippers to the temple, since Wong Tai Sin is very well known in Hong Kong and tourists are prepared to travel in China to interesting destinations. We also wanted to know the extent to which the temple had begun to appeal to Guangzhou urbanites and whether that appeal was mainly confined to the district around the temple (Fangcun) or whether the temple was also drawing visitors from other parts of Guangzhou. The data in Table 2 indicate that most visitors—more than three out of four—come from Guangzhou, and about half of those come from the district around the temple. Only a small proportion of the visitors come from Hong Kong. (Our finding of only a few Hong Kong visitors is an underestimate: tour buses occasionally arrive from Hong Kong and Shenzhen carrying groups of Hong Kong visitors, producing a small temporary surge of Hong Kong visitors, but we did not observe many such visitors on our several visits to the temple.) This result is quite important: It rules out the hypothesis that most visitors are already familiar with the deity through previous active worship at the Hong Kong temple. It also suggests that the temple is not purely a neighborhood or district temple but draws worshippers from across the city.

The 16% of visitors who said that they came from other provinces appeared to be mostly migrants living in Guangzhou for work or business reasons. It is likely that some of them visit the temple seeking help with problems that are particularly acute for migrants, and that some of them will attribute their successes, in their struggles as migrants, to help from this deity. Indeed, this was one of the reasons for the success of the Hong Kong temple: its appeal to insecure migrants living near the temple in the 1950s and 1960s (Lang and Ragvald 1993). Further research on these Guangzhou migrants and their religious activities and needs would be valuable and would give us a better understanding of this portion of the visitors to the Guangzhou Wong Tai Sin temple. We also expect that some of the migrants who achieve success in Guangzhou will eventually carry the worship of this deity back to their home provinces, seeding this sect into other cities in mainland China. (Previously, it was the economic successes of the Hong Kong temple and of Hong Kong worshippers that seeded the cult into Guangdong and Zhejiang. Further spread of the cult in the mainland is now likely to occur as a result of the experience of migrants with the new Guangzhou temple.)

Second, we wanted to know whether the temple's advertising and promotion, described above, had led to a rise in the number of first-time visitors; so we asked how many times visitors on the first day of the New Year had previously visited the temple. The responses are not likely to be precise, except for first-time visitors, and we have data only for the people who were interviewed (not those accompanying them). The results in Table 3 show that one-third of the interviewees were first-time visitors, about another third had visited several times, and the rest had visited the temple repeatedly in the past. If these data were based on a reasonable sample of the 60,000 visitors on the first day of the Chinese New Year, we could estimate, very roughly, that 20,000 people visited the temple for the first time

Table 2. *Original Residence of Visitors to the Temple*

	%	N
1. Guangzhou:*	77	153
2. Other provinces**	16	31
3. Pearl River Delta	6	11
4. Hong Kong:***	2	3
Total:	100	198

 * Includes 34% (68) who said "Fangcun," "live near," and "pass near," the temple.
 ** Most "other provinces" respondents reside in Guangzhou for work-related reasons.
*** The figure for Hong Kong is probably too low. When tour buses arrive from Hong Kong or Shenzhen, there is a temporary surge in Hong Kong visitors that this sampling did not include.

on that day, while 40,000 of the worshippers had visited the temple previously. If the last three categories, 36% of the total, represent 'frequent' visitors, we guess that more than 20,000 of the people who came to the temple at the New Year festival had made the temple a regular part of their religious activities in the two years since it had opened in the city in 1999.

Third, we recorded the age and sex of the 198 people in the groups that we surveyed in the study. We can use these data to answer some important questions. First, it has commonly been observed that women visit temples more than men do in Hong Kong and other parts of 'greater China,' and that middle-aged and elderly women are more commonly found at temples than are young women. Hence, determining the age and sex distributions among the worshippers at the Guangzhou temple allows us to say whether the temple is attracting men as well as women, and young as well as middle-aged and elderly visitors. The data in Table 4 suggest that there are indeed more women than men at the temple, but that worshippers represent all ages, including those in the 20–29 and 30–39 age categories for both men and women. We were not surprised by the age distribution of female worshippers, including a substantial minority of women over age 65.

The biggest surprise was that 51% of the men appeared to be in the age bracket 30–39. Some were accompanying a wife or girlfriend, but others arrived alone or with male friends. From research on the Wong Tai Sin temple in Hong Kong, we know that worshippers ask about current problems, dilemmas and troubles, and that they seek peace of mind through consulting the deity by divination for predictions

Table 3. *Number of Times Visiting the Temple*

	%	N
First time:*	32	39
2–3 times:	33	41
4–6 times:	20	24
7+ times:	7	8
"Many times":**	9	11
Total:	100	123

* January 24, 2001.
** "Many times" includes "1st and 15th of each month."

or advice. We expect that the help or reassurance against the inse-
curities of work, business, and careers in market-economy Guangzhou
make up a substantial part of the appeal of a temple visit, for both
men and women. Our data suggest that middle-aged men might be
especially pressured in this environment. Perhaps they are also attracted
by the idea that Wong Tai Sin is a god of wealth, and that he has
helped Hong Kong people to achieve the economic successes that
have been envied for so many years by their Guangzhou-based com-
patriots. But further interviews with these men and women would
be needed to determine whether the expectations, hopes, and needs
of these urbanites are similar to those of the urbanites who have
made the Hong Kong Wong Tai Sin temple such a great success.
We should also note that in the Hong Kong Wong Tai Sin temple,
businessmen often appear at the temple during the New Year period
to thank the deity for a prosperous and successful year but do not
often visit at other times of the year. The unexpectedly large proportion of male visitors in the 30–39 age group at this Guangzhou
temple on the first day of the Spring Festival in 2001 might represent a similar practice, hence not be typical for other periods.

To conclude this section on our survey of worshippers at a large
Guangzhou temple: We have determined that the temple has succeeded in attracting many new (first-time) worshippers and that within
two years, between its opening in 1999 and our survey in 2001, it
had established itself in the religious worship of tens of thousands of
Guangzhou citizens. Although many of them come from the district
around the temple, it is not only a district temple and has attracted
urbanites from across the city. We also know that it has attracted

Table 4. *Temple Visitors by Age and Sex*

Age*	Female (54%)	N	Male (46%)	N	Total (100%)	N
16–19	4	4	0	0	2	4
20–29	30	31	15	13	23	44
30–39	29	30	51	45	39	75
40–49	18	19	14	12	16	31
50–59	5	5	16	14	10	19
60+	15	16	5	4	10	20
Total:	100	105	100	88	100	193

* Age estimated by interviewers

large numbers of male and female worshippers in all adult age categories, including a large number of middle-aged men. While this might seem to be an unsurprising or mundane result, it does rule out the hypothesis that it is mainly elderly women or tourists who patronize folk religion temples in a modernizing Chinese metropolis such as Guangzhou. The appeal of these temples is much wider.

Finally, we have demonstrated that such research is possible, and that it can answer important questions, even though each interview might last only a few minutes as visitors are entering or leaving the temple. Of course, this kind of survey is possible because this temple attracts such a large number of visitors during a festival. It would be highly inefficient to try to do such research among the trickle of worshippers who visit some of the other temples in our study or some of the small rural or suburban temples that are patronized mainly by people from the neighborhood.

Religious Services and Religious Specialists

Before we conclude, we should note that all the major temples we have discussed in this chapter have, or had, Daoist priests or priestesses in residence. However, although Wong Tai Sin is supposedly a Daoist immortal, we have barely mentioned these specialists in our account of the reasons why these temples succeed or fail. What is the role of Daoism and Daoist specialists in these temples? We can offer here an outline based on our experience, observations, and interviews at these large temples.

First, it must be noted that much of what worshippers do at such temples does not require or benefit from the presence of Daoist clergy. Worshippers bow to the deity or to several deities at a temple, ask for help or advice, make offerings, perhaps donate money or buy religious icons or paraphernalia from shops next to the temple, and leave. None of these activities requires or is mediated by professional clergy. Worshippers can petition the deity directly, without doctrinal or ritual guidance from specialists.

Outside mainland China, worshippers at many temples also commonly ask for advice or predictions using a set of 'fortune-poems' (*qian*) at the temple, by shaking a container of numbered bamboo slips until one of the slips falls to the ground. (The procedure is called *qiu qian*, 'seek [the deity's answers through] fortune-poems'.)

The number on the slip corresponds to the number of one of the fortune-poems, and the poem provides the god's answer to the worshipper's question or problem. Professional fortune-poem explainers provide explanations of the meaning of the poem, in relation to the worshipper's problems, for a fee.[6] These fortune-poem explainers are not clergy, and this service can now be obtained in or near many smaller temples in China, although it is officially considered to be feudal superstition.

Since worshippers can bow before the deity, petition for advice or help, receive the deity's answers (in the form of fortune-poems), and seek explanations of those allusive answers without resorting to the services of a Daoist priest or priestess, what is the role and significance of Daoist clergy in these large temples? From our observations, they play two main roles in such temples.

First, they perform daily rituals before the altar to the principal deity on a schedule that is determined by agreement with the temple's managers. These rituals might have little to do with the deity and are based on Daoist texts and performances that are available within the sects and ritual traditions of contemporary Daoism. Worshippers, according to our observations, pay no attention to the specific content of these rituals, which involve chanting obscure texts that are uninteresting to most ordinary worshippers. However, the clergy wear colorful robes, engage in coordinated chanting, singing, and bowing before the altar, and sometimes accompany their performances with percussion instruments. Thus they provide periodic solemn spectacles for the visitors, adding to the temple's veneer of religious observance with ceremonies which are at least superficially impressive.

In addition to these regular performances by the clergy, visitors can also 'commission' a special ceremony for their personal benefit as they seek the favor of the deity for their own needs. The money earned from such special ceremonies will usually be split between the priests and the temple's general accounts, according to an agreed-upon formula.[7] But few visitors seek (or can afford) such services. In some temples, priests may also be available for personal consultations, usu-

---

[6] For an account of how this works in the Hong Kong Wong Tai Sin Temple, see Lang and Ragvald 1993: ch. 6.

[7] However, there is obviously room for disputes over the division of these performance fees between the priests and the temple's management, and this is not uncommon.

ally outside of the regular activities at the temple as a private and unofficial arrangement.

In any case, the priests do not actually manage these temples, but instead are paid by the temple management to perform rituals according to the schedule. The head priests are also sometimes expected to meet and brief important religious visitors and government officials, and must provide annual reports on their religious activities. The rest of their time may be taken up with reading, study, training, some temple maintenance, or 'outside practice.'[8]

The second important function of these clergy is to legitimize the temple by associating it with an officially recognized religion and with a religious organization that is properly registered with the state. Thus, the Daoist clergy at a temple are supposed to be registered with a branch of the official Daoist Association, to which they report. There is little doubt that some temple managers consider the priests to be an expensive item in the temple's staffing budget, relative to their contributions to the temple's activities and success, but they cannot avoid paying for these priests from temple income, because this is the only way to gain the necessary legitimacy with the state for a large temple. Complaints about the clergy, however, can be heard among some temple managers. The manager of one temple found that the priests in that temple, although well-paid, could not even manage to perform the chants in unison. The manager hired a music instructor to teach them how to do it and noted the irony that a secular manager was teaching priests how to sing!

The methods of recruitment and the certification of Daoist priests, hence the quality of their religious instruction and religious understanding, appear highly variable. In Zhejiang, for instance, it seems that priests and priestesses have considerable freedom to move between temples, and that some of them can gain the qualifications to serve as a priest in a temple with minimal or no formal training. One of the priests whom we interviewed had grown up in a poor village, and first entered a temple with only a letter of introduction from

---

[8] To earn additional income, some temple-based priests provide services to selected worshippers outside the temple and keep the resulting fees, and temple managers may be unable to prevent or control such 'outside practice'. For the priests, however, such activities take them outside the temple—an undoubtedly welcome diversion from temple routine—and provide a way to extend their networks as well as to increase their income.

his local residence committee, stamped by the local police to indicate that he did not have a criminal record. He stayed in a number of temples for various periods, eventually settling in Temple G in Jinhua, after discovering that the conditions were much better there than at other temples in the region. Despite his lack of formal training, however, he seemed to us to be a sincere seeker of esoteric knowledge and of immortality (a classic Daoist preoccupation). Daoist priests in other temples, however, appear to include refugees from the harsh life of some poor villages in north China or from the fierce competition and insecurity of unskilled labor in the cities.

In other parts of southern China, the head priests at major temples are appointed by the local Daoist Association, which may also get a share of the annual payment to the temple's priests. This payment to the priests usually goes to the head priest, who allocates it among his subordinates, and who may also select his subordinates from among candidates for positions at the temple. The head priest thus has considerable power among the priests. For example, at Temple F, near the top of Jinhuashan, candidates can arrive at any time from other temples, sometimes unannounced, and are allowed to stay for a few days while the head priest assesses them (impressionistically rather than through formal evaluation) in regard to their personal qualities and abilities. At Temple E in Lanxi, however, the priestesses were recruited from a Hangzhou temple through a contract arranged through the Daoist Association, and at Temple G, the priests are screened and selected by the entrepreneur who runs the temple who has managed to acquire her own Daoist credentials. Thus, there is a variety of ways in which priests are screened and appointed, even within this small sample of temples in two provinces.

However, the priests are a kind of 'world within a world' in the temple—an enclave of expertise in ritual activities who have little impact on the overall success of the temple in attracting worshippers. No doubt the situation is different in some temples in Shanghai and elsewhere that are more directly controlled and managed by the priests. But in the temples we have observed, the priests are neither the shapers of the temple's fate nor the source of the temple's attractiveness to believers; they are more like bit-players in a drama that is under the direction of the officials, temple managers, or entrepreneurs who are the real sources of decision making and of innovation.

As the religio-entrepreneurial abilities of the priests develop, they might increasingly take the initiative within as well as outside of temples. But the Daoist priests and priestesses whom we have seen in Guangdong and Zhejiang do not yet seem able to develop their own independent sources of funds for temple building and for innovation; hence, for the success of temples at which they serve, they are still dependent on the initiatives and funds of the skillful entrepreneurs who now manage all but one of these major temples. Therefore, we have largely ignored the Daoist clergy in our account of the success and failure of these temples. They are not entirely irrelevant, but it seems that they have little real impact.

Village Temples

We have confined our analysis to the large temples because they are highly visible to everyone and because their successes (and failures) can be spectacular. However, the most vivid and interesting religious phenomena often occur not within these large public temples, but in the small rural or village temples. Although we do not intend to offer a detailed analysis here, we wish to indicate briefly how these smaller temples operate in relation to the religious market, and how the activities in these temples both extend and challenge the reach of the religious economy model.

First, we should note that in regard to supervision or regulation by the state, these rural and village temples often appear to operate below the radar of formal state scrutiny and control. One can observe phenomena at some of these smaller temples that would be considered intolerable if they occurred at most major urban temples. For example, fortune-telling is common inside the smaller temples, spirit-mediums are possessed by deities and deliver greetings and oracles, and animal sacrifices are conducted as part of the ceremonies at some special events.

For many of these events, local officials know what is happening but choose not to interfere. In some cases, they know that they can do little—except to antagonize villagers—if they try to ban or interrupt events that have attracted the support of a large fraction of people in the village. In one village in Guangdong, for instance, local cadres, faced with the imminent opening of an unregistered and thus illegal temple, scheduled a study trip to Macau so that they would not be present when the new shrine was inaugurated (Aijmer and Ho 2000: 233). In some areas, cadres have closed or even demolished illegal rural temples. We think that this is exceptional, rather than typical.

The intensity that accompanies some of the events at these smaller rural temples is much greater than what is typically observed in the grand urban temples. To give an example: in one village near Lanxi, we observed the eye-dotting ceremony for a new and expensive statue to a deity that had just been installed in the village temple. The villagers had collected funds for several days of opera performances to coincide with the event and had hired an opera troupe from the province. The members of the opera company were housed and fed within the village during the several days of performances, and took some of their meals in the village temple. The eye-dotting ceremony (which brings down the spirit of the deity into the statue) was held before six o'clock on a cold December morning. But inside the temple, the atmosphere was intense, yet joyful. A chicken was sacrificed, and its blood dripped into a basin of water, which was then sprinkled over the worshippers. A local spirit-medium was present who is periodically possessed by the deity, offering advice and remedies. (Indeed, the deity possessed her during one of our visits to the temple, and the god greeted us in a gruff voice and welcomed us, "the visitors from afar.") These kinds of events are very important for understanding the state of Chinese popular religion in the countryside. Although they cannot normally be observed in the large urban temples, they must be included among the variety of religious activities and services that makes up the religious market.

In a village where there is only one temple, with no comparable temples nearby offering a similar mix of activities, can we speak of pluralism, competition, innovation, and success or failure? There is no general answer to that question. But it is frequently the case that a variety of religious options is available to worshippers, and the people who offer these services, or design the sites at which the services are offered, often take careful note of the competition and innovate when they see a way to do so that will attract the people whom they wish to serve. For example, the village temple where we observed the eye-dotting ceremony sits within ten minutes walk of a much larger suburban temple in Lanxi (Temple E), which was languishing with few visitors. As we mentioned above, the managers of that larger temple installed three Buddhist statues in the temple and invited the spirit-medium to conduct her consultations from an office in the temple in their attempts to draw worshippers from the village and the nearby communities back to the main temple. The fact that this has not been notably successful does not undermine our contention that in this particular setting, there is some pluralism, competition among the providers of religious services, innovation resulting from this competition, and evidence that religious consumers are aware of these options and choose among them according to their own preferences and needs.

The other smaller temples in our sample are also in competition with nearby temples, and whether the temple managers compete actively, or instead passively wait for worshippers to decide the fate of their temples by either visiting or bypassing them, they occupy a niche in the religious market for smaller temples that draw worshippers mainly from local districts.

For example, Temple A, built on a scenic mountain in southeastern Guangdong in 1989 by a Hong Kong-based believer, sits near several other temples on the same mountain. All of these temples are designed to appeal to tourists and weekend visitors from the nearby town and the surrounding villages. The temple is not large enough to be a major attraction on its own, but many visitors to the mountain also have relatives in Hong Kong and are aware of the deity Wong Tai Sin. The temple is intended to draw some of them to worship as they visit the mountain for recreation or spiritual nourishment. We could theorize a temple niche within the religious market for tourists visiting mountains and other scenic spots who are also willing to worship deities during such visits.

The calculations and strategies that we have observed in the most successful of the large temples can also be observed among some managers of these midsize temples. The man who founded Temple A on the mountain near his ancestral village also carefully cultivates his relationships with local cadres and officials, donates some of the temple revenue to local schools and other local organizations, promotes the temple carefully in the district, and decorates it for maximum appeal within his resources.

We could imagine the religious market for temples as comprised of several levels, the higher-level temples being intended to draw visitors from a wide area with their outstanding and diverse features, while the small village temples are intended to draw only a trickle of local patrons from the neighborhood and are sustained by such moderate patronage because the costs of running those small temples are very low. Mid-size temples such as Temple A, on the mountain, occupy an intermediate position and compete with other nearby midsize temples. They may also draw patrons away from smaller nearby village temples.

Finally, we should note one other feature of some of the small village temples, which constitutes a kind of cultural capital that could be exploited in the future if their managers become aware of it. We have observed that several of these village temples have preserved an earlier version of the cult of this deity, which existed before the great success of one version of the cult of Wong Tai Sin in Hong Kong. This earlier version of the cult involves two deities—the person who achieved immortality and came to be known as Wong Tai Sin and his brother, also surnamed Wong, who is not venerated in the Hong Kong version of the cult and has been forgotten in Hong Kong. The two-saints version of the cult of Wong Tai Sin (i.e., venerating both Wong and his brother) once existed in village temples in both Guangdong and Zhejiang. Those temples were destroyed by the 1960s, and the statues of the deities were smashed or discarded during the Cultural Revolution. But the villagers remembered, and in the 1990s, when they found that they could revive the cult in their villages without repression, they resurrected the two-saints version of the cult in Temple D. All the other temples to Wong Tai Sin in mainland China reflect the Hong Kong version of the cult—that is, the version which was brought from Guangzhou to Hong Kong in 1915 (Lang and Ragvald 1993: ch. 3).

This small village temple thus preserves original iconography, but the temple-keepers seem unaware that the temple is like a museum, a window into the past and an earlier version of this cult. Hence, this small village temple has historical value that is not captured by variables such as size, the number of visitors, or the flow of donations. Thus, it attracts anthropologists and historians as well as peasants. But alas, only the peasants are reliable patrons.

Conclusions

The religious economy model can be usefully applied to the study of temples in Chinese societies. These temples are not passive shrines, but active players. The successes and failures among new temples can be at least partly understood by looking at such factors as location, promotion, innovation, and successful adaptation to the religious interests of potential visitors and worshippers. It should be added that the two most successful temples in our study are operated by entrepreneurs who are also very successful in secular enterprises and who have used some of the same kinds of calculations and strategies in their successful religious enterprises.

Research at a successful temple on a festival day, when large numbers of people visit the temple, helps to provide a picture of these worshippers in regard to age, sex, residential location, and frequency of visiting the temple. We have shown that the Guangzhou temple has attracted worshippers from all age groups and both sexes, and from areas far beyond the immediate neighborhood of the temple, and that the temple's advertising and promotion attract a substantial number of new worshippers, while also drawing previous worshippers back for repeat visits.

We have not investigated as many of the smaller suburban or village temples, but outside of the major cities, these smaller temples also serve the religious market and may compete with each other and with the larger temples, albeit more subtly, as worshippers seek the best experiences and outcomes in their search for supernatural aid, social support, and psychological rewards. Because these smaller temples are less easily controlled, they provide some experiences and services that are not available at the large urban temples. Some of these phenomena can be observed *only* in these smaller temples. Thus their relative obscurity, compared to the grand urban temples, is one of their principal advantages.

Our conclusions, however, are based on only a small sample of temples devoted to one particular deity in two coastal provinces. Further research on the significance and impact of other temples in the religious economy in other provinces and cities of China will help to expand and no doubt modify the preliminary view described in this chapter.

REFERENCES

Aijmer, Goran and Virgil K. Y. Ho. 2000. *Cantonese Society in a Time of Change*. Hong Kong: The Chinese University Press.

Chau, Adam Yuet. 2004. "Hosting Funerals and Temple Festivals: Folk Event Productions in Rural China." *Asian Anthropology* 3: 39–70.

Dean, Kenneth. 1998. *Lord of the Three in One*. Princeton, NJ: Princeton University Press.

———. 1993. *Daoist Ritual and Popular Religion in Southeastern China*. Princeton, NJ: Princeton University Press.

Jing, Jun. 1996. *The Temple of Memories*. Stanford, CA: Stanford University Press.

Kuah Khun Eng. 2000. *Rebuilding the Ancestral Village*. Aldershot: Ashgate.

Lang, Graeme. 1997. "Sacred Power in the Metropolis: Shrines and Temples in Hong Kong." Pp. 242–65 in *Hong Kong*, edited by Grant Evans and Maria Tam. Richmond, UK: Curzon Press.

Lang, Graeme and Lars Ragvald. 1993. *The Rise of a Refugee God*. Hong Kong: Oxford University Press.

———. 1998. "Spirit Writing and the Development of Chinese Cults." *Sociology of Religion* 59: 309–28.

Perry, Elizabeth J. 1985. "Rural Violence in Socialist China." *China Quarterly* 103: 415–40.

Peters, F. E. 1994. *The Hajj*. Princeton, NJ: Princeton University Press.

Stark, Rodney and William S. Bainbridge. 1987. *A Theory of Religion*. New York: Peter Lang.

Stark, Rodney, and Roger Finke. 2000. *Acts of Faith*. Berkeley, CA: University of California Press.

Thogersen, Stig. 2000. "Cultural Life and Cultural Control in Rural China: Where is the Party?" *China Journal* 44: 129–44.

Zhu, Jonathan Jian-Hua and Ke Huixin. 2001. "Political Culture as Social Construction of Reality: A Case Study of Hong Kong's Images in Mainland China." Pp. 188–217 in *Chinese Political Culture, 1989–2000*, edited by in Shiping Hua. Armonk, N.Y.: M. E. Sharpe.

CHAPTER SEVEN

HELPING PEOPLE TO FULFILL VOWS: COMMITMENT MECHANISMS IN A CHINESE SECT

Paul Yunfeng Lu

When studying religious commitment, social scientists have mainly focused on religions in Western societies, stressing membership, exclusivity, and institutional strictness (see Kanter 1972; Kelley 1972; Rudy and Greil 1987; Iannaccone 1994; Stark and Finke 2000). Religious commitment in a polytheistic setting has been rarely studied. This chapter, by contrast, examines how Yiguan Dao increases the commitment of members in Chinese society where religions have not been mutually exclusive and thus where people attached little importance to religious commitment.[1]

Yiguan Dao is a very important sect in Chinese societies. It was the largest sect in mainland China in the 1940s, recruiting more than ten million believers, but nearly disappeared there in the 1950s because of the suppression of religion under the Maoist regime (Lu 1998). The sect has begun to spread in Taiwan since the 1940s. Though the Kuomintang government also suppressed Yiguan Dao, the sect became the biggest sect on Taiwan and finally gained its legal status on Taiwan in 1987 (Song 1983, 1996; Lin 1990; Lu 2005).[2]

The aims of this chapter are two-fold: The first aim is to examine certain types of activities employed by Yiguan Dao to gain commitment. Kanter (1972) proposes that institutionalized mechanisms, including sacrifice, investment, renunciation, communion, mortification, and transcendence, were crucial for nineteenth-century American communes to generate and sustain the commitment of their members. This study finds that Yiguan Dao has also developed specific

---

[1] Strictly speaking, there is no corresponding Chinese word for the term "commitment," and Fenggang Yang (Stark and Finke 2004: 25) had to create a new Chinese word to translate it.

[2] For an extensive English introduction to Yiguan Dao, see Jordan 1982; Jordan and Overmyer 1986: 213–323. Deliusin (1972) offers an English analysis of the Chinese Communist Party's suppression of Yiguan Dao in mainland China.

ways to implement some mechanisms identified by Kanter. In addition, Yiguan Dao adopts a new mechanism, namely progressive strictness, to make committed members. The second aim of this chapter is to probe how Yiguan Dao accommodates Chinese traditional culture in the design of these activities. Yiguan Dao holds a very open attitude toward Confucianism, Taoism, and Buddhism, incorporating many elements of these traditions into the sect's practices. The sect also borrows some popular religious practices, such as vows, to guide its activities.

Methodologically, this study is based primarily on the analysis of field data on Yiguan Dao in Taiwan collected from September to December 2002. During that period, the author visited several important Yiguan Dao temples in Taiwan, participated in the sect's activities, collected spirit writings and other pamphlets written by the sectarians, and interviewed more than forty Yiguan Dao believers.

From Popular Religion to Yiguan Dao

Yiguan Dao mainly recruits its members from popular religion. This statement is more than an impression I gained during the fieldwork; it also can be supported by quantitative research. An island-wide survey on Taiwan in 1994 indicated that among 1682 respondents, there were 49 Yiguan Dao believers. Among these 49 people, there were 43 persons who came from other religious traditions (see Table 1). In detail, among these 43 sectarians, 12 previously belonged to Buddhism, 13 came from popular religion, and 13 had no previous religious belief (see Table 2). Furthermore, none of the twelve persons who said they were Buddhists had held a ritual of conversion to Buddhism. This suggests that most of these people were actually participants in popular religion.

There is no clear distinction among self-defined popular religion believers, Buddhists, and atheists. A study of Taiwan (Zhang and Lin 1992: 102) showed that 87% of Taiwanese who claim to have no religious belief actually believed in or worshiped gods; only 6.3% of the population really had no religious belief and did not believe in or worship gods. Qu Haiyuan (1997: 241) also pointed out that about 70% of those who claim to be Buddhists are actually practitioners of folk religion since they do not perform a ritual of conversion. These studies show that most of those self-defined Buddhists or atheists actually are adherents of popular religion. For this reason, we can hold that Yiguan Dao believers mainly come from popular religion.

Many ethnographers (Jordan 1972; Wolf 1974; Sangren 1987; Weller 1987) find that in China the consumers of popular religion put primary emphasis on a deity's reputation for efficacy (*ling* or *lingyan*). They usually ask for divine help from a god when personal crises or desires emerge. If the god satisfies their wish, they would reward the god with incense, delicious foods, beautiful images, new temples, spectacular plays, or adulatory inscriptions. If the god fails to perform miracles, however, they will not feel obligated to make offerings to the god, and they will usually turn to another deity who is believed to be more responsive and more efficacious. In short, these efficacy-oriented popular religionists tend to establish a temporary exchange relationship with specific spirits when they want to achieve practical ends.

Since folk religionists have been relatively indifferent to religious identities (Tamney and Chiang 2002), it is not difficult for the Yiguan

Table 1. *Religious Switching on Taiwan in 1994*

Different Religions	Number of Believers	Number of Converts
Buddhism	717	164
Daoism	169	18
Folk Religion	577	45
Yiguan Dao	49	43
Islam	1	1
Christianity	99	57
No belief	242	27
Others	11	5
Total	1682	360

Source: Taiwan Social Change Survey, 1994.

Table 2. *Components of Yiguan Dao converts*

The Current Belief	The Previous Belief								
	Buddhism	Taoism	Folk Religion	Yiguan Dao	Islam	Christianity	No Belief	Others	Total
Yiguan	12	2	13			3	13		43

Source: Taiwan Social Change Survey, 1994.

Dao sectarians to recruit them. These folk religionists, however, are also easily attracted by other sects. As Susan Naquin had noted, switching one's religious affiliation was common within China's sectarian tradition: "There were some people who went from sect to sect, joining first one and then another, always searching for the 'best' system" (Naquin 1976: 37). So, the question arises: How can Yiguan Dao keep these efficacy-oriented new recruits and increase their commitment?

Yiguan Dao sectarians themselves use the term *Cheng-quan* to summarize the process of making committed members. Literally, the word *Cheng-quan* means 'helping people to fulfill their wishes,' but the sect prefers the translation of 'supporting and encouraging people to cultivate Dao.' Indeed, *Cheng-quan* involves tremendous organizational endeavors and a long period of training and education that encourage the sectarians to increase their commitment step by step. Two forms of educational activities are practiced by the sect: the research courses (*Yanjiu ban*) and the dharma assembly (*Fahui*). Together with the two educational activities, there is also a mechanism of vows employed by Yiguan Dao. In the following, I will examine these activities by analyzing data collected from the *Fayi Lingyin* division of Yiguan Dao.[3] Although there are minor differences among divisions of Yiguan Dao with regard to the educational activities, we can get a basic understanding of Yiguan Dao's educational efforts from the case of *Fayi Lingyin*.[4]

Research Courses of Yiguan Dao

In her classic *The Making of a Moonie*, Eileen Barker (1994: 94) finds that there are "several stages through which the potential recruit normally has to pass as part of the conversion process." This is also true for Yiguan Dao. Usually, the Yiguan Dao sectarians establish an initial contact by inviting the potential converts to 'worship gods' (*Bai-bai*) at their home. The potential sectarians will next be persuaded to attend a family gathering or 'ordinary research courses'

---

[3] There are 19 divisions within Yiguan Dao. They are: *Jichu, Wenhua, Fasheng, Qianyi, Tianxiang, Jingguang, Tianzhen, Huiguang, Huaoran, Zhongyong, Andong, Baoguang, Mingguang, Puguang, Changzou, Fayi, Xingyi, Chande, Zhengyi* (Mu 2002: 80–127).

[4] For example, the names of research courses are different in different divisions. The courses conducted by the *Baoguang Jiande* division are *Xin-jin-li-jie* course, *ji-chu* course, etc. (Yang 1997: 69).

(*Putong ban*), which are held in family Buddha halls (*Jiating fotang*).[5] In the family gathering, the lecturer would share some religious stories with the guest and persuade him to be initiated into the sect. After the ritual of initiation, or 'pointing out Dao' (*Diandao*), people formally become Dao relatives (*Daoqin*), and they will be invited to attend the *Ming-de* course, a regular and formal workshop which is held once a week and lasts five months.[6] If the initiates survive the

Table 3. *Research Courses Conducted by the* Fayi Lingyin *division in 1992*

Name	Time	Number of Participants
Ordinary research courses	No limitation	No data
The *Mingde* course	Five months; once a week; 7:30 p.m.–9:30 p.m.	About 3000
The *Xinmin* course	Five months; once a week; 7:30 p.m.–9:30 p.m.	About 2000
The *Zhishan* course	Five months; once a week; 7:30 p.m.–9:30 p.m.	No data
The *Xuande* course	Five months; once a week; 7:30 p.m.–9:30 p.m.	No data
The *Jingdian* course I	One year; once a week; 7:30 p.m.–9:30 p.m.	About 1200
The *Jingdian* course II	Two years; once a week; 7:30 p.m.–9:30 p.m.	About 800

Source: Lin 1992: 162.

---

[5] Yiguan Dao's Buddha hall has two forms: the family Buddha hall and the public Buddha hall (*Gong-gong fotang*). While the former is small and located in their private homes, the latter is usually big and serves as a center for holding the large-scale activities.

[6] Yiguan Dao attaches much importance to the ritual of initiation which transfers three treasures (*Chuan Sanbao*): 'Opening the mysterious gate' (*Kai xuanguan*), 'offering the pithy formulas' (*chuan koujue*), and 'giving the hand sign' (*shou hetong*). According to the sect, the mysterious gate, which locates approximately the central point between eyebrows, is the gate through which one's spirit could enter Heaven at the time of death; 'opening the mysterious gate' is equal to getting salvation. As for the pithy formulas, they are five Chinese words which, from the sect's point of view, originate from the Mother. The sect holds that it is a kind of 'secret teaching' (*Xinfa*, literally mind-dharma) that is only imperfectly given expression by the existing religions but completely received by the sect. The pithy formulas can also function as an amulet when in danger. The hand sign is a gesture of cultivation.

Ming-de course, they will be encouraged to progress to the *Xin-min* course, and then to the *Zhi-shan* course, and finally to the *Jingdian ban*, the highest level (see Table 3).

Like the Moonies' workshops in which theology is "the central focus" (Barker 1984: 19), the research courses by Yiguan Dao are also devoted to teaching its theology and dogma. The *Ming-de* course introduces the basic doctrines of Yiguan Dao, including an introduction to the Eternal Venerable Mother (*Wusheng laomu*), the Yiguan Dao's cosmos theory, and the theory of three in one.[7] The *Xin-min* course mainly focuses on the sect's regulations, rituals, missionary skills, testimonies, and spirit writings. The *Zhi-shan* course and *Xuan-de* course further probe Yiguan Dao's doctrines and try to improve the attendees' ability of speech. The purpose of the courses is to train potential lecturers. Their content involves twenty books of five religions, namely Confucianism, Buddhism, Daoism, Islam, and Christianity.

When probing Yiguan Dao's education, Jordan and Overmyer (1986: 237) conclude that:

> Within the idiosyncratic limitations of its system of exposition, the Unity Sect [i.e. Yiguan Dao] is perhaps second only to the public school system in its pursuit of education for its members, and the bulk of almost every Unity meeting is in fact devoted, not to worship, but to the study of and commentary on moral books.

This observation is still valid. Yiguan Dao provides opportunities for working-class and less-educated sectarians to access a range of Chinese heritage. During the fieldwork, I once spent seven days in a huge temple building together with sectarian workers. My job was to plant trees, and my partner was Mr. Zheng, a forty-seven year old believer who was initiated into Yiguan Dao in 1976 in the Philippines where he worked as a foreign worker. Mr. Zheng had the typical appearance of peasants: a sun-darkened face, deep wrinkles, and coarse hands. But when Mr. Zheng tried to convert me during the work, he told me many interesting stories available in such Chinese clas-

---

[7] Like many Chinese sects, Yiguan Dao regards the Mother as its main deity. As the creator and savior of the world, according to the Mother myth, the Mother created ninety-six billion original spirits (*Yuan-ling*) and sent them down to earth. However, these spirits lost their primary spirituality because of the world's temptation. To save these primordial spirits, the Mother sent three Buddhas to the world. The Maitreya Buddha will preside over the future world and save the rest ninety-two billion primordial spirits. For extensive introduction to the myth, see Overmyer (1999).

sics as *The Platform Sutra of the Sixth Patriarch*. Sometimes, he could even recite some classic sentences. It seems that Mr. Zheng indeed knew something about traditional culture although he had only a primary education. He said that all of this knowledge was learned from the research courses held by the *Bao-guang Jian-de* division. When answering why he took part in the courses, Mr. Zheng told me that he had liked to listen to stories since he was young, and thus he likes attending courses held by Yiguan Dao. Before he attended a course, he would first read the materials offered by the lecturer with the help of a dictionary. At the same time, as a master of Buddha hall, Zheng also acted as a lecturer when he paid family visits to neophytes. Thus, after each course, he had to spend some time to prepare for the talks through reading more related materials. Obviously, such training helped Mr. Zheng grasp Yiguan Dao's doctrines as well as parts of Chinese traditional culture.

Another person who impressed me during the fieldwork is Mr. Jian. According to his description, he was a little intellectually disabled in his childhood. Not only did his peer group always make fun of him but also his family regarded him as a fool. After attending three years of elementary school, Jian gave up going to school. In 1971 when he was nineteen years old, his elder sister introduced him to the Dao. From then on, he became interested in courses held by the *Jichu* division of Yiguan Dao, although he could not understand the contents. Gradually, his wisdom grew and his family found that he was smarter. Now he is an excellent lecturer of the *Jichu* division, especially expert at *Dao-de Jing*. When describing his transformation, Mr. Jian especially stressed the function of research courses. He said:

> Yiguan Dao is without any constraints and very open. It is fit for every one to cultivate, no matter whether you are an intellectual or an idiot like me. You know, research courses held by the Dao play an important role. These courses are helpful to activate wisdom. They are divided into different levels and the attendees in a course are usually in the same level of understanding of the Dao teachings; through discussing with each other, they can enlighten each other and bring out inner wisdom. In addition, the attendees often develop a close relationship with each other after attending the courses.

These two cases can support the view that studying Chinese traditional culture not only attracts many working-class and uneducated people to enter Yiguan Dao but also changes their lives by introducing them to a traditional and spiritual world. But the functions of research courses are more than these; the activities also bring the individual into continual and intensive contact with other members and the group as a whole. These regularized group contacts, according to Kanter, are helpful to serve a communion function which can bring out higher commitment, "because they bring together the entire collectivity and reinforce its existence and meeting, regardless of the purpose of the gathering" (1972: 99). Frequent attendance at research courses make sectarians more involved in the group and gives them a stronger sense of belonging and 'we-feeling.' In short, by conducting research courses to promote Yiguan Dao's ideology, Yiguan Dao has generated a successful and lucrative recruitment and education vehicle.

Dharma Assemblies of Yiguan Dao

As mentioned above, the research course usually last a long time and the attendees must be present regularly. Some sectarians, however, are quite busy and cannot take part in such courses. For these people, 'dharma assemblies' are good choices. Dharma assemblies are irregularly conducted in a big temple where a large space is available; and the activities usually last one to three days. Thus, those who do not have time to attend the research courses can spend a weekend taking part in the dharma assemblies held by Yiguan Dao.

The dharma assemblies of Yiguan Dao can trace their origin to 'stove meetings' (*Lu-hui*) which were held in the 1930s.[8] According to Lu (1998: 137–52), stove meeting was very strict. The spirit mediums, who were regarded as the spokesmen of Buddhas and gods, acted as the trainers. They usually utilized dilemmas to test the trainees. For example, they asked the trainees to drink alcohol. If the trainees obeyed, they would violate the sect's regulation which requires the sectarian not to drink; but if the trainees refused to drink, they would be regarded as disrespecting gods. In any case, the trainees would be beaten! Through stove meetings, a lot of pious missionaries were trained, and this partly accounted for the sect's success in the 1940s in mainland China.

---

[8] In China, the stove is a utensil used by alchemists to make pills of immortality. The sect names its training course as 'stove meeting,' perhaps, to show the training is very strict and that the trainees will be powerful if they pass the training course.

Today, most of dharma assemblies of Yiguan Dao have given up using spirit mediums.[9] But some dharma assemblies are still very strict; 'the training course for young cadres' (*qingnian ganbu xunlian-ban*) is a typical one. The following analyses are based on the data on the training course conducted by the *Jichu Zhongshu* division.

According to the informants' descriptions, they did not know the detailed contents of the training course before attending it. After reaching the remote temple where the course was held, they found that the trainers became very strict, although they were very kind previously. The main trainer, who was called an 'administrant' (*Zhi-xing guan*), would ask people to obey him unconditionally. The trainees could not speak, laugh, or even wash hands without his permission. One part of training was to learn some details of Yiguan Dao rituals, such as how to place the shoes, how to wash and place fruits offered to gods, and such. Though the trainees could conduct rituals properly, the 'administrant' would find some minor mistakes, scold the trainees, and ask them to repeat the same action until it was perfectly conducted. Usually, the trainees would spend half an hour to learn how to place shoes.

Another important part of such a training course is to simulate the situations which one may encounter when doing missionary work. I was told that:

> The trainer would ask you to do some ridiculous things. For example, he asked me to find ten ants, five male and five female. How could I do that? It is impossible. The trainer just created difficulties for us purposely. He also asked us to put dust on our faces. I would not do such things usually. But at that time, I had to do it. The trainer was very strict and seemed terrible. I was scared of him. Many trainees cried so did I. We wanted to, but dared not, leave the temple because the temple was so remote. These things were without any significance to me at that time, but now I know that it is to remove our self-centered orientation and educate us to be humble when doing missionary work.
>
> In addition, the trainers would ask you to buy an egg, with a dirty face and bizarre dress. It is really a test. Many people would look at you strangely, and no one would sell an egg to you because eggs were sold in terms of kilograms. This suggests that, if you do missionary work overseas, maybe the foreigners will regard you as a weird person.

---

[9] The *Fayi Chong-de* division is an exception and still keeps the practice of spirit writing.

> So, you should learn to deal with such awkwardness. I think that the training course strengthened my character. In addition, I made many good friends.

The training is related to the idea of testing, which is emphasized by the sect. According to Yiguan Dao, in the process of 'cultivating the Dao' (*Xiu-dao*), one must experience tests: no tests, no improvement. Yiguan Dao identifies several kinds of tests, such as the inner test (*nei-kao*, afflictions such as illness, pain, fire, flood, and robbery), the outer test (*Wai-kao*, ridicule from relatives, friends, and neighbors, and oppression and violence from government officials), the test of anger (*qi-kao*), the unusual test (qi-*kao*), the test of success (*shun-kao*), the test of adversity (*ni-kao*), the test of confusion (*Dian-dao kao*), and the test of Dao (*Dao-kao*). In training courses, the trainers simulate these tests and then make use of them to train the sectarians.

According to Kanter, those nineteenth-century communes exacting sacrifices survived longer because sacrifice is functional for their maintenance. "Once members have agreed to make the 'sacrifice'," Kanter argues, "their motivation to remain participants increases." The tests emphasized by Yiguan Dao can serve a 'sacrifice' function. For example, the training courses ask attendees to give up self-esteem and bear the simulated abuses and tribulations. Since these sacrifices can increase "their motivation to remain participants" and "keep commitment strong", it does not surprise us that so many attendees become the core members of Yiguan Dao (Kanter 1972: 78).

The Mechanism of Vows

In addition to the research courses and dharma assemblies, there is another dynamic mechanism tightly integrated with these educational activities: to make vows (*Xu yuan*) and fulfill vows (*Huan yuan*). As the basic behavior forms of adherents of Chinese popular religion, *Xu yuan* and *Huan yuan* play important roles in Chinese religious life. C. K. Yang (1991: 87) writes:

> *Xu yuan* was the making of a wish before the god with the vow that, if the wish should come true, one would come again to worship and offer sacrifice. *Huan yuan* was worship and sacrifice to the god as an expression of gratitude after the wish had come true, whether it was recovery from sickness, the bringing of prosperity, or the begetting of a male heir. One might thank the god for the fulfillment of a wish during the past year, and then make a new wish for the coming year.

Yiguan Dao borrows the practice of making vows and fulfilling vows from popular religion. When discussing why vows should be made, the sectarians explain that:

> As we strengthen the faith in ourselves and in Dao, we should all make a lifelong plan for ourselves, which is our holy mission in this world. And what can we do to accomplish this mission? As the saying goes, 'Without making vows, one sails without guide.' So only when one makes the great vows can he or she get more driving force from the bottom of the heart (*English Reference Manual for Tao Propagation*: 76).

The ritual of making vows is usually held when a research course or a dharma assembly is over. A big bundle of incense is burned in the ritual; the attendees will receive a form which lists the vows which include 'removing bad habits and refining bad temper' (*gai-piqi qu-maobing*), 'prioritizing holy affairs over worldly matter' (*Zhong-sheng qingfan*), 'contributing material wealth and spreading Dao' (*cai-fa shuang-shi*), 'leading people to receive the Dao' (*duren qiudao*), 'becoming a vegetarian' (*qing-kou ru-su*), 'establishing a Buddha hall' (*she-li fo-tang*) and 'doing missionary work overseas' (*haiwai kaihuang*); the attendees are required to choose a vow to fulfill and sign the form; then the form recording the vow will be burned (Yang 1997). In the following, I will selectively analyze the significance and practice of these vows.

Removing Bad Habits and Refining Bad Temper

It is a basic requirement for the sectarians to 'remove bad habits and refine bad temper.' This vow involves abstinence from bad habits, such as smoking, drinking, eating areca nuts, and speaking dirty words; it also asks them to correct a sign of bad temper such as impatience and pride. These moral requirements are quite in accordance with Chinese traditional values, but Yiguan Dao reinterprets these issues from the perspective of Mother Theology. This theology holds that the primordial spirits sent by the Mother were pure; but they gradually lost their true nature and became ruthless and crafty, full of bad habits and tempers; so, in order to return to the true nature, the sectarians must get rid of such bad things. Through the reinterpretation, 'removing bad habits and refining bad temper' is more than a moral requirement people are familiar with; it becomes salvation-oriented.

How do the sectarians remove bad habits and tempers? From the sect's perspective, one cannot expect to remove bad habits in the short term. It is a long process to get rid of bad habits which are formed over a long time (Guo 1996). The sectarians should learn to reflect on their inner world according to Yiguan Dao's doctrines and engage in constant self-criticism; then they should try to alter the bad habits with the help of the sect's rituals, especially the ritual of kowtow. In his excellent thesis, Yang (1997: 98) tells us a story about this issue. Yang's father was formerly a very bad-tempered person, but he changed a lot after joining Yiguan Dao. Influenced by his father's transformation, Yang became an Yiguan Dao sectarian and attended the courses by the sect. He continues:

> At that time, I could not fully remove my bad habits and temper according to the doctrines I learned in the research courses. One day, after completely reading *The Platform Sutra of the Sixth Patriarch*, I proudly made use of the 'superior' theories of this book to test my father and other Dao relatives to show off. Then I disputed with my father on some issues and my father left angrily. After a while, I realized how ridiculous it was for me to cite *The Platform Sutra* to argue with others who have better religious practices than me. After criticizing myself, I decided to make an apology to my father. However, when I caught my father, he apologized to me before I opened my mouth, telling me that he was very angry after the disputation and so he went to the Buddha hall, knelt before the Mother, told her about his complaints, and kowtowed. During the process of kowtow, he gradually realized that he also should be responsible for the disputation since he was impatient and bad-tempered. Thus, complaints became self-confession. After hundreds of kowtow, he was not angry any longer.

Kowtow is the core practice of ancestor worship in China. But with the trend of democracy, kowtow is associated with authoritarianism by young people in current Taiwan who would reluctantly perform such a ritual (Yang 1997). Facing this situation, the sect reinterprets the significance of kowtow, arguing that kowtow is not to worship authority but to show respect to saints and gods who are examples. These saints and gods also encountered many difficulties; but they conquered these difficulties and finally achieved a high moral and spiritual status. So they are worthy of respect. In addition, kowtow is a best way to conquer pride (Guo 1997). Due to these reinterpretations, those who are formerly reluctant to kowtow accept the ritual (Yang 1997). As we have seen in the above story, kowtowing and confessing to the Venerable Mother actually become powerful tools for the sectarians to criticize and improve themselves spiritually.

In addition to redefining the meaning of the kowtow, Yiguan Dao ritualizes the practice. Though kowtow is widely practiced by adherents of popular religion, it is unsystematic and seems chaotic, without any guidance. Yiguan Dao also ritualizes the practice of 'burning incenses.' Most people unconcernedly burn incense and then throw the incense into the stove. The ritual of burning incense is quite different from the way it is performed by adherents of popular religion. First, the ritual is performed communally rather than individually; and the number of incense for each deity is strictly defined. Second, the ritual of offering incense is presided over by two senior persons; if one says "offering three bundles of incense," the other people would follow: "first offering," "second offering," "third offering." Finally, when the sectarians offer incense, they raise up the incense to the level of their eyebrows to show their respect and piety; they use the left hand which represents 'goodness' to put the incense into the stove orderly and vertically; and the location of each incense has its special meaning (Yang 1997).

Worshiping gods, kowtowing, and burning incense are main practices of popular religion. Unlike Christianity, Yiguan Dao welcomes these traditional symbols and practices with which Chinese people are familiar. At the same time, the sect redefines and rearranges these old elements in a new ritual system in which new religious meanings are added. Through the creative transformation, the ritualized old practices not only are helpful to keep the sectarians' religious capital, but also become a useful tool for the sectarians to remove their bad habits and temper.[10] Every time the sectarians meet problems in life, they kowtow, burn incense, and confess to the Mother, as Yang describes. Through such practices, the sectarians gradually learn to deal with problems through self-reflection and self-criticism, rather than by expecting the gods to give immediate resolutions. By exerting influence on people's thoughts, feelings, and the way of viewing the world, the practice of 'removing bad habits and refining bad temper' conforms the sectarian's inner feelings and evaluations to the group's norms and beliefs.

---

[10] Such traditional practices as burning incense exert great influences to Chinese people although these practices seem to be unsystematic and chaotic. For example, the adherents of popular religion on Taiwan always use the term of "those who do not take incense" to refer to Christians (Yang 1997). Taking incense or not becomes a criterion distinguishing 'us' from 'the other.' This shows traditional religious practices are still influential.

Aside from the self-criticism emphasized by the practice of 'removing bad habits and refining bad temper,' there are confession courses conducted by the sect. In such courses, the attendees are required to admit their shortcoming, failings, faults, and imperfections. "Religious groups often attempt to erase the 'sin of pride,' the fault of being too independent or self-sufficient, substituting instead a self that identifies with the influence of the collectivity." So does Yiguan Dao. Both the confession courses and self-criticism emphasized by the vow of 'removing bad habits' contribute to mortification which "facilitates a moral commitment on the part of the person to accept the control of the group" (Kanter 1972: 103, 105).

Prioritizing Holy Affairs over the Worldly

Yiguan Dao makes a distinction between the sacred and the secular. But Yiguan Dao does not implement the mechanism of renunciation. Renunciation, according to Kanter, requires people to abandon relationships that are potentially disruptive to group cohesion. Successful nineteenth-century communes placed clear-cut barriers and boundaries between the member and the outside; they also tried to weaken exclusive relations among members. Yiguan Dao, however, attaches much importance to family and secular life by emphasizing 'the simultaneous cultivation of the sacred and the secular' (*Shengfan Jianxiu*). Yiguan Dao rarely uses professional clergy; both ordinary members and leaders are lay; thus they must work in secular businesses.[11] At the same time, all Yiguan Dao sectarians should work as missionaries; the priesthood returns to the people. So how to balance the sacred and the secular in practice is difficult. We can get a sense of this from the following words.

> The cultivation of Dao is after all half-sacred and half-secular (*Bansheng Ban-fan*). Every sectarian has to deal with secular affairs, so the cultivation cannot be too rigid. Cultivating Dao should not become a burden. We should know how many times each sectarian attends Dao activities every week. If a person just stays home and watches TV rather than attending Dao activities, it is not good, and we should have a family visit [to encourage people to attend the activities]. But

---

[11] In Yiguan Dao, there are a small number of professional celibate clergy who do not have secular work and devote themselves to the missionary work. They are usually supported by the sect, living and eating in Yiguan Dao temples, but they do not get a salary from their religious services.

if a member's economic situation is not good, then we should let the person earn money. The stomach is of primary importance, the Buddha is second. If we urge him to spend too much time attending activities of Yiguan Dao, it might influence his life and later his children might not cultivate Dao. In short, if you cannot support yourself and your family, people will laugh at you and distrust you when you say the cultivation of Dao is good (Yang 1997: 80).

These words show that the sect is very considerate and flexible in dealing with the relationship between the secular and the sacred. One principle that is always emphasized by the sect is that in different life stages, people should put different ratios of energy to sacred affairs and secular maters; the sectarians should gradually shift their life focus from the secular to the sacred as they grow older. When their children are young, parents should put more emphasis on secular life; when the children grow up and can support themselves, people should devote themselves to the religious life. In any case, the sect does not ask followers to give up secular life exclusively, although it encourages people to attend sect activities as much as possible. Thus Yiguan Dao does not implement the mechanism of renunciation.

Leading People to Receive the Dao

The idea of merit is popular in Chinese society due to the influence of Buddhism. Many Chinese people in Taiwan believe that karma results in illness and suffering, and merit is useful to reduce karma, hence to cure illness. Yiguan Dao accepts these ideas and further argues that, with enough merit, one not only can be free of the circle of birth and rebirth, but also can gain a high status in Heaven. In addition, merits can also be transferred to others such as the sectarians' ancestors. So, people can save their ancestors' spirits through accumulating merits. This interpretation is in accordance with Chinese people's ancestor worship and can be easily accepted by them.

Yiguan Dao utilizes the idea of merit to encourage people to do missionary work, arguing that the more members one recruits, the more merit one accumulates. Encouraged by this argument, the sectarians of Yiguan Dao are very active in 'recruiting neophytes' (*duren*, literally, 'saving people'). Especially when one's relatives are suffering illness, they would try their best to persuade people to receive Dao. A young female sectarian leader told me that sometimes they knocked at the door one-by-one to propagate Dao, just

like Mormons, and then they transferred the merits they gained from
the missionary work to the sectarians who were ill.[12] Encouraged by
the idea that doing missionary work can accumulate merit, new sectarians devote themselves to doing missionary work immediately. This
enables the sect constantly to recruit neophytes in a large scale.

In addition to encouraging people to spend time in recruiting neophytes, the sect also encourages its believers to make financial contributions to the group or work as volunteers. This is what 'contributing
material wealth and spreading Dao' means. As a rule, one must sub-
mit an amount of money, usually 100 NT$ (about 3 US$), to the
sect as the 'merit fee' (*Gongde fei*) when he becomes an Yiguan Dao
sectarian. The process of becoming core members includes more
investments in the sect, requiring the sectarians to perform such activities as publishing morality books, building temples, and even making business investments. When I did my field work in a temple
building in Gaoxiong, I found that dozens of volunteer workers
worked there every day and hundreds of volunteers on the weekend. The land is provided by a sectarian for free, and most of the
building materials are donated by the sectarians. Donation is regular and popular among the Yiguan Dao sectarians. Commitment is
further promoted by the mechanism of investment because it makes
individuals integrated into the group, and because it ensures that the
sectarians' time and resources have become part of the sect's economy, as Kanter has pointed out.

Becoming a Vegetarian

Abstinence from meat is highly stressed and justified by Yiguan Dao's
theology. From the point of view of Yiguan Dao, a genuine sectarian becomes a vegetarian (Guo 1996). Influenced by Buddhism, the
sect believes that killing and eating animals is immoral and harmful because it not only builds a bad relationship with all beings (*yu
zhongsheng jie e-yuan*) but also accumulates karma. To get salvation,
according to the sect, one should not eat meat. In practice, Yiguan
Dao follows a flexible way in trying to persuade people to become

---

[12] Here, the informant uses the term 'they' to refer to the sectarians in *Tianhui*
unit of the *Jichu* division. I do not know whether the same situation occurs in other
divisions or not. But 'transferring merits to others' (*Gong-de Hui-xiang*) is widely
accepted by various Yiguan Dao divisions.

vegetarian. For example, if a student sectarian wants to get a good mark in exams, he is encouraged to make a vow to the Mother, promising to eat no meat for certain period, or to be a vegetarian forever when having breakfast.

Becoming a vegetarian is helpful to promote commitment in two ways. On the one hand, it can function as a sacrifice mechanism which can generate commitment, as Kanter argues. On the other hand, abstinence from meat is helpful to weaken extra-cult affective bonds, because it is quite inconvenient for vegetarians to interact intensively with non-vegetarians (Song 2002). Sectarians usually develop a new life style and new social networks as well. After they become vegetarians, most of their close friends are Yiguan Dao vegetarians too. Thus, becoming a vegetarian is helpful to weaken extra-cult affective bonds and facilitate interaction among members. Since individuals with weak extra-group affective bonds could more easily engage in activities with the ideological organization (Lofland and Stark 1965), abstinence from meat is useful to promote commitment to Yiguan Dao.

Discussion and Conclusion

Yiguan Dao has developed specific ways to implement some of the commitment mechanisms pointed out by Kanter. Abstinence from cigarettes, alcohol, and meat contributes to sacrifice. Yiguan Dao also employs a new way to implement the mechanism of sacrifice: That is the tests introduced by the training course. These tribulations are temporary and simulated but make membership become more valuable and meaningful. Making material contribution and spending time in recruiting neophytes also contribute to investment. The regularized and intensive contacts strengthened by the research courses and dharma assemblies serve a communion function. The practices of self-criticism and confession support mortification. The sect's theology, which serves to legitimate the individual's surrender to the group by providing a set of explanations and a sense of meaning, has a transcendence function. All of these practices generate and promote commitment.

But Yiguan Dao does not emphasize renunciation. Kanter finds that successful nineteenth-century communes placed clear-cut boundaries between the member and the outside. "One is either 'in' or 'out'," Kanter (1972: 80) says. Following Kanter's idea, Iannaccone (1988: 257) argues "[t]he sect naturally creates two classes: the members (or 'true believers'), who fully embrace the sect norms while rejecting the society's, and the nonmembers (both 'heathen' and 'heretics'), who reject the sect and are in turn rejected by it." These observations may be historically true, but they are not applicable here. Miller (1997: 36) also finds that some 'new paradigm' churches, such as the Calvary Movement, do not draw "a hard line on who is 'in' and who is 'out'." Membership in these movements is instead a matter of whether or not one is in regular communication with the movement.

Yiguan Dao resembles those 'new paradigm' churches studied by Miller. Membership in Yiguan Dao is a continuum, falling outside the 'in-or-out' model. According to the data offered by the *Tianhe* unit of *Baoguang Jiande*, from 1953 to 1999, 146,411 people had been recruited by the unit, and 3,367 people became vegetarian.[13] This means that about one out of forty-four new recruits became a vegetarian believer. Table 3 shows that there are 3000 *Fayi Lingyin* attendees in the *Mingde* course while the number of the *Jingdian* course attendees is 800. Since graduates of the *Jiangdian* course will normally be invited to become vegetarian members, we can estimate that among those involved in the primary Yiguan Dao workshop, 29% of attendees will survive the workshop system and finally become vegetarians. Considering *Tianhe*'s data and *Fayi Lingyin*'s data simultaneously, we can guess that about 8.6% of Yiguan Dao neophytes would get involved in Yiguan Dao's workshop system, by attending the *Mingde* course; 5.7% would remain in the *Xinmin* course, following the vow of 'removing bad habits and bad temper;' and less than 2.3% of recruits would like to become vegetarian. Although these estimations are imprecise, they indicate that the commitment in Yiguan Dao is a spectrum ranging from doubtfulness to devoutness, rather than a dichotomy of members and nonmembers.

The sect also develops a new mechanism which goes beyond Kanter's discussion: progressive strictness. Iannaccone (1994) makes a distinction between strict churches and liberal churches, arguing that strictness increases commitment through reducing free-rider problems.

---

[13] From http://www.yitkuant.com.tw/chinese/default.htm

But Yiguan Dao is both liberal and strict, permitting a range of commitment. New recruits are rarely restricted, while the veteran sectarians are expected to conform completely to established rules, such as abstinence from cigarettes, alcohol, meat, and even sex. Both liberality and strictness exist in Yiguan Dao simultaneously. But Yiguan Dao is not unique in this respect. Barker (1984) reveals that there is a type of stratification system in the Unification Church and that potential recruits must pass several 'hurdles' before becoming full-time Moonies. 'New paradigm' churches adopt flexible ways to approach potential converts, allowing them to participate in many activities but restricting membership to those who pass various tests. These churches cannot be easily classified into 'traditional categories,' such as 'liberal church' or 'strict church,' they are both (Miller 1997).

In the design of its activities, Yiguan Dao pays close attention to Chinese traditional culture. Unlike Christianity which stresses monotheism and asks its followers to give up previous beliefs immediately, Yiguan Dao has a very open attitude when it recruits neophytes. Since its potential recruits are adherents of Chinese popular religion, the sect keeps, ritualizes, and utilizes many elements of popular religion, such as burning incense, kowtowing, and making and fulfilling vows. These efforts are helpful to keep the believers' religious capital. After recruiting new members, the sect devotes itself to generating and sustaining the commitment of sectarians through conducting research courses and dharma assemblies. These practices, together with the mechanism of vows, guide the new recruits to becoming core members step by step. In this process, the sectarians fulfill more and more strict requirements, if they are willing to. The Buddhist saying that "first using desirable things to attract people and then bringing them into the wisdom of Buddha" (*xian yiyu gouqian, hou lingru fozhi*) is quite applicable to explaining the process of religious commitment in Yiguan Dao (Yang 1997).

REFERENCES

Barker, Eileen. 1984. *The Making of a Moonie*. Oxford: Basil Blackwell.
Deliusin, Lev. 1972. "The I-Kuan Tao Society." Pp. 225–33, in *Popular Movements and Secret Societies in China 1840–1950*, edited by Jean Chesneaux. Stanford, CA: Stanford University Press.
Guo, Mingyi. 1996. *Yiguan xiuchi [The Cultivation of Yiguan Dao]*. Taiwan: Ciding Press.
———. 1997. *Xiudao baiwen [One Hundred Questions about Yiguan Dao]*. Taiwan: Ciding Press.

Iannaccone, Laurence. R. 1988. "A Formal Model of Church and Sect." *American Journal of Sociology* 94: S241–68.
———. 1994. "Why Strict Churches Are Strong." *American Journal of Sociology* 99: 1180–1211.
Jordan, David K. 1972. *Gods, Ghosts, and Ancestors*. Berkeley: University of California Press.
———. 1982. "The Recent History of Celestial Way. A Chinese Pietistic Association." *Modern China* 8: 435–62.
Jordan, David K. and Daniel L. Overmyer. 1986. *The Flying Phoenix*. Princeton, NJ: Princeton University Press.
Kanter, Rosabeth Moss. 1972. *Commitment and Community*. Cambridge, MA: Harvard University Press.
Kelley, Dean. M. 1972. *Why Conservative Churches Are Growing*. New York: Harper & Row.
Lin, Benxuan. 1990. *Taiwan de zhengjiao chongtu* [*The State-Religion Conflict on Taiwan*]. Taipei: Daoxiang Press.
Lin, Rongze. 1992. *Taiwan minjia zongjiao zhi yanjiu: Yiguan Dao Fayi-lingyin de ge-anfenni*. [Popular Sects on Taiwan: A Case Study of Fayi Lingyin Division of Yinguan Dao] M. Phil. thesis. Taipei: Taiwan University.
Lofland, John, and Rodney Stark. 1965. "Becoming a World-Saver: A Theory of Conversion to a Deviant Perspective." *American Sociological Review* 30: 862–75.
Lu, Yunfeng. 2005. *Chinese Traditional Sects in Modern Society*. Ph D. dissertation. Hong Kong: City University of Hong Kong.
Lu, Zhongwei. 1998. *Yiguan Dao neimu* [*The Inner Story of Yiguan Dao*]. Nanjing: Renmin Press.
Miller, Donald. 1997. *Reinventing American Protestantism*. Berkeley: University of California Press.
Mu, Yu. 2002. *Yiguan Dao gaiyao* [*An Introduction to Yiguan Dao*]. Tainan: Qingju Press.
Naquin, Susan. 1976. *Millenarian Rebellion in China*. New Haven, CT: Yale University Press.
Overmyer, Daniel L. 1999. *Precious Volumes*. Cambridge, MA.: Harvard University Press.
Qu, Haiyuan. 1997. *Taiwan zongjiao bianqian de shehui zhengzhi fenxi* [*A Social-political Analysis of Religious Transformation in Taiwan*]. Taipei: Guiguan Press.
Rudy, David R. and Arthur L. Greil. 1987. "Taking the Pledge: The Commitment Process in Alcoholics Anonymous." *Sociological Focus* 20: 45–59.
Sangren, P. Steven. 1987. *History and Magical Power in a Chinese Community*. Stanford, CA: Stanford University Press.
Song, Guangyu. 1983. *Tiandao goucheng* [*An Investigation of the Celestial Way*]. Taipei: Yuanyou Press.
———. 1996. *Tiandao chuandeng* [*The Development of the Celestial Way*]. Taipei: Chengtong Press.
———. 2002. *Song Guangyu Zongjiao Wenhua Lunwenji* [*Ten Years Works on Chinese Religion and Culture*]. 2 vols. Yinan: Foguang University Press.
Stark, Rodney and Roger Finke. 2000. *Acts of Faith*. Berkeley: University of California Press.
———. 2004. *Xin yang de fa ze* [*Acts of Faith*], translated by Fenggang Yang. Beijing: Renmin University Press.
Tamney, Joseph B and Linda Hsueh-Ling Chiang. 2002. *Modernization, Globalization, and Confucianism in Chinese Societies*. Westport, CT.: Praeger.
Weller, Robert P. 1987. *Unities and Diversities in Chinese Religion*. London: Macmillan.
Wolf, Arthur P. 1974. "Gods, Ghosts, and Ancestors." Pp. 131–82, in *Religion and Ritual in Chinese Society*, edited by Arthur P. Wolf. Berkeley: University of California Press.
Yang, C.K. 1961. *Religion in Chinese Society*, Berkeley: University of California Press.

Yang, Hongren. 1997. *Linglei shehuiyundong: Yiguandao de shengfanjianxiu yu duren chengquan* [*An Alternative Social Movement: Cultivation and Missionary Work of Yiguan Dao*]. M.Phil. thesis. Taiwan: Qinghua University.

Zhang, Maogui and Lin Benxuan. 1992. "The Social Imaginations of Religion: A Problem for the Sociology of Knowledge." *Bulletin of the Institute of Ethnology Academia Sinica* 74: 95–123.

CHAPTER EIGHT

MORALITY BOOKS AND THE MORAL ORDER: A STUDY OF THE MORAL SUSTAINING FUNCTION OF MORALITY BOOKS IN TAIWAN

Chi-shiang Ling

'Morality book' translates the Chinese term *shanshu*, which literally means 'good book.' It is a generic term referring to texts that exhort people to do good deeds and abandon evil ways. However, morality books are not just compilations of moral examples or principles; these texts also employ religious terms to recommend ethical norms. Therefore, morality books not only prescribe the moral duties that people should do, but also provide a religious worldview, in which these moral duties acquire their religious meaning and justification, and are also associated with rewards and punishments. Since the thirteenth century, morality books have been an important medium to spread religious beliefs and ethical instructions to the masses in Chinese society.[1] People for various reasons voluntarily fund the printing, reprinting, and distribution of morality books, so that they can be free of charge and displayed in places where people have easy access: everyone can take them home to read.

Although morality books boast high visibility in popular culture and a long history of almost a millennium, only in the last several decades did they begin to receive attention from academia.[2] Recent studies have explored various aspects of morality books, such as the content

---

[1] The extant oldest morality book, the *Tract of the Most Exalted on Action and Response* (*Taishang ganying pian*), was first published in the twelfth century (c. 1164), though its composition might be even earlier. A century later, this book was endorsed by an emperor of the Southern Song dynasty, who printed thousands of copies and distributed them throughout his empire. From then on, this book has continued to enjoy great popularity, and numerous other morality books have also been composed and published.

[2] One reason for this lack of attention is that most morality books have traditionally been looked down upon by the educated elite in the Confucian or humanistic tradition, for they think morality books contain superstitions and diverge from autonomous ethics.

and composition of a single morality book (Song 1984; Zheng 1988a; Pas 1989), types of morality books in their social-historical contexts (Zheng 1988b; Brokaw 1991), the histories of the 'phoenix halls' that publish morality books (Wang 1995), the activities, texts, and historical backgrounds of spirit-writing cults in Taiwan (Jordan and Overmyer 1986), how morality books reflect their contemporary social conditions and problems, as well as social changes (Song 1993; Clart 2003), and the ritual context of morality books (Clart 1997). Moreover, morality books have also been used as a means to study other cultural features, such as the relationship between printing and religion in China (Bell 1992), the expressions of Taiwanese identity in popular religion (Katz 1999), and the concepts of ghosts and gods in Taiwanese popular religion (Wang 2003).

These studies have greatly advanced our understanding of the history, composition, religious ideas, and ethical views of morality books, as well as their interaction with their social milieux. Nevertheless, many questions about the actual influence of morality books on the masses remain unanswered. How large is the readership of morality books? How successful are morality books in instilling their beliefs and values in the reader? Are morality books really, as their authors and those who fund their printing believe, effective in sustaining the moral order? If yes, then what are the ideas in morality books that serve this function? Without a large-scale survey, what we can achieve is at best an educated guess at these questions.

Thanks to the data from the Taiwan Social Change Survey, some of these questions can be answered for the first time in the context of present-day Taiwan, where morality books continue to be popular and where they may still play an important role in the moral and religious lives of Taiwanese people.[3] In this chapter, I will first depict in broad strokes the ethical and religious views in the morality books currently circulated in Taiwan. This not only is meant to

---

[3] Today in Taiwan, one can find morality books in the corners of temples, clinics, hospitals, bus and train stations, vegetarian restaurants, and even some shops and telephone booths; these books are all free of charge. Many of them are printed on high quality paper, and some are also published in hardback. In recent years, morality books take not only the forms of books and booklets, but also the forms of audiotapes, CDs, and video CDs. Many popular morality books have also been put on the Internet. Every month there are new morality books being composed, printed, and distributed.

give an introduction of morality books to the reader unfamiliar with their contents, but also serves to identity the beliefs I find most representative of the morality-book literature, so that they can later be used to examine the effectiveness of morality books. Second, the data from the 1999 Taiwan Social Change Survey will be used to show the readership of morality books. Third, by analyzing the survey data, I will examine whether there is any positive relationship between reading morality books and holding specific beliefs presented in them. Finally, I will investigate whether holding these beliefs has any impact on people's moral thinking.

The Moral-religious Vision in Present-day Taiwanese Morality Books

In order to assess the impact of morality books on people's moral consciousness, I will treat the present-day Taiwanese morality books as a whole, rather than explore just one or a few particular texts. The attempt to present a common thinking that may epitomize thousands of morality books currently circulating in Taiwan not only takes a high degree of generalization, but is also unavoidably subject to personal bias. Here I would like to reveal my criteria for selecting morality books and the reasons for giving some of them special emphases.

A variety of publications fall under the definition of morality books given in the beginning paragraph. For example, the scriptures of major religious traditions could also be regarded as morality books, for these scriptures all contain moral teachings embedded in religious worldviews. Indeed, today in Taiwan, many Buddhist sutras and tracts are distributed along with morality books, and in some temples, even the New Testament and Christian evangelical booklets are put side-by-side with morality books of other religious traditions. Nevertheless, the writings of institutional religions will not be counted as morality books in my discussion, since traditionally—and even nowadays—these writings are considered more often as pertaining to other categories of literature than to morality books.[4] However, this does not mean that the beliefs contained in these religious texts

---

[4] An exception will be made for the *Tract of the Most Exalted on Action and Response*, for while this book is included in the Daoist canon, *Daozang*, it is better known as the oldest and most famous morality book.

are also to be excluded from this study, for some of these beliefs (such as the Buddhist idea of karma) have found their way into morality books and have gained a strong foothold in them. Based on this criterion, the morality books in this study are primarily coming from the 'popular religious tradition' in Chinese culture, by which I mean a religious tradition that inherited ancient Chinese religious beliefs and practices, and has been in constant exchange with Confucianism, Buddhism, and Daoism. This tradition is shared by people across denominational and social boundaries, and also unceasingly shaped and reshaped by them.

The morality books currently circulating in Taiwan include not only newly composed texts, but also those written centuries ago, such as the *Tract of the Most Exalted on Action and Response* (*Taishang ganying pian*),[5] the *Precious Records Copied from the Jade Emperor's Calendar* (*Yuli baochao* [n.d.]), and the *Four Admonitions Given by Liaofan* (*Liaofan sixun* [2004]).[6] They are often reprinted with vernacular translations, prefaces, commentaries, and allegedly real stories that serve to illustrate or testify to the ideas presented in them.[7] Since these texts have passed the test of time and become the prototypes of many later morality books, and moreover, since there have been continuous efforts to make them accessible to the modern reader, they will be considered as typical morality books and hence weigh more heavily than others.

Among the morality books composed in recent decades, *Records of a Journey to Hell* (*Diyu youji* [2000]) will receive special attention, for it is the most popular and renowned morality book in Taiwan.[8] After its publication, many morality books with similar motifs have been produced. Therefore, although in these years the popularity of this book has decreased in Taiwan, its influence can still be seen through the morality books that follow it as an example.

---

[5] For English translations of this book, see Suzuki and Carus (1906), Legge (1980), Coyle (1981).

[6] For an English translation of this book, see Lai (1997). Brokaw (1996) translated the first chapter of this book, titled "Determining Your Own Fate."

[7] Suzuki and Carus's translation of the *Tract of the Most Exalted on Action and Response* (1906) also includes stories that exemplify the principles taught in it. For more such stories, see Bell (1996).

[8] This book was composed from 1976 to 1978 by means of spirit-writing, and was first published as a booklet in 1978; see Pas (1989). Within five years of its first publication, three million copies were printed (Song 1995: 7–8). In recent years, this book even has a comic version for children.

Wang (1995: 10–11) points out that morality books, especially those produced in Taiwan over the past decades, are characterized by constantly reiterating traditional moral values and extensively imitating and plagiarizing from one another. This characteristic makes the generalization of the ethical and religious views found in a few typical morality texts much less dangerous and more reliable. Nevertheless, the moral views and religious beliefs presented in the following discussion should not be regarded as essential features shared by all morality books but rather as attributes that define the family resemblance for this kind of literature. In other words, not every morality book propagates all these views; nevertheless, by holding various combinations of these views, morality books resemble one another and are seen as belonging to the same category.

Confucian Ethics

As many authors have pointed out, the moral norms and standards in morality books are predominantly derived from Confucian ethics, which are concerned with building a harmonious society in which each person can develop oneself and become a fully human being. Therefore, family, the basic unit of Chinese society, holds a very important place in Confucian ethics, because it is in a family that one is nurtured and first experiences social relationships. A person should obey and honor parents and take care of them when they are old, respect elder brothers and sisters and care for younger ones, treat one's spouse with love and respect, and take responsibility for raising and educating one's children. Moreover, one ought to extend the virtues cultivated in the family to other social relations. A person should be loyal to country, show respect to elders, teachers, employers, etc., treat others with sincerity, honesty, and fairness, and help those who are in need. These moral norms are advocated in morality books, with some focusing on external behaviors and some also emphasizing inner attitudes. By the same token, morality books also condemn any conduct that would prevent one from fulfilling one's humanity or undermine social relations, such as being unfilial, licentiousness, infidelity, gambling, ingratitude, trickery, and unkindness.

While the Confucian virtues upheld in morality books are millennia old, present-day Taiwanese morality books also demonstrate notable efforts to redefine these virtues in ways that take modern social conditions into consideration. By comparing two morality texts written in 1921 and 1989 respectively, Clart (2003) gives an excellent example of how the husband-wife relationship and the expression of female virtue have been reinterpreted to adapt to new social reality. Indeed, this trend to reformulate traditional values can also be found in the treatment of the parent-child relationship in modern morality-book literature.[9]

Similarly, the authors of present-day morality books also notice that in modern Taiwanese society, the opposites of traditional virtues take new forms as well. Some of the manifestations of these vices become much more harmful than before, and thus should be clearly pointed out and vehemently condemned. According to the Taiwanese scholar Song Guangyu (1993), the most frequently mentioned social problems in recent morality books are injustice of the wealthy, fraud and perfidy, corruption, and such sexual immoralities as pornography, adultery, rape, and prostitution.

Although the moral code prescribed in morality books is of Confucian origin, it nonetheless has long been incorporated into Daoism and Chinese Buddhism and embodies the fundamentals of Chinese ethics widely accepted by both Confucians and non-Confucians. It is the popularized form of Chinese ethics furnished with religious beliefs that is advocated in morality books.

Love and Compassion for Living Beings

Confucian ethics characterize ideal human relationships in society. Nevertheless, they offer people little guidance on how they should treat nonhuman beings, especially animals. In morality books, this is complemented by the Buddhist virtue of compassion toward sentient beings, as well as the Daoist attitude of tender care for nature and all living things. Buddhism sees that humans are trapped in a world of suffering due to their ignorance of the fact that they are not self-contained entities separate from other beings. This ignorance leads to and is strengthened by one's mistreatment or cruelty to animals, which will produce bad karma and make the individual more

---

[9] For example, in the 1981 morality book *Records of a Journey to Heaven* (*Tiantang youji* [2002]), chapter 10, parents are instructed to rear children in a loving and self-involving way without expecting any material gain. When parents give unselfish love to children, children will naturally show filial piety in return. Construed in this way, filial piety is part of an ideal parent-child relationship that is characterized by mutuality, rather than just a unilateral demand on children.

bound to suffering. According to Daoism, humans should follow the Dao, which creates and nurtures everything without trying to dominate or exploit anything. Therefore, protecting animals and preserving the natural environment is essential to one's moral and spiritual cultivation. While Buddhist compassion and Daoist love for nature are based on different worldviews, in practice there is a great affinity between them. As a result, most morality books denounce unnecessary killing of animals as a vice and recommend being compassionate toward all creatures.[10]

Moral Retribution

The morality presented in morality books appeals to the reader not only through examples and expositions, but also to a large extent through the idea of moral retribution, that is, the belief that the virtuous will be rewarded, and the wicked will be punished. This belief is shared by many religions; indeed, it is arguably inherent in the deep structure of religion's moral reasoning (Green 1988). Nevertheless, the ways moral retribution is brought about differ among religions. In monotheistic faiths, it is actualized by the supreme God, since God is conceived to be omniscient, omnipotent, and morally concerned. In Chinese popular religion, however, the idea of a supreme God in the monotheistic sense does not exist. So how is moral retribution brought about? In morality books, there are basically two strands of thinking: divine retribution and karmic retribution.

Divine retribution. Passed down from China's antiquity and shared by both Daoist and popular religious traditions is a belief that there exists a divine bureaucracy consisting of many gods and spirits presided over by a highest God. They perform various duties and functions, and some of them are designated to scrutinize human thoughts and deeds. These deities are ubiquitous and always observant; no single act can escape their eyes. An old Chinese saying goes: "Gods and spirits are three feet above your head [and watching what you do]." They take notes of humans' merits and faults and make periodical

---

[10] In the oldest morality book, the *Tract of the Most Exalted on Action and Response*, there are already injunctions against injuring insects, animals, and trees. A recently composed and widely circulated morality book that is primarily dedicated to this theme is *Suffering and Wretchedness of Sentient Beings (Shengling de beiqi* [1998]). During his stay in Taiwan from 1994 to 1995, Pas (1996: 147) also observed that a lot of morality books discourage hurting and killing animals.

reports to Heaven or the gods who are in charge of reward and punishment. These divine beings will then execute moral retribution according to the reports they get. The rewards include health, longevity, and prosperity, and the punishments include illness, short life, and misfortune.[11]

Karmic retribution. The doctrine of karma becomes part of a popular Chinese belief system through Buddhism. This doctrine asserts that every action will produce a reaction, and every event in the world is in a complex web of cause and effect. Any act of mind, speech, or body will inevitably bring an effect consonant with the act to its doer. The Buddhist karma doctrine also involves the belief of reincarnation, which holds that the karmically-bound ego will experience successive rounds of death and rebirth. Therefore, if the karmic effect does not happen in this life, then it will happen in the lives to come. Besides, one's karma also determines the form of one's next existence— one may be reborn in the human realm, in the animal realm, in the divine realm as a god, or in the hell realm suffering enormous torments, and so on. The operation of the karmic law is natural, automatic, without having to involve spirits or gods in the retributive process.

In both theories, there is a concept of sin as violation of the moral code or the moral law. However, in divine retribution, the punishment executed by the divine beings does not necessarily formally correspond to the sin with which it is associated, while in karmic retribution, the punishment is inherently connected with the sin and an automatic consequence of it. Moreover, in divine retribution, the idea of reincarnation is not involved, and reward and punishment are meted out mainly in this lifetime. Today in Taiwan, most morality books incorporate these two seemingly different theories and make them work together seamlessly. Therefore, for example, the punishment of an evil person is understood as being brought by gods as well as by the karma the individual produces. But how do gods and the karmic force actually collaborate? Generally speaking, first the nature and the amount of punishment and reward one deserves are determined

---

[11] The *Tract of the Most Exalted on Action and Response* presents a theory of divine retribution not influenced by the doctrine of karma. According to this book, there are gods in heaven and on earth overseeing people's misdeeds. One's lifespan will be reduced by hundred-day units or twelve-year units according to the gravity of his transgressions. As his lifespan diminishes, poverty, illness, calamity, misery, and such will also come to him. If one does good deeds, then he will be protected by Heaven, have good fortune and success, and even become an immortal.

by the karmic law, which is universally binding and unbreakable. Consequently, the law followed by gods to distribute reward and punishment is regarded as identical to the karmic law. Second, the idea of reincarnation is affirmed, so moral retribution does not need to happen in this lifetime or in the human realm. When punishment and reward take place in other worlds (such as hell or heaven), gods and spirits are almost always on the scene, acting as judges of conduct or executors of retribution in accordance with the impersonal karmic law. When punishment and reward take place in this world, whether in one's current life or future lives, seldom are gods and spirits explicitly mentioned, unless the emphasis is on the miracles performed by a particular god; it seems as if the karmic law simply works itself out. Nevertheless, it might be assumed that gods and spirits are still watching and keeping records of what one does, and assisting in administering the karmic law.[12]

According to the Buddhist doctrine of karma, the recipient of moral retribution is the agent of the action, either in his present incarnation or in his future incarnations. Nevertheless, in morality books, the recipient needs not to be the agent. It can be his family or descendents. A virtuous person's family and descendents will be blessed, and a wicked person's will be cursed. In other words, moral retribution operates also on a family basis.[13] To be sure, this belief must be understood within the context that in many premodern cultures (such as the ancient Hebrew culture), solidarity among family members and the bond between ancestors and descendents are much stronger than conceived in the modern West. Knowing that one's

---

[12] I interviewed by phone the personnel and chairs of several institutions that publish morality books, and most of the interviewees agreed that divine retribution and karmic retribution are two sides of the same coin: retribution is brought about by karma as well as executed by gods. A few of the interviewees told me that in this world, gods and spirits can reveal to humans how they acquired bad karma in their previous lives and how they could make amends for it in this life, and in the underworld gods and spirits can make known the faults of sinners and the punishments they deserve, but gods and spirits do not punish people; people are punished by their own karma.

[13] This thinking comes from an ancient Chinese belief and is recorded in the *Book of Changes*: "The family that accumulates good will have abundant fortune; the family that accumulates evil will have abundant misfortune." This saying is quoted in many morality books, some of which also contain stories illustrating this principle. Without directly quoting it, the *Tract of the Most Exalted on Action and Response* teaches that if a person dies with unexpiated sin, the misfortune he deserves will be transferred to his descendents.

deeds have impact on one's family and descendents may provide additional incentives to do good and avoid evil.

In morality books, the idea of moral retribution is closely associated with the belief that one's fate is not totally predetermined, but can be changed by one's deeds.[14] If one has done evil things in the past but wants to reduce punishment or even improve life, one should repent, change the evil ways, and start to do good deeds. By accumulating merit, a person may have a better fortune in this life or in the lives to come. One easy yet effective way to generate merit is to sponsor the printing and distribution of morality books, for it is believed that they are capable of teaching and inspiring people to live a moral life, and hence more good deeds will be done as a result of the dissemination of morality books. Therefore, many morality books teach that one's bad karma can be canceled by sponsoring the printing of morality books.[15] This might also be a reason that they have continued to thrive. In addition to accumulating merit for oneself, the individual can also transfer merit to others—often to parents, children, siblings, and even deceased ancestors—by praying or simply willing that blessings come to them. As a result, sponsoring the printing of morality books can also be used as a way to transfer merit to others.

Syncretic Outlook

The syncretic nature of morality books is evident in the fact that in these texts, Confucian, Buddhist, and Daoist ideas are interwoven and their incompatibilities are overlooked. Traditionally, morality books advocate the 'Three Teachings' and see them as a unified one. Today, this trinitarian paradigm is explicitly broadened by some modern Taiwanese morality books to include Christianity and Islam (and other religions). While borrowing little from Christianity and Islam, these texts affirm the morally exhorting function and transforming power of these two religions and grant them a place within the religious vision of Chinese popular belief.[16] In such a vision, conduct is more important than beliefs. The meaning of a person's life and that

---

[14] This belief is very powerfully presented in the *Four Admonitions Given by Liaofan*.

[15] For example, the *Precious Records Copied from the Jade Emperor's Calendar* and *Records of a Journey to Hell* repeatedly instruct the reader not only to repent and do good, but also to explain the teachings or distribute the copies of these two books to others, so that he may receive less or no punishment in hell.

[16] For example, in *Records of a Journey to Hell*, chapter 4, the reader is introduced to a building named "All Teachings Return to Unity" (*Wanjiao guizong*) in the under-

person's final fate are not determined by the doctrines embraced, but by the mind cultivated and the deeds done. It is due to this vision that in morality books, the concern for ethical living generally outweighs the concern for doctrinal correctness and consistency, and that is also why in some temples texts of differing religious traditions can be displayed together with morality books.

Data and Measurements

The data used in this study are drawn from the 1999 Taiwan Social Change Survey sponsored by the Taiwan National Science Council and conducted by the Institute of Sociology and the Office of Survey Research, Academia Sinica. The year 1999 is chosen because it is the latest survey that includes questions directly related to morality books and some other variables suitable for this study. The survey contains two sets of questionnaires, focusing on culture/values and religion respectively, and thus has two data sets. The respondents were adults aged 20–70 in the first data set (culture/values) and aged 20–64 in the second data set (religion), chosen by an island-wide stratified (levels of urbanization) probability sampling method, and the data were collected through in-person interviews. The first data set consists of 1948 observations and the second data set consists of 1925 observations. In this study, observations with missing values in terms of the variables being analyzed are deleted.

Table 1 and Table 2 contain the major questions from the survey that are used in this study. The questions listed in Table 1 are from the religion questionnaire, and those in Table 2 are from the culture/values questionnaire. Each question is given an abbreviation to stand for the variable measured by that question. The response options and their assigned values are provided in the footnotes to the tables.

---

world. This is not a place for punishing sinners, but an education center for believers who during their lifetime belittle and slander other religions. In this center, they are instructed that the five world religions are all from the same source—the Way (Dao) and have the same goal—to teach people to do good. If believers fail to treat those of other religions with love and respect, these believers will exclude themselves from the perfect world they hope to enter. Another example is found in the morality book, *The Sagely Thearch Wenheng's Statutes of Merit and Demerit* (*Wenheng Shengdi gongguo lü* [1985–86]), produced by a very active temple in central Taiwan by means of spirit-writing. Interestingly, the 'gods' that descended on and communicated through the spirit medium included Confucius, the Daoist deity Heavenly Worthy of Primordial Beginning (*Yuanshi tianzun*), the Buddha, and even Jehovah and Mohammed.

Table 1

Questions from the Religion Questionnaire	Abbreviations
Do you read morality books?[a]	Read
Did you fund the printing of morality books or sutras last year?[b]	Fund
Do you go to temples to worship gods?[b]	Temples
Do you go to Buddhist temples to worship or venerate Buddhas?[b]	Buddhas
Do your family worship ancestors?[b]	Ancestors
Do you consider yourself a devout believer?[b]	Devoutness
Do you believe that there is a highest God in the universe?[c]	God
Do you believe in the idea of karma and reincarnation?[c]	Karma
Do you believe there really are heaven and hell?[c]	Hell
Do you believe that one's moral and immoral deeds have impacts on the happiness of one's descendents?[c]	Descendents
Do you believe that one's moral and immoral deeds have impacts on the fate of one's next life?[c]	Next fate
Do you believe that one's fate can be changed by doing good and accumulating merit?[c]	Change fate

[a] Never (1); I browse them once in a while (2); I've read several of them (3); I've read a lot (4).
[b] No (1); Yes (2).
[c] Strongly disbelieve (1); Not quite believe (2); Somewhat believe (3); Strongly believe (4).

Table 2

Questions from the Culture/Values Questionnaire	Abbreviations
Is it right to leave one's parents unattended and uncared for?[a]	Unfilial
Is it right to have extramarital affairs?[a]	Affairs
Is it right to litter (a public place)?[a]	Littering
Is it right to evade payment of taxes?[a]	Tax evasion
"Those who do evil are to be punished by Heaven." Do you agree?[b]	Punished
"Good-hearted people are to be rewarded." Do you agree?[b]	Good-hearted
"Those who do good will go to heaven; those who do evil will go to hell." Do you agree?[b]	Good to heaven
"Those who do good deeds will live a prosperous life in their next incarnation." Do you agree?[b]	Next incarnation

[a] It is right (1); It is wrong (2); It is quite wrong (3); It is very wrong (4).
[b] Strongly disagree (1); Disagree (2); Agree (3); Strongly agree (4).

There are several variables that need to be controlled in this study: age, gender, religion, and education. Their measurements are described in the appendix.

The Readership of Morality Books

To assess the influence of morality books, one initial step is to find out how many people actually read them. Table 3 shows that around 60% of Taiwanese people aged from 20–64 have read some sort of morality books, and about 15% of Taiwanese people have read several or lots of morality books.

Who are the people that read morality books? Table 4 displays a summary of their profile. As can be seen, those who funded the printing of morality books or sutras in the previous year are also more likely to read morality books, and more women than men read them. Among the people with college or higher degrees, more than two-thirds of them are readers of morality books.

The Effectiveness of Morality Books in Instilling Religious Beliefs

Since morality books have been used for centuries to spread religious and moral instructions, these texts might effectively instill the ideas contained in them in their readers. During the last few decades, they may also have become more and more effective in this regard for the following reasons: first, owing to the policy of nine years compulsory education implemented since 1968, the literacy rate above age 15 in Taiwan had been significantly increased to 96.03% by 2003 (GIO 2003), thus making written texts no longer a barrier to but a useful vehicle for conveying information. Second, in the past,

Table 3. *Survey Responses to the Question Regarding Reading Morality Books*

Do you read morality books? (N = 1923)	
Never	41.6%
I browse them once in a while	43.3%
I've read several of them	10.6%
I've read a lot	4.5%

Table 4. *Profile of the Readership of Morality Books*

| | | Read morality books? | | |
		Never	Yes	Total
Ever Fund printing of morality books (N = 1919)	No	39.3%	47.9%	87.2%
	Yes	2.3%	10.5%	12.8%
Gender (N = 1923)	Male	22.5%	27.5%	50%
	Female	19.1%	30.9%	50%
Education (N = 1911)	No formal education	4.2%	0.5%	4.7%
	Elementary school	11%	7.2%	18.2%
	Junior high school	6.6%	8.2%	14.8%
	Senior high school	10.5%	21.1%	31.6%
	Junior College	4.7%	11.1%	15.8%
	Bachelor and graduate degree	4.6%	10.4%	15%

most morality books were written in classical Chinese, which is not easily comprehensible to the common people, even if they are literate; now, almost every recently composed morality book is in the vernacular. As to the classical morality books that are still circulated today in Taiwan, they are usually printed with vernacular translations and/or commentaries. Third, since morality books are popular religious literature, they do not need to be constrained by certain strict canonical rules or forms. Therefore, morality books tend to be responsive and adapted to social change and cultural taste, and hence are free to adopt various literary formats and incorporate modern language and thinking. As a result, the ideas of morality books may become more impressive and sound more persuasive.

The religion data set is used to examine whether there is a relationship between reading morality books and holding certain religious beliefs. Based on the foregoing discussion of the moral-religious vision in morality books, six beliefs are chosen from the survey as representative of the teachings of the morality-book literature, such as "Do you believe that there is a highest God in the universe?" ('God'), "Do you believe the idea of karma and reincarnation?" ('Karma'), "Do you believe there really are heaven and hell?" ('Hell'), and so on. The means and standard deviations of these variables, and their correlations with reading morality books are presented in Table 5.

Table 5. *Correlation between People's Beliefs and Reading Morality Books*

	God	Karma	Hell	Change fate	Descendent	Next fate
Correlation	.161***	.128***	.251***	.170***	.118***	.150***
Mean	2.65	3.04	2.85	3.13	3.41	3.24
S.D.	.958	.900	.922	.786	.728	.850

*** $p < .001$ (two-tailed tests). N = 1322.

Table 5 shows that there are significant positive relationships between reading morality books and believing in the existence of a highest God, the idea of karma and reincarnation, and the existence of heaven and hell, and believing that doing good will change one's fate in this life as well as that one's conduct will influence the fate of one's descendents and one's next life. In other words, reading morality books is a significant predictor of holding these beliefs.

To isolate the effect of morality books on each of these beliefs, multiple regression analyses were conducted in which several variables were controlled, such as worship performances ('Temples', 'Buddhas', 'Ancestors'), religious devoutness ('Devoutness'), religion (Popular religion, Buddhism, etc), and major demographic factors (Age, Gender, Education). The results of the regression analyses are presented in Table 6.

As can be observed in Table 6, after controlling for the variables that may have effects on people's beliefs, the positive relationships between reading morality books and holding these beliefs still remain significant. That is to say, regardless of their religious faith, education, gender, age, and whether or not they worship any deity, readers of morality books are significantly more likely to hold the beliefs presented in them. The results suggest that reading morality books has a significant impact on people's beliefs.

While morality books may be effective in instilling the above-mentioned beliefs into their reader's mind, this does not mean that morality books are thus also effective in disseminating *any* beliefs or practices. Comparing the ritual instructions prescribed in the many widespread scriptures and morality texts associated with the stove god with the actual stove god rituals practiced in most households, Chard (1995) finds that the textual teachings have failed to exert any significant influence on the popular observances to the stove god.

Table 6. *Multiple Regression Coefficients (Beta) for the Effects of Reading Morality Books on People's Beliefs*

	God	Karma	Hell	Change fate	Descendent	Next fate
Read	.052*	.076**	.165***	.129***	.075**	.105***
Temples	.118***	.074*	.093**	.072*	.085**	−.013
Buddhas	.018	.046	.057*	−.022	.039	.032
Ancestors	−.012	−.006	−.009	.047	.007	−.013
Devoutness	.184***	.152***	.163***	.089***	.092***	.115***
Popular religion	.106*	.112**	.087	.067	.099*	.093*
Buddhism	.058	.222***	.164***	.193***	.186***	.243***
Daoism	.089*	.135***	.085*	.069	.063	.072*
Christianity	.411***	−.228***	.235***	.013	.106**	−.023
Sects	.124***	.098***	.070*	.064*	.039	.053
Other religions	.055	.092***	.120***	.067*	.066*	.086**
Age	−.001	−.034	−.145***	−.013	.081**	−.047
Gender	.102***	.055*	.120***	.083***	−.009	.055*
Education	−.055	−.097***	−.120***	−.033	−.082**	−.178***
R^2	.193	.235	.179	.086	.077	.122
F	23.559***	31.728***	21.053***	10.246***	9.239***	14.712***
N	1396	1463	1365	1542	1566	1496

* $p < .05$; ** $p < .01$; *** $p < .001$ (two-tailed tests).

For instance, despite the texts' advocacy of the stove god's monthly ascents and reports, people still believe that he ascends to Heaven to report the family's merits and faults only at the New Year. Chard suggests that the rituals prescribed in the stove texts are probably intended by the educated elite to modify popular practices. Why have the scriptures and texts on the stove god had no effect on people's practice? One possible reason is that with regard to the New Year observances to the stove god, the texts are propagating practices that are at variance from some generally-accepted concepts and widely-observed customs. In other words, the ineffectiveness of these texts may be accounted for by the lack of cultural resonance with the practices they advocate. By contrast, in my current study, the beliefs in a highest God, karma and reincarnation, heaven and hell, and so on are all already well-established in Chinese and Taiwanese religious cultures. Therefore, morality books may not be successful in introducing *unconventional* beliefs and practices, but may nevertheless be effective in instilling and reinforcing *traditional* ones.

Morality Books and the Moral Order

Morality books may be effective in upholding various religious beliefs, as shown in the previous section, but this is not the major purpose of morality books. The major purpose is to influence their reader's moral thinking and conduct. By introducing people to certain religious beliefs, morality books may change their value systems and their perspectives on their lives, hence induce the virtues encouraged and inhibit the vices condemned by these religious beliefs. Traditionally, morality books are supposed to be capable of achieving this purpose. It is due to this supposed effectiveness that morality books continue to exist, and why sponsoring their printing and helping their distribution are considered meritorious. While the morally transforming power of morality books may be sincerely believed and anecdotally evidenced, it remains to be tested and explained.

The survey used in this study has two sets of questionnaires, administered to two different samples of respondents. The religion questionnaire contains questions regarding morality books and religious beliefs, but does not include questions about moral values or practices, whereas the culture/values questionnaire has questions concerning religious beliefs and moral values, yet does not ask about morality books. Because of this design, the impact of morality books on people's moral thinking cannot be directly examined by analyzing the survey data. Nevertheless, since morality books are effective in instilling and reinforcing certain beliefs, if these beliefs can be shown to have strong correlations with morality, then the function of morality books to sustain the moral order may be at least indirectly affirmed.

Four beliefs in the culture/value questionnaire are chosen for examining the relationship between beliefs and morality; they are 'Punished', 'Good-hearted,' 'Good to heaven,' and 'Next incarnation.' They are chosen because they represent the beliefs about moral retribution found in the present-day morality texts. To measure morality (or disapproval of immorality), four behaviors in the questionnaire are selected: 'Unfilial,' 'Affairs,' 'Littering,' and 'Tax evasion.' The first two behaviors are explicitly condemned by many morality books because not taking care of one's parents and having extramarital affairs seriously undermine Confucian family values. While littering and evading taxes are not often mentioned in morality books, these two acts may be considered as deviating from one's duty to the public and to one's country, and hence are also at odds with the ethics presented in morality books. The means, standard deviations, and zero-order correlations for these eight variables are presented in Table 7.

The correlation coefficients in Table 7 indicate that the four beliefs all positively correlate with each of the four measures of morality in a significant way. Multiple regression analyses need to be performed in order to see whether the positive relationships are merely due to other relevant factors, such as religion, age, gender, and education. Since the culture/values questionnaire does not include questions regarding common religious practices (such as worship, prayer, and so on), these factors cannot be controlled in the analyses. Table 8a–d reports the results of multiple regression analyses.

As one can clearly see, these four beliefs are all shown to have significant correlations with people's moral judgments. That is to say, when judging the morality of not taking care of one's parents, having extramarital affairs, littering, and evading taxes, people with these beliefs are significantly more likely to consider these behaviors as wrong than those who do not hold these beliefs. The results suggest that these four beliefs influence the moral behavior of Taiwanese people.

In the previous section I have demonstrated that morality book readers are more likely to believe in the existence of a highest God, the idea of karma, the existence of heaven and hell, and the idea

Table 7. *Means, Standard Deviations, and Zero-Order Correlations for Variables Regarding Beliefs and Moral Attitudes*

	1.	2.	3.	4.	5.	6.	7.	8.
1. Punished	1.00							
2. Good-hearted	.570***	1.00						
3. Good to heaven	.560***	.491***	1.00					
4. Next incarnation	.578***	.559***	.579***	1.00				
5. Unfilial	.071**	.083**	.064*	.071**	1.00			
6. Affairs	.174***	.173***	.125***	.115***	.260***	1.00		
7. Littering	.105***	.128***	.065*	.086***	.221***	.419***	1.00	
8. Tax evasion	.148***	.155***	.084**	.106***	.226***	.386***	.467***	1.00
Mean	3.03	3.15	2.83	2.92	3.48	3.26	3.15	2.99
S.D.	.732	.685	.771	.742	.802	.869	.866	.893

* $p < .05$; ** $p < .01$; *** $p < .001$ (two-tailed tests). N = 1371.

Table 8a. *Multiple Regression Coefficients (Beta) for the Effects of the Belief "Those who do evil are to be punished by Heaven" on People's Moral Judgments*

	Unfilial	Affairs	Littering	Tax evasion
Punished	.087***	.158***	.123***	.165***
Popular religion	.051	.019	.009	.015
Buddhism	.028	−.038	−.047	−.071*
Daoism	.025	.006	−.025	.022
Christianity	−.021	.002	.015	.035
Other religions	−.001	.034	−.015	.023
Age	.065*	.021	.161***	.125***
Gender	−.080***	.129***	.089***	.039
Education	−.006	.001	.121***	.105***
R^2	.021	.049	.046	.047
F	4.172***	9.261***	9.154***	9.175***
N	1723	1638	1724	1673

* p < .05; *** p < .001 (two-tailed tests)

Table 8b. *Multiple Regression Coefficients (Beta) for the Effects of the Belief "Good-hearted people are to be rewarded" on People's Moral Judgments*

	Unfilial	Affairs	Littering	Tax evasion
Good-hearted	.101***	.145***	.131***	.157***
Popular religion	.051	.029	.017	.019
Buddhism	.043	−.028	−.050	−.057
Daoism	.043	.006	−.015	.040
Christianity	−.019	.002	.017	.032
Other religions	.005	.042	−.005	.024
Age	.067*	.012	.151***	.096***
Gender	−.083***	.117***	.080***	.038
Education	−.007	−.007	.114***	.097***
R^2	.026	.043	.047	.042
F	5.169***	8.386***	9.668***	8.395***
N	1784	1690	1785	1724

* p < .05; *** p < .001 (two-tailed tests)

Table 8c. *Multiple Regression Coefficients (Beta) for the Effects of the Belief "Those who do good will go to heaven; those who do evil will go to hell" on People's Moral Judgments*

	Unfilial	Affairs	Littering	Tax evasion
Good to heaven	.083***	.106***	.079***	.094***
Popular religion	.046	.037	.010	.027
Buddhism	.043	−.012	−.047	−.053
Daoism	.035	.017	−.009	.034
Christianity	−.018	.000	.024	.039
Other religions	−.003	.050	−.009	.024
Age	.068*	.022	.155***	.111***
Gender	−.076**	.121***	.090***	.047
Education	−.001	.001	.117***	.099***
R^2	.020	.034	.037	.029
F	3.747***	6.045***	7.048***	5.340***
N	1660	1578	1661	1617

* $p < .05$; ** $p < .01$; *** $p < .001$ (two-tailed tests)

Table 8d. *Multiple Regression Coefficients (Beta) for the Effects of the Belief "Those who do good deeds will live a prosperous life in their next incarnation" on People's Moral Judgments*

	Unfilial	Affairs	Littering	Tax evasion
Next incarnation	.077**	.103***	.111***	.125***
Popular religion	.060	.024	.015	.013
Buddhism	.051	−.027	−.051	−.067
Daoism	.041	.013	−.009	.035
Christianity	−.031	.003	.024	.040
Other religions	−.003	.042	.004	.013
Age	.082**	.021	.159***	.109***
Gender	−.078**	.118***	.073**	.033
Education	.005	.008	.117***	.109***
R^2	.025	.031	.041	.035
F	4.660***	5.452***	7.788***	6.344***
N	1649	1569	1650	1605

** $p < .01$; *** $p < .001$ (two-tailed tests)

that one's deeds have influences on the fate of one's next life. Now their related beliefs, which are advocated in morality books as well, have also been shown to have significant impacts on people's moral thinking. This indicates that in present-day Taiwan, morality books are effective in influencing moral consciousness and do function to sustain the moral order.

Conclusion

Being a product special to Chinese popular religion, morality books contain the crystallization of some essential aspects of popular beliefs and provide us a window into the religious mind of Chinese people. Morality books also constitute an important part of the cultural and religious phenomena of Taiwanese society and thus deserve serious attention. This study has shown that morality books are indeed quite popular in Taiwan, for about 60% of Taiwanese adults read morality books. Moreover, their popularity is by no means restricted to the non-elite. In Taiwan, among those with higher education, more than two thirds of them read morality books. As to their efficacy, significant correlations between reading morality books and holding the beliefs typical of them were observed, suggesting that they are effective in implanting and reinforcing these beliefs in the reader's mind. Some of these beliefs were also found to have noticeable impacts on people's moral attitudes. These results demonstrate that morality books exert significant influences on the belief and value systems of Taiwanese people.

Nevertheless, since in this study I included only the beliefs representative of morality books and the behaviors disapproved by the ethics presented therein, the results cannot be used to support the claim that the medium of morality books is also effective in instilling beliefs alien to the prevaling religious views or in sustaining some other forms of ethics. My speculation is that morality books would be much less effective in doing that.

This study not only contributes to our understanding of the morally transforming power of morality books in Taiwan, but also has strong implications for the morality-sustaining function of religion in general. This discussion has recently been revitalized by Stark (2001). Refuting the claims made by the functionalists that religion functions to sustain morality and that religion does so through communal ceremonies, Stark demonstrates that not every religion functions to sustain the moral order. And that when religions do sanction morality, it is not through participation in collective rituals and rites, but due to the belief in a powerful, active, conscious, morally concerned God or gods. In other words, it is the conception of the supernatural as personal and mighty God or gods concerned about humans' conduct toward one another that makes religions effective in sustaining morality. Accordingly, impersonal, amoral, or small gods have no effects on the moral order.

The results of my study testify that beliefs in the supernatural do matter in morality. When making moral judgments, people with certain religious beliefs differ significantly from those without them. Nevertheless, this study also shows that the religious beliefs that are effective in sanctioning morality are not all about personal and powerful gods of large scope. The four beliefs found to have moral impacts center around the idea of moral retribution, which is conceived in morality books as being achieved through the cooperation of gods and karmic law rather than exclusively by gods. In this cooperation, karmic law plays a more pivotal role, for it is the universal and unbreakable law of karma that determines the nature and amount of reward and punishment, and guarantees the ultimate necessity of moral retribution. This is why in the present-day Taiwanese morality books, the idea of moral retribution is usually expressed in the term *yinguo baoying*, which literally means 'cause-effect retribution.' Certainly, gods are also involved in the retributive process, but unlike the law-giving God in monotheistic faiths, they are often merely overseers and executors. The moral norms in morality books are generally considered as less associated with gods' wills than derived from some impersonal principles, such as the Way of Heaven, the Dao, or the Buddha-dharma, to which even gods must also conform. Moreover, most of the gods in Chinese religions are of limited power and scope. Were these gods not equipped with the unfailing and all-embracing law of karma, the belief in them would exert less influence on people's moral thinking. Therefore, in Taiwan, popular religion functions to sustain the moral order at least in part because of the belief in the impersonal principle of karma rather than simply due to faith in powerful, active, conscious, and morally-concerned gods. Future research may investigate the effect of the idea of karma on moral attitudes in other places, especially where the conceptions of gods have been shown by Rodney Stark's research (2001) to have no impact on morality, such as Japan.

APPENDIX

Control Variables and Their Measurements

Age	Computed from: What is your year of birth?
Gender	male = 1, female = 2.
Education	None = 1, Self-educated = 2,
	Elementary school (without graduating) = 3,
	Elementary school = 4, Junior high school = 5,
	Junior vocational school = 6, Senior high school = 7,
	Senior vocational school = 8, Sergeant school* = 9,
	Five-year upper secondary school = 10, Junior college = 11,
	Military/Police preparatory school = 12, Military/Police
	academy = 13, College = 14, Graduate school = 15
Popular religion	Recoded from: What is your religious faith?
	Popular religion = 1, else = 0
Buddhism	Recoded from: What is your religious faith?
	Buddhism = 1, else = 0
Daoism	Recoded from: What is your religious faith?
	Daoism = 1, else = 0
Christianity	Recoded from: What is your religious faith?
	Christianity, Catholicism = 1, else = 0
Sects	Recoded from: What is your religious faith?
	Yiguan Dao, Xuanyuan Jiao, Xia Jiao, etc. = 1, else = 0
Other religions	Recoded from: What is your religious faith?
	Islam, Scientology, etc = 1, else = 0

REFERENCES

Bell, Catherine. 1992. "Printing and Religion in China: Some Evidence from the *Taishang ganying pian*." *Journal of Chinese Religions* 20:173–86.
———. 1996. "Stories from an Illustrated Explanation of the *Tract of the Most Exalted on Action and Response*." Pp. 437–45 in *Religions of China in Practice*, edited by Donald S. Lopez, Jr. Princeton, NJ: Princeton University Press.
Brokaw, Cynthia J. 1991. *The Ledgers of Merit and Demerit*. Princeton, NJ: Princeton University Press.
———. 1996. "Supernatural Retribution and Human Destiny." Pp. 423–36 in *Religions of China in Practice*, edited by Donald S. Lopez, Jr. Princeton, NJ: Princeton University Press.
Chard, Robert L. 1995. "Rituals and Scriptures of the Stove Cult." Pp. 3–54 in *Ritual and Scripture in Chinese Popular Religion*, edited by David Johnson. Berkeley, CA: Chinese Popular Culture Project.

* Sergeant school in Taiwan is a three-year military school that recruits students graduated from junior high schools.

Clart, Philip. 1997. *The Ritual Context of Morality Books: A Case-study of a Taiwanese Spirit-writing Cult.* Ph.D. dissertation, University of British Columbia.
———. 2003. "Chinese Tradition and Taiwanese Modernity: Morality Books as Social Commentary and Critique." Pp. 84–97 in *Religion in Modern Taiwan*, edited by Philip Clart and Charles B. Jones. Honolulu: University of Hawaii Press.
Coyle, Michael (trans). 1981. "Book of Rewards and Punishments." Pp. 71–74 in *Chinese Civilization and Society*, edited by Patricia Ebrey. New York: Free Press.
Diyu youji [*Records of a Journey to Hell*]. 2000 [1978]. Taizhong, Taiwan: Shengxian zazhi she.
G.I.O. (Government Information Office, Republic of China). 2003. "Taiwan at a Glance 2003: Education." *http://www.gio.gov.tw/taiwan-website/5-gp/glance/ch7.htm* (accessed October 27, 2004).
Green, Ronald M. 1988. *Religion and Moral Reason.* New York: Oxford University Press.
Jordan, David K. and Daniel L. Overmyer. 1986. *The Flying Phoenix.* Princeton, NJ: Princeton University Press.
Katz, Paul R. 1999. "Morality Books and Taiwanese Identity: The Texts of the Palace of Guidance." *Journal of Chinese Religions* 27:69–92.
Lai, Chiu-nan. trans. 1997. *Liao-Fan's Four Lessons.* Taipei: Corporate Body of the Buddha Educational Foundation.
Legge, James. trans. 1980. "The Thai Shang Tractate of Actions and their Retributions." Pp. 233–46 in *The Sacred Books of the East*, edited by Max Müller, vol. 39. Oxford: Oxford University Press.
Liaofan sixun [*Four Admonitions Given by Liaofan*]. 2004. Gaoxiung, Taiwan: Gaoxiung jingzong xuehui.
Pas, Julian F. 1989. "Journey to Hell: A New Report of Shamanistic Travel to the Courts of Hell." *Journal of Chinese Religions* 17:43–60.
———. 1996. "Religious Life in Present Day Taiwan: A Field Observations Report, 1994–95." *Journal of Chinese Religions* 24:131–58.
Shengling de beiqi [*Suffering and Wretchedness of Sentient Beings*]. 1998. Taizhong, Taiwan: Xuyuan zazhi she.
Stark, Rodney. 2001. "Gods, Rituals, and the Moral Order." *Journal for the Scientific Study of Religion* 40:619–36.
Song, Guangyu. 1984. "Cong *Yuli baochao* tan Zhongguo sumin de zongjiao daode guannian" ["A Discussion of the Religious and Moral Views of Common Chinese People on the Basis of *Yuli baochao*"]. *Taiwan shengli bowuguan niankan* 27:3–15.
———. 1993. "Cong zuijin shiji nian lai de luanzuo youjishi shanshu tan Zhongguo minjian xinyang li de jiazhiguan" ["A Discussion of the Concepts of Value in Chinese Popular Religion on the Basis of the Spirit-written Travelogues from the Last Ten-odd Years"]. Pp. 35–63 in *Zhongguoren de jiazhiguan—shehui kexue guandian* [*Value Concepts of the Chinese: Social-science Perspectives*]. Taipei: Guiguan chuban she.
———. 1995. *Zongjiao yu shehui* [*Religion and Society*]. Taipei: Dongda.
Suzuki, Teitaro and Paul Carus. trans. 1906. *T'ai-Shang Kan-Ying P'ien.* Chicago, IL: Open Court Publishing.
Tiantang youji [*Records of a Journey to Heaven*]. 2002 [1981]. Taizhong, Taiwan: Shengxian zazhi she.
Wang, Jianchuan. 1995. "Taiwan luantang yanjiu de huigu yu qianzhan" ["A Review of the Studies on the Phoenix Halls in Taiwan and their Future Outlook"]. *Taiwan shiliao yanjiu* 6:3–25.
Wang, Zhiyu. 2003. "Taiwan minjian xinyang de gui shen guan: Yi Shengxian tang xilie luanshu we zhongxin de tangtao" ["The Concepts of Ghosts and Gods in Taiwanese Popular Religion: A Study of the Spirit-written Books Published by Shengxian Temples"]. *Fengjia renwen shehui xuebao* 7:117–40.

Wenheng shengdi gongguo lü, shang, xia [*The Sagely Wenheng's Statutes of Merit and Demerit*, 2 vols]. 1985–1986. Taizhong, Taiwan: Luanyou zazhi she.

Yuli baochao [*Precious Records Copied from the Jade Emperor's Calendar*]. n.d. Taizhong, Taiwan: Fazang wenhua chuban she.

Zheng, Zhiming. 1988a. "*Taishang ganying pian* de lunli sixiang" ["The Ethical Thinking of *Taishang ganying pian*"]. Pp. 41–61 in *Zhongguo shanshu yu zongjiao* [*Chinese Morality Books and Religions*]. Taipei: Xuesheng shuju.

———. 1988b. "Youjilei luanshu suo xianshi zhi zongjioa xin qushi" ["The New Religious Trends Manifested in Spirit-written Travelogues"]. Pp. 413–56 in *Zhongguo shanshu yu zongjiao* [*Chinese Morality Books and Religions*]. Taipei: Xuesheng shuju.

CHAPTER NINE

THE FATE OF CONFUCIANISM AS A RELIGION IN SOCIALIST CHINA: CONTROVERSIES AND PARADOXES

Anna Xiao Dong Sun

Since the turn of the twentieth century, many scholars in the West have treated Confucianism as a religion (Legge 1877; Müller 1900; Weber 1951; Granet 1977; Ching 1977; Tu 1989; Taylor 1990; Teiser 1996; Wilson 2002), and Confucianism is often portrayed as the official or national religion of China in introductory texts on world religions (Smith 1991; Bowker 1997; Oxtoby 2002). It might come as a surprise to many people that Confucianism is not included in the Chinese official classification of religions. In this chapter, I will focus on the formation of the governmental classification of religions in post-1949 China, the ever-increasing tension between the official classification and the academic categorization of Confucianism, and the tension within the academic community over the different interpretations of the religious nature of Confucianism.

There are essentially three positions concerning Confucianism as a religion: (1) Confucian is not a religion; (2) Confucianism is a religion, and as such has a negative impact, for religion itself is intrinsically a negative force in society; and (3) Confucianism is a religion, and it has a positive or neutral impact, for religion is either a positive force in society or a neutral one. The first position is easy to distinguish, but the other two are often conflated with each other, for they differ only in their value judgments. In contemporary China, the second position is based on the Marxist denunciation of any religion, whereas the third one comes from either a favorable or a nonjudgmental view of religious life. The state has been taking the first position, denying Confucianism the status of religion. Among scholars of Confucianism all three positions can be found, and the opposing value judgments between them have become the primary cause of the most recent intellectual debates.

In this chapter I will focus on how the different combinations of the three positions interact with each other, and how such interactions

shape the categorization of Confucianism in China. To some extend
this study touches on the larger issue of articulation, which refers to
"the ways in which ideas are shaped by their social situations and
yet manage to disengage from these situations." Although this chapter centers on how ideas are shaped by their social situations, I will
emphasize how ideas about Confucianism, like many other bodies
of knowledge, "were shaped by and yet succeeded in transcending
their specific environments of origin" (Wuthnow 1989: 5). Although
I am not going to examine how the knowledge of Confucianism
transcends its social environments here, it is important to have this
broad understanding in mind when we look at how certain views
triumph over others in a particular historical moment.

I will first give a brief summary of the conception of Confucianism
as a religion in China in the late ninteenth and early twentieth centuries, shortly before the establishment of the socialist state; I shall
then outline the process of the construction of the official religious
classification, the 'Five Major Religions,' in the 1950s, which includes
Catholicism, Protestantism, Buddhism, Daoism, and Islam, but not
Confucianism. Next I will discuss the contemporary controversy over
the religious nature of Confucianism, an important on-going intellectual debate with potential political implications that has not previously been studied by social scientists. It can be traced to the 1970s
and the work of Ren Jiyu, a leading scholar of the history of Chinese
philosophy and religions, who has also been a high-ranking admin-
istrator in state-controlled academic institutions.

The current controversy reached its height in 2001–2004, with
several dozen participants publishing progressively more heated articles in various academic journals and on much-browsed scholarly
websites. The remaining parts of this paper will be devoted to an
analysis of the current controversy and its potential political impact,
as well as an assessment of the present and future status of Confucianism as a religion in contemporary China.

This study draws on research done between 2002 and 2004, including interviews with officials from the National Bureau of Religious
Affairs, the past and current members of the Department of Confucianism (or Confucian Religion) at the Chinese Academy of Social Sciences
(CASS), and the current head of the Institute of World Religions,
of which the Department of Confucianism is a part.

The choice of interviewing the members of CASS was not an
arbitrary one. Although it is called the Academy of Social Sciences,

CASS is the national academy for the studies of both the humanities and the social sciences, with 31 institutes devoted to disciplines ranging from literature, history, religion, and philosophy to economics, sociology and American Studies. Established in 1977, CASS occupies the most prestigious position on the Chinese intellectual landscape as the highest ranking national research institution.[1] However, despite its close ties to the state (the head of CASS shares the same official rank as a vice-premier, and the current head is in fact a former vice-premier), CASS has had a long history of harboring intellectual dissenters. During the 1989 Tiananmen Square student movement, for instance, many members of CASS helped the students with political ideas and strategies, which led to the commonly shared view of CASS being the think-tank of student leaders.

In the case of the controversy over Confucianism as a religion, CASS again plays an important role for both historical and political reasons. The Institute of World Religions was founded in 1964; it is the only institute at CASS that was established as a result of Mao's direct request, who wrote in a memorandum dated 30 December 1963 that "there hasn't been a research institution led by Marxist scholars" to study the "three great world religions (Christianity, Islam and Buddhism)," yet "one cannot understand world philosophy, literature and history without critically examining and refuting theology" (Mao 1963).[2] The Institute of World Religions was set up only four months after Mao's written instructions; from the very beginning, it was laden with unambiguously political agendas, which have become a highly problematic legacy for its researchers.

'*Rujiao shi*,' the only research facility in China bearing the name Department of Confucianism (or Confucian Religion), was created in 1979 under the Institute of World Religions at CASS. As we shall see, the contemporary controversy centers around both its past and current members, and I will demonstrate that, in this case, CASS is again the crucial cultural location where the state and the intellectuals

---

[1] Although it was officially founded in 1977, CASS was set up on the basis of the Division of Philosophy and the Social Sciences at the Chinese Academy of Sciences, which was created in 1949.

[2] Interview with Jin Ze, deputy director of the Institute of World Religions at CASS, January 13, 2004; and from a speech given by the General Secretary of CASS on the occasion of the Fortieth Anniversary of the establishment of the Institute of World Religions, September 24, 2004.

encounter each other, and the consequences of such interactions reflect both the internal dynamics of this complex institution and the changing political climate of the country.

Clarification of Terms

Before we start investigating the controversies over Confucianism as a religion in socialist China, we need to clarify the different usages and meanings of the term 'Confucianism.' Although the word 'Confucius,' the Latinized name of *Kong Fuzi*, was first used by Jesuit missionaries in China in the late sixteenth century, the word 'Confucianism' did not come into existence until 1862, according to the OED, when it was used in a passage mentioning "Confucianism, the state and national creed." However, the real usage of the word as referring to a religion was in James Legge's pamphlet *Confucianism in Relation to Christianity*, published in Shanghai in 1877. In a later text, Legge (1880: 4) elaborated on the meaning of the word 'Confucianism.'

> I use the term Confucianism as covering, first of all the ancient religion of China, and then the views of the great philosopher himself, in illustration or modification of it, his views as committed to writing by himself, or transmitted in the narratives of his disciples. The case is pretty much as when we comprehend under Christianity the records and teachings of the Old Testament as well as those of the New.

Today 'Confucianism' in English refers to both the philosophical teaching of Confucius (551–479 B.C.E.) and the religion associated with Confucius.[3]

In Chinese, however, it is difficult to find the exact equivalent of the English word 'Confucianism;' one might say that 'Confucianism' is indeed both a translation and an invention. The closest might be *run jiao*, or 'the Confucian religion,' but the word *jiao* does not always mean 'religion' in Chinese. Many of the confusions about Chinese religions are related to the translation and interpretation of *jiao* as 'religion' without further qualifications. Buddhism, Daoism, and Confucianism are commonly referred to in Chinese as *san jiao*, a phrase that first appeared in the ninth century, but the term meant 'three teachings' at the time, rather than 'three religions.'

---

[3] For a detailed account of the Jesuits' translation or creation of "Confucius," see Jensen 1997.

The literary meaning of *jiao* is 'teaching,' and the contemporary usage of *jiao* as 'religion' didn't start until the twentieth century, when *jiao* became the component of a newer term *zong jiao*, which does explicitly mean 'religion.' Scholars have pointed out that *zong jiao* was a loanword imported from Japanese (Liu 1995: 301); the original term in Japanese was first used in treaties between Japan and the West in the end of the nineteenth century (Beyer 1999; Masini 1993). In other words, the term *zong jiao*, or 'religion,' did not exist in the Chinese vocabulary until the turn of the twentieth century, and the contemporary usage of *jiao* as a shortened version of *zong jiao* is a rather recent innovation.

Most current scholarship suggests that the two words, *zong* and *jiao* have in fact been "brought together in the sixth century by one or two scholar-monks who differentiated strands in Buddhist thought as different 'principle-teachings,' combining the two terms, though other similar terms were also current." This "slightly *ad hoc*" combination eventually found its way to Japan among the Buddhist clergy, and it was probably "reintroduced to China as *zongjiao* toward the end of the nineteenth century" (Tarocco and Barrett 2004: 4–5, 14).

In the contemporary Chinese debate over the religious nature of Confucianism, scholars have followed the unspoken rule of distinguishing the confusing terms: *Rujia* (the school of Confucian teaching) and *ruxue* (Confucian learning) are usually used to refer to Confucianism as a philosophy or school of thought, whereas *rujiao* (the Confucian *jiao*, or the Confucian religion) is used to refer to Confucianism as a religion. In this chapter, I will translate *rujia* and *ruxue* as 'Confucianism as a philosophy' or 'Confucian thought,' and *rujiao* as 'Confucianism as a religion' or 'the Confucian religion.'

Confucianism as a Religion in pre-1949 China: A Brief Overview

Although there is no place for Confucianism in the religion category in most of the Qing dynasty local gazetteers, where one can often find estimates of the numbers of Buddhists, Daoists, and Catholics in a given town or county, there are occasional mentions of Confucians in the context of discussions of religion. In a national regulation of foreign missionaries issued in 1871 (the tenth year of the *Tongzhi* reign), presumably authorized by the emperor, the phrase *rujiao renshi*, "the followers of *rujiao*," was constantly referred to in connection with the conduct of missionaries. The first mandate begins with the following imperative: "Missionaries should obey Chinese customs, following the examples set by the followers of *rujiao*." The fifth mandate starts with the following description: "Catholics don't worship the gods, nor the ancestors, unlike the Confucians" (Academia Sinica 1976: 1–2).

Not too long before the Chinese republican revolution in 1911, during which the last imperial dynasty was overthrown, many intellectuals felt that China needed a national religion to strengthen its cultural and political identity (Jensen 1997). In 1895, Kang You-wei, the most influential public intellectual at the time, campaigned for the establishment of *kongjiao* (*kong* being the last name of Confucius), meaning the 'Confucian religion' or 'Confucianity,' which was modeled after Christianity. A reform-minded thinker, Kang wanted to invent a national religion for China in its transition into modernity, and *kongjiao hui*, the Association of Confucian Religion, was set up by Kong and his supporters in 1912, right after the founding of the Republic of China (Chen 1999).

However, their efforts proved to be unsuccessful, at least politically, and in the late 1920s the government ordered the association to change its name into *kongxue hui*, the Association of Confucian Learning. This change of a single word is indeed a crucial one; *jiao* denotes religion in modern Chinese, whereas *xue* denotes learning or education. Although the movement of reinventing Confucianism as a religion faded quickly after that, some of the followers of Kang did continue to advance his ideas. For example, a Confucian Academy was established in Hong Kang in 1929 by Chen Huanzhang, who had been active in the Confucian religion movement, and there were also attempts to make Confucianism a national religion in Taiwan in the 1920s and 1930s, when Taiwan was under Japanese rule. But such efforts had little impact on what was about to happen in mainland China after the People's Republic of China was founded in 1949.

The Birth of the 'Five Major Religions' Category in Socialist China:
1949–1957

The conception of the 'Five Major Religions' took place in the 1950s behind the closed doors of Chinese communist leaders. To my knowledge there has been no scholarly account of what happened during those important deliberations about religious policy. The exclusion of Confucianism in particular has been very much a mystery: Why was it excluded? What were the reasons of the decision-makers?

From various sources, including published materials and interviews with scholars from the Chinese Academy of Social Sciences and an official from the National Bureau of Religious Affairs, which is part of the State Department (*guowo yuan*), I learned that the notion of Five Major Religions was coined in the 1950s, when the concerns for national security and social stability forced the newly formed government to find a way to deal with China's religious population. The religious organizations, especially the Catholic Church and the Protestant churches, were large enough to pose potential threats to the socialist state. In order to gain control of these organizations, the National Bureau of Religious Affairs was established solely for the management of such groups.[4]

In 1953, four religious associations were founded under the titles of 'Patriotic Associations' of Chinese Catholics, Protestants, Muslims, and Buddhists. The Patriotic Association of Daoists did not come into existence until 1957, when a communist general intervened to make it an official religion.[5] Apparently no one spoke out for the Confucians. But who were the Confucians? It seems plausible that Confucianism was left out of the official classification because there was no Confucian population perceived to be posing political threats. Moreover there was no self-identified Confucian population to speak of in the first place.

---

[4] I was turned down repeatedly in my quest to consult the Bureau of Religious Affairs archive in 2003–2004. In my telephone conversations with someone knowledgeable about the archival documents at the Bureau, I was told that the documents related to the establishment of the category of Five Major Religions were stored in the Central Archive in the National Archive, along with other classified political documents. The reason that the documents are not available for research was that "discussions of religion are too sensitive to be open to scholars." The official also expressed her view that "Confucianism is definitely not counted as a religion in our thinking, because it doesn't have supernatural beliefs or rituals. It's natural that it was not included in the Five Major Religions." In the end I did secure an interview with an official working for the Bureau, who shall remain anonymous.

[5] Zhu De, the legendary general and a close colleague of Mao, was at one point in his youth a Daoist priest before he joined the Communist Party. Zhu De must have reasoned that the only way to help the Daoists avoid future prosecution was to make them part of an officially recognized and legitimate religion. But he did not expect the arrival of the Cultural Revolution, which had on its agenda the destruction of anything that had to do with religion.

This was confirmed by Professor Ren Jiyu, who was knowledgeable about the original discussion over the new China's religious policy:

> The Five Religions policy was conceived because of political concerns; the more believers a religion had, the more seats for representatives they would get in the People's Political Consultative Congress. In Buddhism we had (representatives such as) Zhao Puchu; in the Catholic Church we had Ding Guangxun. We knew there were relatively fewer believers of Daoism, but we couldn't find any Confucians at all.[6]

Many Chinese intellectuals might consider themselves living a life based on the Confucian virtues of learnedness and self-cultivation, yet at least in the mid-twentieth century, none would call himself or herself 'a believer of the Confucian religion.' Although the general atmosphere of scientism and atheism, which were part of the ideology promoted by the Enlightenment-minded Chinese communists, must have played a role in people's silence about their religious beliefs, it is important to note that most people would have found the following sentence, "I am a believer of the Confucian religion" (*woshi yige rujiaotu*), deeply problematic, even though it is similar to the sentence "I am a believer of the Christian religion" (*woshi yige jidutu*).

Although they share the exact same grammatical structure, the latter is something that has been uttered countless times by Chinese Christians, whereas the former is rarely uttered, since the statement would not make sense to most Chinese people. Being a Confucian in traditional China means living a certain way of life; it is deeply embedded in everyday practice, and there is nothing in it that is akin to the Catholic or Jewish rites of confirmation during which one declares one's belief or faith. Without a recognizable or identifiable base of believers, Confucianism as a religion has primarily been a matter of academic and political concern.

The Beginning of the Contemporary Confucianism Controversy: Ren Jiyu and His Legacy

Although the contemporary controversy over the religious nature of Confucianism took off for the most part in the 1990s, its origin can

---

[6] Interview, January 8, 2004, Chinese National Library, Beijing. The People's Political Consultative Congress is a so-called democratic association for national policy consultation; it is run by the state in an effort to control different religious associations, several "democratic parties," various mass organizations, and notable individual intellectuals.

be traced to 1978. Two years after the end of the Cultural Revolution (1966–1976), at the founding meeting of the Chinese Association for the Study of Atheism, a state-run organization which counted many intellectuals voluntarily or involuntarily as its members, Ren Jiyu, a renowned scholar of the history of Chinese religion and philosophy who has since become the chairman of the association, made the proclamation that "Confucianism is a religion." His presentation later became the much-debated article "On the Formation of Confucian Religion," which was published in the leading state-supported academic journal *Chinese Social Sciences* in 1980 (Ren 2000). But it was not an endorsement of Confucianism as a religion; far from it, for it was the beginning of a prolonged effort to hold what Ren perceived to be the religious component of Confucianism responsible for many of the grave ills in the long history of China.

The article was controversial due to its bold statement that Confucianism should be considered a religion, like Buddhism or Daoism. As a historian, Ren offered concrete evidence to support his reading of Confucianism as a religion in the long course of Chinese history. But a close reading of this piece also reveals familiar ideas about religion that were part of the communist ideology at the time. Ren believed that Confucianism was a religion just like any other, and its influence in China had been largely negative, in the way Christianity had been the tool of "coercion and oppression" in the Western world. He wrote that, because of its emphasis on "feudal rituals and restrictions," Confucianism as a religion "tortured the Chinese people" in the same way the Inquisition made people suffer in the Middle Ages. He further argued that "Confucian religion limited the development of modern ideas, [and] restricted the growth of technology and science in China" (2000: 15).

It would take a very detailed analysis to unpack the complex meanings of these passages. There is the Marxist denunciation of religion as the "opium of the people." There is also the reiteration of Max Weber's verdict (1951 [1916]) that Confucianism is responsible for China's failure to develop modern capitalism; although this is more likely a coincidence, since it is doubtful Ren had read Weber's treatise on Chinese religions at the time, since the Chinese translation of Weber's *Religions of China* did not appear until 1991. For Ren, Confucian values such as filial piety and reverence toward the ruler are not cultural traditions worth preserving but signs of the harm done by religion. He concluded his essay: "Hence, as history has shown us, the Confucian religion has brought us only disasters, shackles, and poisonous cancers, rather than valuable traditions" (2000: 21).

It became very clear in my interview with Ren, now the director of the Chinese National Library, that he still firmly believes that Confucianism as a religion is a negative force which prevented modernization in China. A lifelong Marxist, he also seems to think that Confucianism was partly responsible for the fanaticism during the Cultural Revolution—too much reverence toward the ruler, for instance. This view was shared by many in the late 1970s and early 1980s, when they tried to shift the blame for the Cultural Revolution from the Party and Mao to the 'feudalistic traditions' in Chinese society, such as Confucianism.

However, it is important to note that, although Ren believes that the Confucian religion has done much harm to modern China, he does not consider Confucianism to be a real, living religion in contemporary Chinese society. This explains his remark about the nonexistence of Confucians when the Five Major Religions policy was being formed in the 1950s. When I asked him whether Confucianism should be regarded as a religion today, he said that it was "a thing of the past," and a revival was impossible because of the "internal limitation of Confucianism due to its emphasis on tradition and filial piety, which is incompatible with modernity." He stated that Confucianism ceased to be a full-blown religion when the last Chinese imperial dynasty was overthrown in 1911 by the republican revolution:

> Because there was no separation between the state and religion in Confucianism, the emperors had been serving as the heads of the religion, like the Pope. When the revolution put an end to the throne, it also marked the end of the Confucian religion. Today Confucianism as a religion no longer exists.

For him, the continuation of certain Confucian ritual practices is simply a part of the folk superstition tradition, which is relatively insignificant; the important task is to uncover the true history of Confucianism as a religion in China before 1911, which is primarily an intellectual project.

Because of his high standing in the Communist Party and his reputation as a leading historian of Chinese religions, Ren was handpicked by Mao to found the Institute of World Religion in 1964. He became its first director, a position he held until 1985, when he took over the directorship of the National Library, although he remains the Honorary Director of the Institute. The establishment of the Department of Confucianism in 1979 was largely due to the influence of Ren and his strong interest in Confucianism as a religion. The department is still the only one of its kind in the entire country, and until 2003 the chair of the department had been held consecutively by three of Ren's former students. It is certainly an institution endorsed by the state, given Ren's political identity and his anti-religion stance toward the religious nature of Confucianism.

The Confucianism as a Religion Debate: 2001–2004

The current 'Confucianism as a Religion Debate' (*rujia shijiao zhizheng*) refers to the controversy over the religious nature of Confucianism that in effect started in 2001. Although there were already discussions about Confucianism as a religion before that, most of them responses to Ren's work, it was not until 2001 that the debate became intense and widespread enough to be labeled "the red-hot topic in Chinese academia" (Wen Li 2002). Even though Ren and his followers remain central figures in the current debate, the controversy is not simply a reevaluation of Ren's legacy. In many ways, it also reflects growing intellectual interest in the study of Confucianism in recent years.

During the so-called 'Culture Fever' of the 1980s, when socialist China finally started to open its door to the West, there was general enthusiasm about Western culture and ideas, and more and more foreign intellectuals were allowed to lecture or attend conferences in China. One of the visitors was Tu Wei-ming, the most influential scholar of Confucianism in the United States and the long-time director of the Harvard-Yenching Institute, whose lecture on Confucianism at Beijing University in 1985 was a legendary event. Being a 'New Confucian,' Tu has long been interested in the religious dimensions of Confucianism (Tu 1989, Tu and Tucker 2003), and his positive appraisal of the Confucian tradition (including its religiosity) as the core of Chinese culture was very inspiring to his audience.

There were also scholarly works on Confucianism from East Asian regions such as Singapore, Taiwan, and South Korea being introduced, which often treated Confucian ethics as the driving force behind the industrial success of the 'Four Little Dragons' of East Asia, the way Protestant ethics were perceived as instrumental in the development of modern capitalism in Europe (Tu 1991). To the

Chinese intellectuals who considered the question of modernization to be the most urgent one, such a Weberian take on Confucianism offered both a new solution and a new perspective on the Confucian tradition. There were also international conferences on Confucianism; one of the first was held in 1987 in Qufu, Confucius's birthplace, jointly hosted by the newly founded Confucius Foundation of China (a state-funded cultural organization to promote Confucian studies and Chinese culture) and the Institute for East Asian Philosophies in Singapore (Ching 1993: 82). Such encounters with new interpretations of Confucianism from both East Asian regions and North America, along with the budding institutional encouragement from the state, indeed facilitated the changing attitude of the younger generation of Chinese scholars.

When Tu visited the Academy of Chinese Culture during his 1985 trip, the Academy was one of the few institutions devoted to the study of Chinese classics, or the 'National Learning' (*guoxue*), at the time. But the number of students who wanted to study Chinese classics was steadily on the rise, and the fervor for 'National Learning' became more prevalent in the 1990s, with many younger intellectuals joining the field, most of whom undertook their academic training after the Cultural Revolution. It should not come as a surprise that they began to question the legitimacy of the politically charged negative assessment of Confucianism as a religion.

But the debate did not become a sensational one until October 2001, when the website *Confucius2000.com* was founded. The site was devoted to the scholarly studies of all aspects of Confucianism, and soon the 'Confucianism as a Religion Debate' dominated the site and brought the controversy to the attention of intellectuals nation-wide.

The storm reached its height in 2002–2003, with hundreds of articles and responses posted on the *Confucius2000* forum. In the postings, the core participating scholars attacked one another with unprecedented candor, and their escalating quarrels were fueled by the speediness of internet publishing. The heated debate captured the attention of many intellectuals, especially those working in the fields of religion, philosophy, and history. In the words of one of the key participants in the controversy, in those two years, the debate "reached a height and intensity that stunned the Chinese academic community" (Han 2004a).

But before we turn to a detailed analysis of the debate, we need first to take a look at the cultural venues where the debate takes place. In today's China, there are two main channels of intellectual exchange for scholars who study religion, as is the case for most Chinese academics. One is the official channel, which includes numerous state-sponsored academic journals, such as *Chinese Social Sciences*, and state-sanctioned conferences. The other is the unofficial channel, which means mostly online publishing, since scholarly independent print journals normally do not last very long due to lack of funding. The internet venue includes independent journals such as *Tracing the Dao*, a print scholarly publication with its own website, as well as internet sites such as *Confucius2000* that are dedicated to specific areas of scholarly interests.

Starting in the 1990s, the internet has been creating a virtual communal space of ideas for Chinese intellectuals, and this space has been expanding ever since, particularly in the category of scholarly websites, which normally refrain from publishing direct criticisms of contemporary Chinese politics, hence are relatively free from state censorship. Many such sites are expertly organized and maintained, and the involvement of leading intellectuals often provides these online ventures with a sense of academic legitimacy. The *Confucius2000* site, for instance, counts many important scholars of Confucianism as its active contributors. About 30 or so similar sites on Chinese philosophy and religion are listed on *Confucius2000* as members of a larger network of websites sharing common intellectual goals, which shows how such forums are thriving for people who wish to carry out a serious exchange of ideas in cyberspace. Although none of these sites is state-sponsored, there are often interactions between official and unofficial channels; for example, relevant papers published in state-run journals often end up on the *Confucius2000* website.

There were various articles debating Ren's view on Confucianism in official scholarly journals in the 1980s, but it was in 2001 that the debate reached a new phase, with many articles published in the official as well as the unofficial venues. The current controversy started when the two-volume *History of Confucianism as a Religion in China* was published in 2000. The author of the book is Li Shen, a former student of Ren who at the time was the head of the Department of Confucianism (Confucian Religion), and his analysis of Confucianism as a religion closely resembles the substance of Ren's arguments. In other words, Li Shen carried out a systematic historical study of

Confucianism as a religion with a similar negative value judgment, depicting the religious aspect of Confucianism as a fundamentally harmful element in Chinese culture and society.

A few months after the publication of the book, a review was posted on the *Confucius2000* website with the title "The Federal Project Made of Tofu Dregs: Reflections on the First Volume of *History of Confucianism as a Religion in China*." The author was Chen Yongming, a colleague of Li's at the Department of Confucianism (Confucian Religion). It also carried the following postscript: "For various reasons this article has been rejected by many journals. The author hopes that a journal with the agenda of resisting academic mediocrity would be willing to publish this review."

But it turned out that the review did not need to be published anywhere else. Within a week, Li posted a furious response on the same site, defending his interpretations of classical Confucian texts, which had been appraised by Chen as "full of nonsense" and essentially a "vulgarization and demonization" of Chinese cultural traditions (Chen 2001: 14). In the months that followed, Li had to respond to dozens of similar attacks, which were often severe criticisms made by scholars who have an entirely different take on the impact and meaning of Confucianism as a religion. One strategy Li adopted was to ally himself with other intellectual authorities by listing well-known scholars as supporters of his work; he wrote that when he first started the project in 1996, "there were only five people in China who supported [Ren's] "'Confucianism is a religion' view." But now, he said, "there are more than thirty scholars who have endorsed my ideas" (Li 2002).

Unfortunately his tactic backfired when several of the people he mentioned posted pieces on *Confucius2000* denouncing such alliance. At least two of them were Li's colleagues at CASS, although the entire debate involved participants from quite a few different institutions. One further twist came when Li allegedly prevented the publication of Chen's review, in the state-run *Confucius Studies*, while publishing his own article attacking his opponent, which caused an outrage among Chen's supporters.

Today under the heading of "The Debate about Confucianism and Religion" on *Confucius2000*, there are at least 200 related postings, although the later ones focus more on articulating the different understandings of Confucianism as a religion than about the actual disagreement between Li and his critics. It seems clear that *Confucius2000* mainly represents scholars who want to restore a positive evaluation of Confucianism as a religion, even though it has also been publishing articles by Li and some of his associates. The overwhelming consensus on the site is that people might not agree with one another about whether or how Confucianism is a religion, but unlike Ren and Li, most of them do agree that there is nothing inherently negative about the category of religion (Han 2004b).

What is at Stake: Reclaiming the Category of Religion

In fact, many scholars have found positive reasons to support the notion of a Confucian religion. The newer generation of scholars of Confucianism is for the most part well-versed in both Chinese classics and Western theories, and they are more interested in a historically and philosophically nuanced understanding of Confucianism, with the religious element as an intriguing part of the Confucian tradition. The younger scholars I interviewed often expressed their desire to go beyond the 'Confucianism as a Religion' debate, which they thought to be ideological, and instead focus on more productive discussions.

Some of them, however, also voiced their interest in locating a source for a stronger culture identity for China in the time of a market economy, commercialism, and globalization. Lu Guolong, a renowned scholar of Daoism and Confucianism who replaced Li Shen in 2003 to became the head of the Department of Confucianism (Confucian Religion), said in our interview that Confucianism "is the host of our culture—all the other religions and traditions are secondary, like guests in our house." Like many other scholars, he also hopes for a revival of Confucian ethics, regardless of whether Confucianism can be revitalized as a religion.

In some ways, the controversy over the meaning of Confucianism as a religion between the older generation of Marxist scholars and the younger, more national-culture minded intellectuals is a battle over the control of an important cultural and political asset. The newer generation has long accepted the notion that religion is an affirmative part of human experience, and now they are rehabilitating *rujiao*, the Confucian religion, from the weight of communist vilification.

What's really at stake is that the category of religion has not been value-free in socialist China, which is what many people sought to

challenge through the Confucianism debate. Indeed, their disagreement with Ren and Li is not primarily about whether Confucianism
is a religion, but about the value judgment that comes with such a
conclusion. They might also speak of Confucianism as a religion,
but their pronouncement comes with different intellectual justifications
and completely opposite values. In this context, the meaning of religion is at the center of the debate; the value of the category is something to fight for, and at the moment the Young Turks seem to
have won the first round.

It is clear from the postings on *Confucius2000* that the overwhelming
majority of the participants disagree with Li Shen and his disparaging
value judgment toward religion. Even though people are divided
about whether Confucianism is a religion, there is no negative con-
notation when the religious aspects of Confucianism are discussed.
But the most telling evidence comes from CASS. The Department
of Confucianism, the symbolic center of the debate, had a changing of the guard in 2003, with Lu Guolong replacing Li Shen as
the director.[7] To my knowledge the other six members of the department have either publicly opposed Li's view or have stayed neutral
throughout the controversy. The fact that Chen Yongming, the author
of the article "The Federal Project Made of Tofu Dregs," which
triggered the most intense episode in the debate, and Cheng Ming,
one of the leading opponents of Li on *Confucius2000*, have stayed on
as members of the department shows CASS's commitment to supporting the newer generation of scholars. Although internal politics
must have played a role in this case, it is unlikely that broader intellectual and political considerations were not taken into account, such
as the issue of the official position concerning the religions nature
of Confucianism.

Confucianism as a Religion: A New Classification in the Making?

What is the official position regarding Confucianism as a religion? There
is no easy answer to the question, although there might be clues to
be found. Besides the heated debates among Chinese scholars, it is
also important to note what has been published in the official venues,

---

[7] Li now holds a professorship in Shanghai, and he is also affiliated with *Science
and Atheism*, a journal published by the Chinese Association of the Study of Atheism.

for it could reflect the impact the intellectual debate might have had on the official religious classification. One of the best places to examine these shifting boundaries is the *Annual of Religious Research in China*, the series of annual volumes reviewing the state of religious studies that first appeared in 1998. It has been published by Religion and Culture Press, a publishing house owned by the National Bureau of Religious Affairs, whose support is acknowledged in the 'Preface' of the latest *Annual* (Cao 2003: 1). The series has been edited by Cao Zhongjian, the deputy director of the Institute of World Religions at CASS when the first *Annual* was published; he is now the Party Secretary of the Institute of World Religions, the *de facto* head of the Institute.

From the beginning of its publication, the structure of the *Annual* closely followed the Five Major Religions classification given by the Bureau of Religious Affairs. However, Confucianism did find its way into the official text. In the very first volume, the *Annual* of 1996, after 300 pages of reviews about scholarly works on Buddhism, Daoism, Islam, and Christianity (both Catholic and Protestant), there was the category of 'Others.' Under 'Others' we find the following classification:

The Studies of Confucianism
The Studies of Chinese Folk Religions
The Studies of Baojuan[8]
A Summary of the Studies of New Religions.

The article on "The Studies of Confucianism" was written by Li Shen. In his short review, he recounted the debate initiated by his teacher, Ren, in 1978, and concluded triumphantly that Ren's view had now been accepted by many scholars. He described a few events which he thought to be markers of the turning point, one being the inclusion of Confucianism as one of the 350 items in the *Dictionary of Religion* in 1994, edited by Ren, and another being a lecture given by Li himself at the inauguration of the Department of Religion at Beijing University in 1996, entitled "There Exists a Confucian Religion in China."

The category of 'Others' was suspiciously missing in the 1997–1998 volume, and when it did come back in the 1999–2000 volume,

---

[8] Baojuan is a form of popular retelling of religious tales.

Confucianism was absent from the category. But in the bibliography accompanying the articles, about a dozen books and articles on the religious nature of Confucianism were mentioned. Then, in the 2001–2002 volume, which was published in 2003 during the heyday of the online 'Confucianism as a Religion' debate, we find Confucianism listed in the following way on the content page:

The Studies of Buddhism
The Studies of Daoism
The Studies of Islam
The Studies of Judaism and Christianity
The Studies of Confucianism

Although 'The Studies of Confucianism' is only a subheading, it seems significant that Confucianism is listed for the first time as one of the major religions in an official document. Given the official status of the *Annual* as the authorized record of the state of religious studies in China, it is hard not to speculate about a possible connection between the intensity of the on-going Confucianism controversy and the government's potential interest in revisiting the existing classification system of religions. But will such a reclassification of the religious status of Confucianism ever happen?

Beyond the Academic Debate: Paradoxes Present and Future

South Korea seems to be the only country where Confucianism as a religious category appears frequently in surveys on religion, and the Confucian religion does appear to play a vital role in the nation's political and cultural life (Rozman 2003). In a 1995 National Statistical Office survey of religious population, 0.5% of Koreans identified themselves as Confucians (Kim 2002: 293), even though there is a similar ambivalence in South Korea about whether Confucianism is a religion (Koh 1996). There are no statistics about the number of Confucian practitioners in China, whatever that category might mean. But perhaps the focus on finding self-identified Confucians is not the most productive way of understanding Confucianism as a religious tradition. It might be more fruitful to view Confucianism from an anthropological perspective and look for Confucian religious practices rather than dogmas or systems of belief. Are there people who practice Confucian rituals in China today? Are there people who worship Confucius in the way a Buddhist might worship the Buddha?

Are there sites of veneration which might offer us clues of a deeply embedded tradition of Confucian ritual life?

In 2003, when I visited the Ancestral Temple in the Southern city of Foshan, which is one of the most popular temples in the region, there was much incense burning in the small courtyard on the Confucian side of the temple. The other parts of the Ancestral Temple were grander Daoist and Buddhist ceremony halls, with statues of the Northern King and Buddhist pagodas among many other multi-religious symbols. This type of syncretistic temple is quite common in China, although it is unusual to have a complete Confucian temple tucked in such a compound.

Traditionally the ritual of burning incense in front of a Confucius statue is said to bring blessings to students in their quest for fame and fortune through learning.[9] In this particular temple, the worshippers normally come during two important dates: The eve of the Chinese New Year and the week of the national college entrance examinations. Yet on the early June day I visited, the incense indicated that the temple was well visited in the rest of the year as well; its proximity to the other religious sites might have made it an easy stop in people's busy lives.

In the Confucian Temple in Beijing, when I failed to detect any scent of incense in the air during my winter visit in 2004, I concluded that it might be because the majestic temple was not a site for worship any longer, but merely another stop for sight-seeing tourists. But a temple manager told me that the opposite is true. Because there are far too many people coming in to worship in certain times of the year, especially during the Chinese New Year and the days of the annual college entrance examinations, the temple administrators have forbidden anyone to burn incense on the ground of the temple at any time, in fear of a fire burning down the invaluable fourteenth-century wood structures.

Does this anecdotal evidence suggest that Confucianism as a religion is indeed experiencing a revival in China? Can we consider the ones praying in front of Confucian statues the followers of Confucius? Such questions can be answered only through extensive research that

---

[9] From the fourteenth century until 1904, men from all social backgrounds competed for official posts within the imperial government by taking the civil examinations, which required them to write essays interpreting the Confucian classics (Elman 2000). It was not surprising that the cultural institution of the examinations solidified Confucius's status as the patron saint of students.

combines survey data and ethnographic research, which will show us how much traditional Confucian ritual practice has persevered among ordinary people today, whether educational level or regional difference matter in people's attitudes toward Confucianism, and whether there are any people who would identify themselves as Confucians. The question of the religious nature of Confucianism is an empirical one, although the right theoretical framework is crucial to a meaningful investigation, such as what constitutes a Chinese religion and what constitutes a Confucian ritual.

Nevertheless, it is obvious that there is a potential tension between the rise of Confucian ritual practice and the existing official classification of religion. The tension is only potential at the moment because even though the Confucian temples are clearly used for ritual purposes in recent years, organizationally they are not controlled by the Bureau of Religious Affairs, hence they are still technically below the radar. Since most of these temples are historical buildings, they are managed by the Bureau of Historical Relics, and the officials working on religious affairs have little to do with the temples, according to the administrators at the two Confucian temples I visited. This seems to be another indication of the ambiguous status of Confucianism as a religion in contemporary Chinese society.

During an interview with the official from the Bureau of Religious Affairs, I was told that the Bureau had been worrying about the current scholarly controversy, for "it might create a new religion." But how worried is the state? Has it started to participate actively in the reshaping and the redefining of the Confucian religion? The most telling sign—a rather surprising one—came in September 2004, during the celebration of the 2,555th birthday of Confucius.

Historically, such as in the Ming and Qing dynasties, there were official rites offered by the court at the Confucian temples in the city of Beijing (Naquin 2000), and government officials were in charge of annual ceremonies in the Confucius temple in Qufu, Confucius's birthplace. The rites were discontinued after the end of Qing Dynasty in 1911, except for the few years when the political reformers attempted to make Confucianism into a national religion. It was indeed a gesture of open-mindedness of the socialist government when the annual ceremony on Confucius' birthday in Qufu was reinstalled in 1993. Kong Deban, Confucius's 77th descendant, had been the chief ceremonial official until 2004.

On 28 September 2004, for the first time since the founding of the People's Republic, the state officially took over, with government representatives presiding over the rites. In fact, they choreographed the entire ceremony of 'The Veneration of Confucius,' with several stage directors orchestrating the events, dozens of actors playing the roles of the disciples of Confucius, and 36 dancers recreating a Confucian ritual dance. Although it was clearly a performance, the organizers wanted to make sure that it was an authentic Confucian ceremony, which they tried to achieve by copying most of the rituals depicted in Qing Dynasty records. The emphasis on 'authenticity' was the prevailing principle, and the 77th descendent of Confucius remarked that he felt more pious than ever during this first official ceremony for Confucius (Xinhua she 2004a).

Several weeks later, on 16 November 2004, the Deputy Secretary of the Department of Education announced to reporters that the Chinese government is planning to found one hundred 'Confucius Institutes' globally in the next few years to promote the study of the Chinese language and Chinese culture. He explained that they are named 'Confucius Institutes' because Confucius is an internationally recognizable symbol of Chinese culture, and the institutes will be teaching primarily language courses rather than classes on Confucian thought (Xinhua she 2004b).

His speech came during a ceremony unveiling a 'holy statue' of Confucius on an university campus in Beijing. It is hard to ignore the quasi-religious undertone of the occasion, even though there was no suggestion of a religious dimension in the ambitious new plan for global Chinese language training. Interestingly, the 'holy statue' was donated by Tang Enjia, the director of the Hong Kong Confucian Academy, who has been promoting Confucianism as a religion for many years. The Chinese name of the academy, Hong Kong Kongjiao Xueyuan, literally means the academy of "Confucian religion" (Confucianity). Tang has donated sixty such statues to leading universities in China, and it is clear from the warm welcome he receives that his donation has been granted approval from high political authorities.

It seems reasonable to suggest that there are indeed conflicting messages about the religious status of Confucianism being offered by the state. On the one hand, the state is not interested in supporting any new religion (it has enough trouble with the existing ones); on the other hand, the state is beginning to recognize the importance of identifying Confucianism (or Confucius) as a unifying element in Chinese society. Such a symbol is needed for the representation of

a Chinese national culture in the global context, and it is also needed
for the centering of the increasingly shaky collective sense of morality
in the country's fast transition into a market economy and capitalism.[10]

The growing number of worshippers at Confucian temples also
suggests an increasing need among ordinary people for a religious
system that is deeply rooted in Chinese tradition, with long-established
customs and rites, such as the blessing of exam-taking students.[11]
Fenggang Yang has pointed out that the religious economy of China
is one of "economics of shortage," and "while some people have set-
tled with the forced substitution of the Communist faith and other
pseudo-religious alternatives, many people have resorted to quasi-
religious substitutes as well as conventional religions" (Yang 2004: 1).
It seems that Confucianism as a religion (or quasi-religion) has the
potential of offering an alternative that could satisfy the religious
needs of many people, and it might have an advantage over the
other religious options because of its time-honored ethical system (as
a moral foundation for the entire society) and its symbolic significance
(as an indigenous tradition).

There have been rumors that, during one of the more dramatic
moments of internal conflict within the Department of Confucianism
at CASS, higher political authorities were appealed to, and their
endorsement was crucial to the settlement of the disagreement. The
current regime has been very pragmatic in its dealings with the possibility of the revival of Confucianism as a religion, and it remains
to be seen how the political climate will affect the academic discourse
about Confucianism as a religion. It also remains to be seen how
the academic categorization might play a role in the possible rein-

---

[10] A recent news report is a good illustration of the latter endeavor. At a "renewal
of marital vows" ceremony taking place in Beijing during the moon festival in 2004,
which is a tradition holiday celebrating familial harmony, 180 couples renewed their
vows in a hotel ballroom among friends and family, with government officials as
special guests. What's highly unusual about this ceremony was that the couples
declared in front of a "holy portrait of Confucius" that they "will never divorce"
(Zhongxin she 2004). This is certainly not a traditional Confucian practice, for the
notion of legal divorce did not exist in China until the early twentieth century.
Today the divorce rate is about 21% (a tremendous increase from 7% in 1980),
according to the Ministry of Civil Affairs, hence this ceremony reflects a societal
need for such promotion of marital stability.

[11] It should be noted that it is difficult to differentiate many folk religious practices
from specifically Confucian ones. Hence I am focusing only on the most obvious
Confucian rituals in this chapter, which are what take place in a Confucian temple.

vention of Confucianism: As a national cultural identity, as a revival of ritual practices, or as a full-fledged religious movement with intellectuals acting as its spokespeople. It is not an overstatement to say that now is indeed an exciting time to be studying the fate of Confucianism as a religion, for its future is about to unfold right before our eyes.

REFERENCES

Academia Sinica, Institute of Modern History. 1976. *Jiaowu jiaoan dang* [*Archival Materials Related to Religious Affairs, 1871–1878*], vol. 3, No. 1. Taipei: Academia Sinica.

Beyer, Peter. 1999. "The Modern Construction of Religions in the Context of World Society: A Contested Category in Light of Modern Chinese History." Paper prepared for the conference "Chinese and Comparative Historiography and Historical Culture" in Wolfenbüttel, Germany.

Bowker, John, ed. 1997. *The Oxford Dictionary of World Religions*. Oxford: Oxford University Press.

Cao, Zhongjian. 1998. *Zhongguo zongjiaoyanjiu nianjian, 1996* [*Annual of Religious Research in China, 1996*]. Beijing: Chinese Academy of Social Sciences Press.

———. 2000. *Zhongguo zongjiaoyanjiu nianjian, 1997–1998* [*Annual of Religious Research in China, 1997–1998*]. Beijing: Chinese Academy of Social Sciences Press.

———. 2001. *Zhongguo zongjiaoyanjiu nianjian, 1999–2000* [*Annual of Religious Research in China, 1999–2000*]. Beijing: Chinese Academy of Social Sciences Press.

———. 2003. *Zhongguo zongjiaoyanjiu nianjian, 2001–2002* [*Annual of Religious Research in China, 2001–2002*]. Beijing: Chinese Academy of Social Sciences Press.

Chen, Hsi-yuan. 1999. *Confucianism Encounters Religion: The Formation of Religious Discourse and the Confucian Movement in Modern China*. Ph.D. dissertation, Harvard University.

Chen, Yongming. 2001. "Guojiaji de doufuzha gongcheng" ["The Federal Project Made of Tofu Dregs: Reflections on the First Volume of *History of Confucianism as a Religion in China*"]. *Confucius2000.com*.

Ching, Julia. 1977. *Confucianism and Christianity*. Tokyo: Kodansha International.

———. 1993. *Chinese Religions*. Maryknoll, NY: Orbis Books.

Confucius2000.com. http://www.Confucius2000.com.

Elman, Benjamin. 2000. *A Cultural History of the Civil Examinations in Late Imperial China*. Berkeley: University of California Press.

Granet, Marcel. 1977 [1922]. *The Religion of the Chinese People*. New York: Harper Torchbooks.

Han, Xing. 2003. "*Dalu rujiaopai de lishi dingwei*" ["The Historical Context of the School of Confucianism in Mainland China"]. *Confucius2000.com*.

———. 2004a. "Guanyu rujiao wenti de zuixin taolun" ["The Latest Discussions about Confucianism as a Religion"]. *Confucius2000.com*.

———. 2004b. *Rujiao wenti* [*The Question of Confucian Religion*]. Shaanxi: Shaanxi Shaanxi People's Publishing House.

Jensen, Lionel M. 1997. *Manufacturing Confucianism*. Durham, NC: Duke University Press.

Kim, Andrew Eungi. 2002. "Characteristics of Religious Life in South Korea: A Sociological Survey." *Review of Religious Research*, 43: 291–310.

Koh, Byong-Ik. 1996. "Confucianism in Contemporary Korea." Pp. 191–201 in *Confucian Traditions in East Asian Modernity* edited by Tu Wei-Ming. Cambridge, MA: Harvard University Press.

Legge, James. 1877. *Confucianism in Relation to Christianity*. Shanghai: Kelly and Walsh.
———. 1880. *The Religions of China*. London: Hodder and Stoughton.
Li, Shen. 2000. *Zhongguo rujiao shi* [*History of Confucianism as a Religion in China*]. Shanghai: Shanghai People's Publishing House.
———. 2002. "Zhongguo rujiaoshi zaokong zhounianji" ["Remarks on the First Anni-versary of the Attack on *History of Confucianism as a Religion in China*"]. *Confucius 2000.com*.
Liu, Dongchao. 2004. "Dangdai zhongguo shifou xuyao rujiao?" ["Does China Need a Confucian Religion Today?"]. *Confucius2000.com*.
Liu, Lydia. 1995. *Translingual Practice*. Stanford, CA: Stanford University Press.
Mao Zedong. 1963. "*Mao Zedong Tongzhi guanyu jiaqiang zongjiao wenti yanjiu de pishi*" ["The Memo from Comrade Mao Zedong Regarding the Strengthening of Studies of Religions"]. http://www.cass.net.cn/chinese/s13_zjs/ceremony/mao.htm.
Masini, Federico. 1993. *The Formation of Modern Chinese Lexicon and its Evolution toward a National Language. Journal of Chinese Linguistics*, Monograph No. 6.
Müller, Friedrich Max. 1900. "Religions of China: I. Confucianism." *The Nineteenth Century* 48: 373–84.
Naquin, Susan. 2000. *Peking*. Berkeley: University of California Press.
Oxtoby, Willard G. 2002. *World Religions*. Oxford: Oxford University Press.
Ren, Jiyu, ed. 2000. *Rujiao wenti zhenglun ji* [*The Confucianism as a Religion Debate*]. Beijing: Religion and Culture Press.
Rozman, Gilbert. 2003. "Center-Local Relations: Can Confucianism Boost Decentralization and Regionalism?" Pp. 181–200 in *Confucianism for the Modern World*, edited by Daniel A. Bell and Hahm Chaibong. Cambridge: Cambridge University Press.
Smith, Huston. 1991. *The World's Religions*. New York: HarperCollins.
Tarocco, Francesca and T. H. Barrett. 2004. "East Asian Religion Unmasked." Unpublished paper.
Taylor, Rodney L. 1990. *The Religious Dimensions of Confucianism*. Albany: State University of New York Press.
Teiser, Stephen F. 1996. "Introduction." Pp. 3–37 in *Religions of China in Practice*, edited by Donald S. Lopez, Jr. Princeton, NJ: Princeton University Press.
Tu, Wei-Ming, ed. 1991. *The Triadic Chord*. Singapore: Institute of East Asian Philosophies.
———. 1989. *Centrality and Commonality*. Albany: State University of New York Press.
Tu, Wei-Ming and Mary Evelyn Tucker, eds. 2003. *Confucian Spirituality*. New York: Crossroad Publishing.
Weber, Max. 1951 [1916]. *The Religion of China*. New York: Free Press.
Wen, Li. 2002. "Guanyu rujiao yu zongjiao de taolun" ["The Confucianism and Religion Debate"], in *Zhongguo zhexue shi* [*The History of Chinese Philosophy*] (Beijing) 2002: 63–75.
Wilson, Thomas A., ed. 2002. *On Sacred Grounds*. Cambridge, MA: Harvard University Press.
Wuthnow, Robert. 1989. *Communities of Discourse*. Cambridge, MA: Harvard University Press.
Xinhua she [Xinhua News Agency] 2004a. "Qufu kongmiao juxing dadian jikongzi 2,555 sui" ["The Grand Ceremony Venerating Confucius on His 2,555th Birthday Took Place in the Confucian Temple in Qufu"], www.news.xinhuanet.com.cn, 9 September.
———. 2004b. "Quanqiu jiangban baisuo Kongzi xueyuan." ["There Will be 100 Confucian Institutes all over the World"]. www.news.xinuanet.com.cn, 16 November.

Yang, Fenggang. 2004. "Religion in Socialist China: Demand-Side Dynamics in a Shortage Economy." Paper presented at the Annual Meeting of the Society for the Scientific Study of Religion, Kansas City.

Zhang, Rongming. 2001. *Zhongguo de guojiao* [*The National Religion of China*]. Beijing: Chinese Academy of Social Sciences Press.

Zhongxin she [China News]. 2004. "Beijing 180 dui fuqi xuanbu yong bu lihun" ["180 Couples in Beijing Vow that They Will Never Divorce"], www.chinanews.com.cn, 28 September.

CONTRIBUTORS

Thomas Borchert is a Ph.D. candidate in the History of Religions at the University of Chicago. He is completing his dissertation on the monastic education practices of the Dai-lue, a Tai minority group of Southwest China that practices Theravada Buddhism. His research interests include disciplinary practices within Buddhism and the effects of nationalism and transnational flows on the formation of religious communities.

Selina Ching Chan has a D.Phil. in Social Anthropolgoy from Oxford University. She taught in the Department of Sociology at the National University of Singapore and is currently an associate professor in the Department of Sociology and Associate Director of the Contemporary China Research Center at Hong Kong Shue Yan College. Her areas of research include the study of Chinese kinship, cultural identity, and religion in Hong Kong, Singapore and China. Her work has been published in international journals such as *Ethnology*, *China Information*, and *Modern China*.

Jainbo Huang received his doctorate in anthropology from The Central University of Nationalities in Beijing and is a postdoctoral fellow at the Institute of Ethnology and Anthropology, Chinese Academy of Social Sciences. He is the author of chapters in various books as well as articles in the *Journal of Christian Culture Studies*, *Journal of Thoughts and Cultures*, and *Journal of Guangxi Ethnic Studies*. His current research focuses on urban Christian churches and migrant Christian churches in China and on Chinese folk religions.

Graeme Lang, Ph.D. (from York University in Toronto) is Associate Professor of Sociology at City University of Hong Kong. He is the author, with Lars Ragvald, of *The Rise of a Refugee God* (1993), and his recent publications include a formal analysis of forms of religious fundamentalism with examples from Southeast Asia, an article on shamanism in Hong Kong, and an essay on challenges for the sociology of religion in Asia.

Chi-shiang Ling holds a B.S. in psychology and an M.A. in philosophy, both from National Taiwan University, and received a Masters of Theological Studies (*magna cum laude*) from Duke University. He is an adjunct faculty member in the Department of Philosophy at Utah Valley State College, teaching courses on ethics and religions. His current research interests include religion in Taiwan and issues in interreligious dialogue.

Paul Yunfeng Lu received his Ph.D. from City University of Hong Kong and is a postdoctoral research scholar at the Department of Sociology and the Center for Religious Inquiry across the Disciplines at Baylor University. His articles are forthcoming in the *Journal for the Scientific Study of Religion* and the *Interdisciplinary Journal of Research on Religion*. Currently, he is interested in Chinese sectarian movements and cross-cultural studies of religiosity.

Lars Ragvald is Professor and Head of the Department of East Asian Languages at Lund University in Sweden. He has been visiting and studying China since the 1960s, and his research includes studies of trends in social and cultural change in southern China, particularly in Guangdong province.

Anna Xiao Dong Sun is a Ph.D. candidate in the Department of Sociology at Princeton University. She was a Mellon Dissertation Fellow at the University of London from 2003 to 2004, doing research for her dissertation, *Confusions over Confucianism: The Emergence of the World Religions Paradigm and the Construction of Confucianism as a World Religion, 1870–1915*. She is currently a Visiting Instructor in the Department of Sociology at Kenyon College.

William H. Swatos, Jr., is completing his first decade as Executive Officer of the Association for the Sociology of Religion, prior to which he served for six years as editor of *Sociology of Religion*, the ASR's official journal. He is also executive officer of the Religious Research Association and senior fellow of the Center for Religious Inquiry Across the Disciplines at Baylor University, serving as managing editor of the *Interdisciplinary Journal of Research on Religion*. He received his B.A. with honors from Transylvania University, his M.Div. *summa cum laude* from the Episcopal Theological Seminary in Kentucky, and his M.A. and Ph.D. from the University of Kentucky, with honors in social theory. He is author, co-author, editor, or co-editor of over twenty books including the *Encyclopedia of Religion and Society* (AltaMira 1998). His most recent book is *The Protestant Ethic Turns 100* (Paradigm 2004), co-edited with Lutz Kaelber.

Joseph B. Tamney is Professor Emeritus in the sociology department, Ball State University (USA). He received his B.S. and M.A. from Fordham University and his Ph.D. from Cornell University. He was a member of the editorial Board for the *Encyclopedia of Religion and Society*, editor of *Sociology of Religion* (1994–2000), and president of the Association for the Sociology of Religion (2003–4). His published works include: *The Resilience of Christianity in the Modern World* (State University of New York Press, 1992), *American Society in the Buddhist Mirror* (Garland 1992), *The Struggle Over Singapore's Soul: Western Modernization and Asian Culture* (Walter de Gruyter 1996), *The Resilience of Conservative Religion* (Cambridge University Press 2002), and, with Linda Hsueh-Ling Chiang, *Modernization, Globalization, and Confucianism in Chinese Societies* (Praeger 2002).

Dedong Wei received his Ph.D. from the People's University of China (Beijing). He is an associate professor of religious studies at the People's University of China. His research focuses on the sociology of religion and Buddhist studies. His publications include *The Essence of Buddhist Yogacara Philosophy* and "The Buddhist View on Ecology."

Der-Ruey Yang received his doctorate from London School of Economics and Political Science in 2003 and was a post-doctoral fellow in the National University of Singapore. Currently he teaches the anthropology of religion at Nanjing University (China). His research interests include the education of Daoist priests, comparisons of Daoist practices in mainland China, Taiwan and Singapore, and Daoist demonology, theodicy and spatial consciousness.

Fenggang Yang received his B.A. from the Hebei Normal University (Shijiazhuang, China), M.A. from Nankai University (Tianjin, China), and Ph.D. from The Catholic University of America (Washington, DC). He is an assistant professor of sociology at Purdue University. He is the author of *Chinese Christians in America: Conversion, Assimilation, and Adhesive Identities.* (Penn State University Press 1999) and the co-editor, along with Tony Carnes, of *Asian American Religions: The Making* *and Remaking of Borders and Boundaries* (New York University Press 2004). His articles have been published in various books and in the *American Sociological Review*, *Journal for the Scientific Study of Religion*, *Sociology of Religion*, and *Journal of Asian American Studies*. His current research focuses on the political economy of religion in China, Christian ethics and market transition in China, and Chinese Christian churches in the United States.